Energy and Environment in Architecture

Energy and Environment in Architecture

A Technical Design Guide

Nick Baker and Koen Steemers

E & FN SPON

An Imprint of the
Taylor & Francis Group
London and New York

First published 2000 by E & FN Spon, an imprint of
the Taylor & Francis Group
11 New Fetter Lane, London EC4P 4EE

Simultaneously published in the USA and Canada by Routledge
29 West 35th Street, New York, NY 10001

Typeset in Gill Sans by Stephen Cary

Printed and bound in Great Britain at the University Press, Cambridge

British Library Cataloguing in Publication Data
A catalogue record for this book is available from the British Library

Library of Congress Cataloguing in Publication Data
Baker, Nick.
  Energy and environment in architecture: a technical design guide /
  Nick Baker and Koen Steemers.
      p. cm.
  Includes bibliographical references and index.
  ISBN 0-419-22770-9 (pbk.)
   1. Architecture and energy conservation. 2. Public buildings
   - Design and construction. I. Steemers, Koen. II. Title.
NA2542.3.B34 1999
720'.472–dc21   98-54418 CIP

ISBN 0-419-22770-9

Contents

About this book   vii
Acknowledgements   viii

Foreword   ix
Max Fordham

Part One: Energy and environment

Chapter 1
Introduction   2

Chapter 2
Low-energy strategies   4

Chapter 3
The provision of comfort   8
  3.1 Thermal comfort   9
  3.2 Indoor air quality   12
  3.3 Visual comfort   12
  3.4 Acoustic comfort   13
  3.5 Adaptive opportunity and control   14

Chapter 4
Heating   18
  4.1 Useful solar gains and thermal mass   20
  4.2 Thermal balance of glazing   22
  4.3 Orientation and overshadowing   23
  4.4 Insulation and cold bridges   24

Chapter 5
Prevention of overheating   26
  5.1 Cooling load reduction   30
  5.2 Shading and orientation   31
  5.3 Reduction of other heat gains   33

5.4 Ventilation cooling   35
5.5 Thermal mass   36
5.6 Night ventilation   39

Chapter 6
Daylighting   42
  6.1 Daylight as energy   42
  6.2 Daylight factor   44
  6.3 The sky as a light source   44
  6.4 Interaction of shading with daylighting 45
  6.5 Lighting control systems   46
  6.6 Daylighting and thermal function of glazing 48

Chapter 7
Ventilation   52
  7.1 Ventilation regimes   54
  7.2 Natural ventilation   55
  7.3 Ventilation configurations   57
  7.4 Use of stacks and ducts   58
  7.5 Mechanical ventilation   60
  7.6 Air-conditioning   62

Chapter 8
The passive zone concept   64

Chapter 9
Atria and sunspaces   66
  9.1 Daylighting and atria   67
  9.2 Winter performance   70
  9.3 Summer performance   76
  9.4 Heating in atria   78

Chapter 10
Energy systems   82
  10.1 Energy sources   82
  10.2 Renewable sources of heat   83
  10.3 Electricity generation   84
  10.4 Heat production and distribution   86
  10.5 Heat emitters   87
  10.6 Heat recovery   87
  10.7 Controls   88
  10.8 Management issues   89

Bibliography   90

Contents

Part Two: The LT Method

Chapter 11
Introduction to the LT Method   92
  11.1 Technical background   93
  11.2 Limitations of the LT Method   94

Chapter 12
How to use the LT Method   96
  12.1 Step 1: the passive zone   96
  12.2 Step 2: the glazing ratio   99
  12.3 Step 3: the LT curves   99
  12.4 Step 4: the LT worksheet   103
  12.5 Primary energy and CO_2 103
  12.6 Interpretation of cooling energy   104
  12.7 Step 5: the Urban Horizon Factor   104
  12.8 Step 6: atria and sunspaces   106

Chapter 13
LT Method worked examples   110
  13.1 Five-storey office building   110
  13.2 Four-storey office building with atrium   113
  13.3 School with conservatory   115
  13.4 Nucleus hospital   117

Chapter 14
LT data and worksheet   120
  14.1 LT data   122
  14.2 The LT worksheet and notes   165

Bibliography   166

Part Three: Case studies

Introduction   168
  1 Ionica Headquarters, Cambridge   170
  2 St. Mary's Hospital, Isle of Wight   180
  3 Netley Abbey Infants' School, Hampshire   188
  4 Department of Electrical Engineering, Norwegian University of Science and Technology, Trondheim   196
  5 BRF Headquarters, Copenhagen   206

Appendices   214
  A.1 Glossary   214
  A.2 The LT model   215
  A.3 LT default values   216
  A.4 Design checklist   218

Illustration acknowledgements   219
Index   220

About this book

The objective of this book is to fill in the gap between the prescriptive design guide and the building science textbook. Prescriptive guidelines are vulnerable in a field as broad as non-domestic building design, becoming unwieldy if every guideline carries too many qualifications and limitations. Understanding the principles behind such guidance allows the designer to apply his or her own qualifications, and increases the robustness of the advice. The guide is technical in that it deals with the processes and mechanisms which influence environmental performance and energy use in non-domestic buildings.

Stephen Hawking, the famous theoretical physicist, in his book *A Brief History of Time*, wrote on some of the most fundamental issues in the physics of the universe, using almost no equations or formulae. In Part One we have set ourselves a more modest task of discussing the use of energy in buildings making only minimal use of mathematics. It does not then, set out to provide the means of detailed quantitative analysis – other sources must be referred to for this purpose. A selected bibliography lists sources cited in the text.

In Part Two, the LT Method 2.0 is presented. This method offers a way to quantify the potential energy performance of non-domestic buildings at an early design stage. Data is read off from pre-computed graphs and together with a small data set of building parameters such as plan areas and façade glazing ratios, the annual energy use for heating, lighting, ventilation and cooling, can be predicted. The output is in primary energy which relates well to both cost and CO_2 emissions. Case Studies in Part Three give a critical account of real buildings which demonstrate good energy design practice. They also illustrate the principles set out in Part One and in some cases the LT Method is applied to analyse the energy performance of the building retrospectively.

A view prevails that the architectural process tends to be isolated from the analytical support of the engineering and building science professions. Rather, the latter provide support in a reactive way, accepting the basic concept and enabling it to be realised. However, there is growing evidence that the environmental performance of buildings is determined, to a considerable extent, at the conceptual stage. It is hoped that this book will provide support to the architect directly, and assist in a dialogue with the other professions, at this strategic phase in the design process.

Acknowledgements

The authors wish to acknowledge the financial support provided by the Energy Efficiency Office for earlier versions of this work and the contribution made by BRECSU staff. Important contributions were also made at these early stages by Bill Bordass, John Doggart, Max Fordham, Brian Ford, Kevin Lomas, Pat O'Sullivan, and David Turrent. The original version of this document was produced by Cambridge Architectural Research Ltd, with contributions from Helen Mulligan and Simon Ruffle and Janet Owers.

Graphics by Mike Baker, Colchester CO3 4BZ

Foreword

This book, *Energy and Environment in Architecture*, has been produced by Nick Baker and Koen Steeemers at The Martin Centre for Architecture and Urban Studies. The Martin Centre was founded by Professor Sir Leslie Martin in Cambridge in the 1960s. Early in its history the Centre became interested in how buildings use energy (in particular the relationship between energy and architectural form), developing analytical tools and computer models for analysing a wide range of factors to predict the performance of a building. The Martin Centre has never jumped on the "glass is a wonderful material" bandwagon, but Nick Baker and Koen Steemers have now collected together their experiences to produce this book.

Part One provides a mostly non-quantitative explanation of the factors in physics which describe the performance of a building. This will give architects an understanding of the principles involved and it will give engineers an insight into the kind of information which is needed to enter the architectural debate and have some influence on the form of a building. The advice should not be taken as prescriptive.

The LT Method, which is covered in Part Two of the book, may seem to be prescriptive, but when I first read it as part of the brief for an ideas competition for a building in Europe, it represented a breakthrough. The idea of the passive and non-passive zones of a building is coupled with calculations where the amount of total energy use has a minimum value when the light admitted by windows offsets the extra heat loss of those windows. I was able to explain the ideas to my co-worker architect. We then developed the ideas outside the prescribed calculations of the LT Method, but modified the calculations to show exceptionally low energy use, and won the competition. Not only that, but for me (and I hope now for everybody else), the LT Method provides a means of designing buildings with reduced energy consumption.

Read the book and then extend its thinking so that we can design buildings which need no electricity for lighting if the sun is above the horizon, need no fossil fuels for heating and no fossil fuels for cooling.

Max Fordham

Energy and environment

Chapter 1

Introduction

The energy consumption of non-domestic buildings varies over a wide range, even for buildings of similar-use types as illustrated in Figure 1.1. A well-designed daylit and naturally ventilated office building such as the BRE Low Energy Office (building no. 92 on the graph), with efficient and well-controlled plant, will have an annual energy cost less than £3.0/m²yr. On the other hand, an air-conditioned, deep-plan, overglazed building, with poor services design and control, could cost more than £45.00/m²yr.

This suggests that for many designs there is the need for significant improvement. But just what are the parameters which lead to this wide variation in performance, and to what extent are they in the control of the building

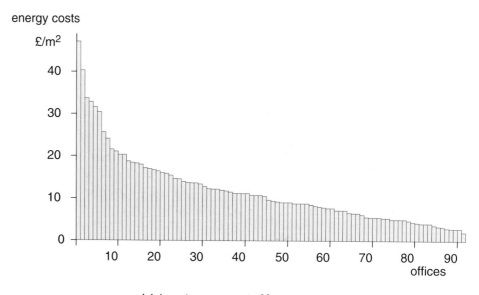

energy costs
£/m²

1.1 *Annual energy costs in 92 individual office buildings. Source: BRECSU(1).*

designer? And furthermore, can these parameters be optimised for energy performance without compromising the
comfort and well-being of the occupants?

Nearly half of the UK's energy use is accounted for in
buildings, and of this about a third is used in non-domestic
buildings (Figure 1.2). The growing awareness of the environmental effects of energy use, and the commitment to
respond by reducing energy consumption and the associated CO_2 emissions, places conservation in non-domestic
buildings high on the agenda. Equally topical is the concern
for the health and well-being of the occupants of these
buildings, in which many spend almost as great a part of
their lives as in their homes.

The purpose of this book is to reconcile these two
aims – the design of low-energy buildings without reducing the internal environmental quality. It provides the principles upon which recommendations for low-energy
design are based, and by using the LT Method, described in
Part Two, a way of testing the initial design proposals.
Whilst primarily addressing the design of new buildings,
many of the principles can be applied when refurbishing
and remodelling existing buildings.

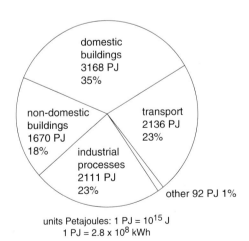

units Petajoules: 1 PJ = 10^{15} J
1 PJ = 2.8 x 10^8 kWh

1.2 *Energy by end use in the UK.*
Source: Digest of UK energy
statistics 1991.

Low-energy strategies

We have already referred to the wide range of energy consumption in buildings of similar-use type. It is important to point out that the energy consumption is by no means an indicator of the degree of comfort in buildings – indeed complaints relating to comfort are more prevalent in air-conditioned buildings which generally consume more energy than non-air-conditioned ones. Thus we have the situation where buildings which apparently achieve the same end result are consuming energy over a tenfold range. We would be somewhat surprised to find two family saloon cars returning fuel consumption figures differing as widely as 6m.p.g and 60m.p.g.! We might reasonably conclude that if the first car could get the family from A to B for ten times less than the second, then the design of the second car is seriously suspect, showing an almost immoral disregard for the environment. Why then do we tolerate this situation in buildings?

First, let us consider the factors upon which the energy performance depends. From case studies, energy audits and studies using mathematical models, a picture is beginning to emerge which provides some explanation for this. Three types of factor can be identified, as in Figure 2.1:

2.1 *Building, system and occupant factors affecting energy consumption in non-domestic buildings.*

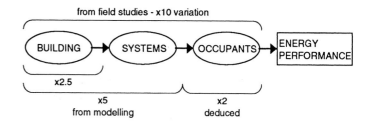

1 building design;
2 services design and performance (systems);
3 occupant behaviour.

2.2 *The original Low Energy Office at the BRE, built in 1983 and refurbished in 1991, now returns an energy cost of approximately £3.00 per annum, the lowest in the examples shown in Figure 1.1. It is a shallow-plan heavyweight building, naturally ventilated, and daylit.*

LT : LIGHTING + THERMAL

A fourth factor could be the presence of a particular activity or process in the building, such as the use of a large computer in an office building, a heavy use of energy for a swimming pool in an institutional building, or the process energy in a factory. When assessing a building's performance it is essential to be aware of these cases, and account for them separately from the energy for environmental conditioning.

The next question is – what is the relative contribution of these factors to the tenfold range in performance? From studies using the LT Method it has been found that allowing building design parameters such as plan, section, orientation and façade design to vary over a plausible range, energy use varies by about 2.5 times. If we allow the services system parameters, such as lighting efficacy, boiler efficiency, etc., to vary, this range is extended to about 5 times. Thus we can conclude that occupant factors account for the remaining twofold variation bringing the total to 10 as observed in the real data in Figure 1.1. It must be stressed, however, that these are not precise figures and contain many assumptions.

To explain this concept further, let us consider a worst case compared with a best case. A building of poor design creates a demand 2.5 times greater than one of the best design. If the bad building is equipped with services of bad design the mechanical systems will consume 2.0 times as much as the same building with good services design. If the occupants of this badly designed, badly serviced building manage the building in a wasteful way, this will create a further factor of two compared with optimum building

2.3 *Office buildings such as this, relying heavily on air-conditioning systems, often use 10 to 15 times more energy than the most energy-efficient buildings.*

are extremely important for the long-term energy and environmental performance of the building. Firstly, it is the building design factors that are the least likely to be changed. Only major refurbishment could do this, whereas services systems can be improved and may be replaced as a matter of course relatively frequently. And better management can persuade occupants to use the building more efficiently.

Secondly, there is growing evidence that the three factors (building, services and occupants) do not operate independently, that certain low-energy strategies for building design are more likely to result in better system performance and more favourable occupant behaviour.

For example, buildings with carefully controlled solar gains, moderate fabric losses and good thermal inertia require much less intervention from services systems and there is thus less opportunity for them to operate inefficiently. Furthermore, in simple shallow plan buildings, where most occupants sit close to openable windows, it is found that the occupants are much more tolerant of temperature swings and environmental conditions in general, making much less demand on the mechanical systems.

Thus it seems that strategic decisions for design have a knock-on effect and therefore much wider implications for the actual performance of a building over its lifetime than the initial energy analysis might suggest. There is also growing evidence that buildings which gain their good energy performance by adopting passive design solutions, such as daylighting and natural ventilation, also show higher occupant satisfaction. This suggests that the initial strategic moves by the designer are very important, and that it may be more appropriate to use simplified energy tools to predict performance early in design development than to use detailed simulation studies later.

The following baseline design advice could be applied at the beginning of the design development, and for most non-domestic buildings will ensure a robust solution which will probably attain 75% of the performance of a carefully optimised design. It will go some way to meet the aims of energy conservation, global environmental protection, and internal environmental quality (Figure 2.4). The purpose of the remaining material in this technical guide is to explain these strategies more fully and use them to give quantitative design guidance.

management. The commuting of the factors leads to the worst case consuming 10 times more than the best case (Figures 2.2 and 2.3).

At first sight, however, this analysis might seem rather disappointing in respect of building design guidance – why should the architect take on new constraints if the major contribution to energy performance is jointly held by the engineer and the occupants?

There are two good reasons why the strategic decisions made by the architect early in the design development

2.4 *The new BRE Low Energy Office incorporates many of the same characteristics of the earlier BRE building, but in a far more sophisticated form.*

Avoid the need for air-conditioning by employing shallow plans. This permits natural ventilation and daylighting, but unwanted solar gains must be avoided in summer by shading and correct orientation. The use of passive solar gains, particularly for ventilation pre-heat, can make modest reductions on heating load. Natural ventilation eliminates fan power; night ventilation (naturally driven or mechanical) can reduce daytime temperatures, typically by 3°C.

Controls should be easy to use and compatible with the occupant needs. Ideally controls should incorporate a 'caretaker' function, returning the building to a low-energy mode after occupant intervention. Condensing boilers, heat recovery and heat pumps can make savings in heating demand. Low-energy light sources reduce electricity demand. Combined heat and power (CHP) is a highly efficient option for larger buildings. If mechanical cooling is unavoidable, minimise load by adopting passive means (e.g. shading) or operate in mixed mode.

3

The provision of comfort

In the pursuit of energy conservation we must not forget the Vitruvian principles of commodity, firmness and delight. In this context, we read comfort for commodity; and the second underlying theme of these guidelines is that comfort should not be compromised, but in many cases improved. The pursuit of comfort is a basic drive in human behaviour, evolved for the purpose of survival (Figure 3.1), and is not just a sign of wimpishness! If the occupants of a building are subjected to discomfort for substantial periods no amount of architectural delight will compensate, nor will reduced energy bills.

However, in stressing the importance of comfort, we are not advocating an obsessive application of narrow 'optimised' environmental parameters. Providing temperatures of 21°C ± 1°C and 60% RH ± 5% does not guarantee comfort. Comfort is a far more holistic experience, being dependent upon the interaction of many environmental factors, the variability and options that the environment offers, and the ability of the occupant to determine those options. We only have to look at how people spend their holidays to realise that the feeling of well-being is not prescribed by narrow environmental limits.

This is particularly applicable to passive buildings, where conditions are naturally more variable, and it is becoming apparent that this natural variability may be a positive attribute, provided the variation remains within limits. A further requirement is that variations relate to natural or outdoor conditions, and not a fault in the control system or a quirk of the management.

Although this is good news for passive and low-

3.1 *Cave dwellings in Tunisia. The comfort-seeking behaviour of humans led primitive man to utilise the thermal stability of the ground to survive the most extreme desert climates.*

3.2 *Food is converted into work and heat. The heat has to be lost to the environment to maintain long-term equilibrium.*

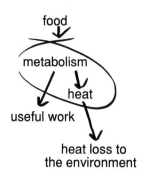

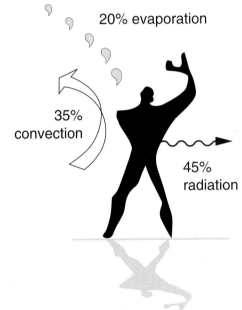

3.3 *Heat loss from the body in typical conditions.*

energy design, it makes the formulation of guidelines less straightforward than the simple 'engineering' definition of comfort conditions. Thus, the guidelines we give below stress the *avoidance* of discomfort sources, particularly those where the occupant is likely to find them unavoidable by actions such as changing position, or opening a window.

3.1 Thermal comfort

Thermal comfort is related to the thermal balance between heat gains due to the metabolism of the body and heat losses from the body to the environment (Figure 3.2). Figure 3.3 indicates the breakdown of the heat-loss mechanism: 20% by evaporation, 35% by convection, 45% by radiation. The environmental parameters controlling these components are, respectively, (a) humidity and air movement, (b) air temperature and air movement, and (c) mean radiant temperature.[1] These individual components can vary in proportion up to certain limits, provided the medium-term heat loss balances the metabolic rate. For example, we may be comfortable on a sunlit snow slope because the high radiant temperature compensates for the low air temperature and consequent high convective losses.

Most of the causes of discomfort can be explained by long-term imbalance of losses and metabolic gains, or extreme values of one of the environmental parameters.

It is also helpful to understand the influence on comfort of a person's activity (described by their metabolic rate) and their clothing level. This is indicated in Figure 3.4, which shows the thermal comfort zone as a function of metabolic rate and clothing level. It underlines the wastefulness of, for example, heating a department store in winter to generous indoor temperatures when the majority of people will be in outdoor clothing. Similarly, stairways and circulation areas should be at lower temperatures to allow for the higher activity levels.

A number of particular areas where care must be taken to avoid conflicts between passive and low-energy measures, and comfort, are listed below. Many of the technical design solutions are discussed in more detail later in this book, as indicated by the references in square brackets.[2]

1   Avoid underheating of the space by providing sufficient heating plant and emitter capacity. Do not underestimate the heating load during the pre-heating period.

---

1 The Mean Radiant Temperature (MRT) is approximately equal to the average temperature (area weighted) of all the surfaces surrounding the point of interest.

2 There are three kinds of referencing in this volume. Numbers in square brackets, e.g. [2.3], cross-refer to other sections. Numbers in parentheses, e.g. (6), refer to sources found in the list of references (see pp. 96, 172). Footnotes are indicated by superscript numbers. Reference is also made in the text to documents listed in the Select Bibliography (see p. 227).

3.4 *The influence of activity and clothing on thermal comfort zones.*

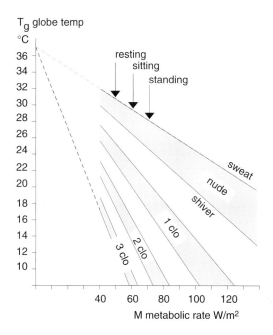

a normal suit has insulation
approximately equal to 1 clo unit

2   Avoid overheating the space in relation to occupant activity level and clothing.

3   Avoid local radiant heat loss and down-draughts due to proximity to large areas of glazing (Figure 3.5) by attention to room layout, use of multiple or low-e glazing, and careful positioning of heat emitters.

4   In air-conditioned buildings, consider the positioning of inlet and outlet grilles to give good air distribution without local draughts – more important in low-energy buildings where delivery temperatures may be low.

5   Avoid overheating the space from solar [5.2] and casual gains [5.3], by use of shading, ventilation [5.4], and providing local thermostatic control [5.2]. Avoid lightweight internal surfaces [5.5].

6   Avoid local overheating of occupants by direct sunlight by providing shaded areas. There can be a conflict between local overheating and the desire to maximise thermal and daylighting benefits of solar radiation (Figures 3.6 and 3.7).

3.5 *Radiant heat loss and cold down-draughts can cause thermal discomfort.*

3.7 *Continuous glazing provides no opportunity to avoid direct sun in the perimeter zone. Intermittent glazing results in patches of shade.*

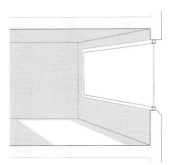

3.6 *Interior showing sunlight penetration together with large areas of shade (Darwin College Library, Cambridge).*

3.8 *Elements used for natural ventilation were often celebrated in Victorian school architecture.*

3.2 Indoor air quality

Indoor air quality has always been a proper concern for the architect. Indeed, the Victorian architects addressed it very explicitly, and ventilation chimneys, cupolas and grilles became part of the architectural vocabulary, especially evident in school and hospital buildings (Figure 3.8). A century ago, the concern was to get rid of products of human occupancy, and from combustion, and the prevailing principle was 'the more ventilation the better'.

In the last few decades however, the situation has changed, since concerns for energy conservation have encouraged both lower controlled ventilation rates and far-lower uncontrolled infiltration rates. Meanwhile new and more sinister pollution sources have appeared, especially in the workplace. These include ozone from photocopiers and laser printers, volatile organics from cleaning materials, paints and adhesives, plastic furnishings, etc., and faecal particles from the house dust mite. Furthermore, although the Clean Air Act has visibly cleaned up outdoor air, pollution from transportation has increased enormously, creating carbon monoxide, oxides of sulphur and nitrogen, and the most recently discovered hazard – PM10s; that is, carbon particles less than 10 microns in diameter.

The outdoor conditions are not usually within the scope of the designer to control, although it is as well to be aware of them in choosing fresh air inlets, whether for natural or mechanical ventilation. Indoor air quality, on the other hand, is influenced by design and specification.

It is often claimed that the only way of obtaining guaranteed air quality is to mechanically ventilate. This is only partly true – whilst specific rates cannot be guaranteed at any particular instant, the performance of a natural ventilation system has to be assessed on a probabilistic basis, i.e. the average air quality is satisfactory provided the ventilation rate drops below a minimum value only rarely. Ventilation is dealt with in more detail in Chapter 7. Listed below are a number of strategic objectives.

1   To reconcile the conflict between air quality (high rates of ventilation) and energy conservation (low rates of ventilation) consider heat recovery [10.6] or solar ventilation pre-heat [9.2].

2   Consider seasonal use of windows – i.e. permit casual window opening by occupants at times of the year when this will not seriously impair comfort or energy performance.
3   When providing natural ventilation for winter conditions, avoid causing local draughts and temperature gradients by appropriate design of the openings.
4   Natural ventilation may be impractical in noisy sites, such as adjacent to a motorway or under the flight path to an airport, but with careful design may be possible in most urban environments [3.4].

3.3 Visual comfort

It is common experience that visual performance is in some way dependent upon the lighting level. Both too little and too much light result in eye strain and discomfort. When specifying artificial lighting, illuminance standards can be met quite precisely. However, due to the variability of the sky as a light source, ensuring adequate illuminance under daylighting conditions is more complex, as are all aspects of visual comfort.

The designer must be aware that there are other parameters which affect visual comfort. These include freedom from glare, freedom from veiling reflections (Figure 3.9) and, particularly in the case of artificial lighting, colour rendering. Furthermore, both daylighting and

3.9 *Daylit rooms for VDUs present particular problems. Veiling reflections of windows or sunpatches may cause both discomfort and disability.*

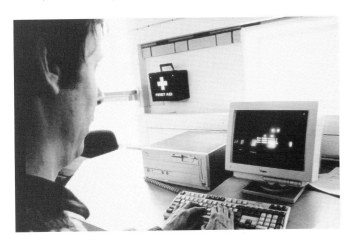

artificial lighting have an important role in expressing the architectural intentions of the building, and hence may affect the pleasure and well-being of the occupants. Windows usually have the dual function of providing daylight and views out. The association of these in the mind of the occupant is positive – i.e. the limitations of daylight may be more readily accepted if the window provides pleasant views.

Daylighting design is dealt with in more detail in Chapter 6. Here we list a number of strategic objectives.

1. The design should ensure that all permanent workplaces are daylit for the majority of the hours of daylight.
2. Sufficient illumination must be provided to enable the occupants to carry out their particular tasks in comfort.
3. Large areas of vertical glazing for deep daylight penetration will need careful detailed design, possibly including redirecting elements such as light shelves, to avoid glare from direct sunlight and bright diffuse sky.
4. Consider the positioning and reflectance of surfaces both inside and outside the building to minimise the risk of glare.
5. Artificial illumination should be low in glare and of good colour rendering, especially in areas where occupants spend long periods. This consideration should influence choice of both lamp and luminaire.
6. Where automatic light-switching controls are used, ensure that they do not create irritation and interfer-

ence to occupants. Dimming controls may be preferable to on/off controls.

7. Both daylighting and artificial lighting should be designed with recognition of the tasks to be carried out in the space. For example, special consideration will have to be given to the growing use of VDUs in all kinds of non-domestic buildings.

3.4   Acoustic comfort

There are three major areas of conflict between acoustic comfort and passive building design. Firstly, the use of heavyweight surfaces to provide thermal mass [5.5] will reduce the acoustic absorption and lead to a reverberant space. This allows noise levels to build up and affects speech intelligibility. Secondly, the provision of ventilation paths through partitions and internal windows [7.3] may lead to noise propagation and privacy problems. Thirdly, outdoor conditions, e.g. heavy road-traffic noise, may prevent openable windows from being used.

For internally generated sound much knowledge exists, gained largely from interest in the open-plan office. However, much of this knowledge applies to air-conditioned spaces, and this has to be carefully adapted for naturally ventilated spaces. For example many open-plan offices have highly acoustically absorbent suspended ceilings and carpeted floors and rely on the ventilation systems to provide masking noise to maintain privacy. Detailed design for noise control is beyond the scope of this book and it is recommended that specialist sources are consulted and advice sought. Some publications are listed in the bibliography (see p. 227). Listed below are a few initial recommendations.

1. Provide 'free-standing' acoustic absorption by partitions, drapes, baffles, etc., whilst maintaining access to thermal mass (Figures 3.10 and 3.11). This is especially relevant, also, in large volumes such as atria [9.3].
2. Place acoustic absorbers at critical positions in air-flow paths to reduce reflections of noise between zones via hard surfaces (Figure 3.11).
3. Care should be taken to avoid excessive absorption at

3.11 Provision of both acoustic absorbent surfaces and exposed thermal mass.

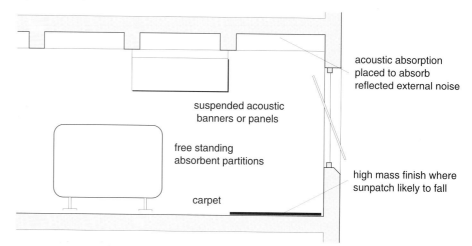

acoustic absorption placed to absorb reflected external noise

suspended acoustic banners or panels

free standing absorbent partitions

high mass finish where sunpatch likely to fall

carpet

3.10 Acoustic absorbing ceiling treatment which allows thermal coupling to the massive floor slab (Lycée de Blain, France).

desk level without ensuring that ceiling reflections are minimised. Otherwise local quiet conditions will lead to a loss of acoustic privacy by unattenuated reflections from the ceiling.

4   Consider the detailed design of window openings in order to reduce transmitted sound whilst providing adequate air-flow (Figure 3.12).
5   Staggered opening double windows, acoustic-attenuating ventilators, and glazed angled reflectors, provide varying degrees of attentuation and will be appropriate for sources of external noise (Figures 3.13 and 3.14).

3.5 Adaptive opportunity and control

There is a growing body of evidence to show that people are comfortable in environments where conditions fall well outside the strict comfort limits used by engineers to specify air-conditioned buildings. This is especially true in summer conditions. There is also considerable evidence that even in highly controlled environments, quite poor levels of occupant satisfaction still persist.

Explanations of this phenomenon generally refer to 'adaptive behaviour'; that is, where the occupant takes some kind of action which improves his or her comfort. This could include, for example, moving out of a patch of sunlight, deploying a blind, or removing an article of clothing.

It has been suggested that the necessity to do this is not a bad thing, provided that the opportunity to take the action exists. Figure 3.15 shows a workspace rich in adaptive opportunity. This opportunity would be eliminated by continuous ribbon glazing, absence of sunblinds, and strict dress code respectively. Note that the first two are design-dependent.

The satisfying nature of these adaptive actions can be explained by our evolved response to the natural physical environment. This trait which first drove man into the thermally stable environment of the cave, ultimately led to the colonisation of the entire globe (apart from Antarctica) without the use of fossil fuel.

3.13 *Proprietary window system with glass panel to reflect traffic noise away from ventilation opening.*

3.12 *The influence of window design on noise transmission when open.*

3.13 *Proprietary window system with glass panel to reflect traffic noise away from ventilation opening.*

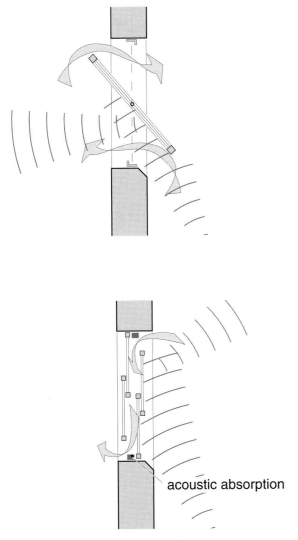

acoustic absorption

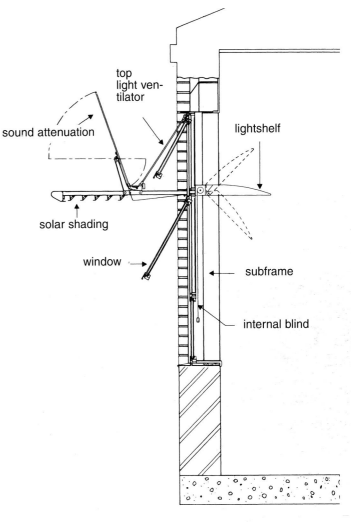

top light ventilator

sound attenuation

lightshelf

solar shading

window

subframe

internal blind

Furthermore, it has been observed that people sitting close to windows, and therefore being able to experience the outdoor climate visually, seem to be more tolerant of variations in the indoor climate provided they relate logically to outdoor conditions – i.e. people expect to feel hotter on a sunny day. Conversely an occupant will feel very intolerant if they know that the sensation of hotness is due to a faulty air-conditioning system about which they have no control.

The provision of adaptive opportunity seems to have the effect of expanding the conventional comfort zone, as indicated in Figure 3.16. It is also suggested that the opportunity for adaptive behaviour makes a positive contribution to the occupants' overall satisfaction with the building, even if the adaptive action is not taken. This explains why people tolerate far less strict conditions in their homes, where they have total control, than in their workplaces. Engineers, on the other hand, resist personal control mainly on the

3.14 *Proprietary ventilator providing 47 dBA of sound reduction compared with 10 dBA of a partially open window.*

220 mm

260 mm

perforated sheet facing to acoustic lining

140 mm

casing

steel plate baffle

pre-formed mineral wool acoustic fitting

47mm diameter perforated tube

steel plate baffle

outer baffle assembly

exterior louvred plate

grounds of energy conservation. This is ironic since in most cases it is highly controlled air-conditioned buildings which are amongst the highest energy users.

Whilst most of the discussion above has made reference to the thermal environment, the broad principles can be applied to other environmental aspects such as lighting and acoustics.

The main strategic objectives are:

1 Limit extreme conditions by the inherent properties of the building (in the case of thermal comfort by thermal mass, ventilation and shading).

2 Where possible give the occupant the option to control his/her local environment, but interaction between occupants must be considered.

3 User controls should have 'caretaker' functions which return the building to a status optimised for energy conservation and average comfort conditions. This could be achieved by a building energy management system (BEMS) or local 'intelligence' (e.g. occupancy-detecting light switch).

4 Design the controls to be ergonomically convenient and easily understood.

3.15 *A workspace rich in adaptive opportunity (Housing 21, London).*

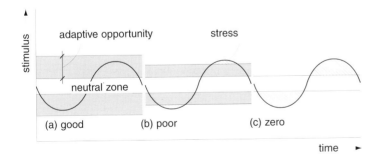

3.16 *The comfort zone is in effect extended by the presence of adaptive opportunity.*

Comfort in buildings should be considered as the absence of long-term extreme values of environmental comfort parameters, rather than the maintenance of precise and close limits. The overall satisfaction of the occupants will be influenced by the building's own climate-modifying performance, the occupant's ability to adapt the building by means of controls, and the freedom of the occupant to take adaptive behavioural actions.

Heating

Non-domestic buildings tend to be more densely occupied than domestic buildings and, being deeper in plan, have to rely more on artificial lighting. This leads to high levels of internal heat gain. However, the surface area to volume ratio tends to reduce in larger buildings, thus reducing fabric losses in relation to floor area.

Two important points follow from this – firstly the insulation value of the envelope becomes less important, and secondly the internal gains alone are often sufficient to meet the heating demand for prolonged periods.

When the heating load is equal to the internal heat gains the thermal balance point is said to have been reached. For buildings of high insulation and high gains this point can be at a very low temperature. This is indicated in Figure 4.1 which shows a graph of the heating demand of a building as a function of external temperature. It shows

4.1 *The thermal balance point: the external temperature at which the heat losses from the building equal the heat gains. The graph shows the net heating demand (kW) plotted against external temperature °C.*

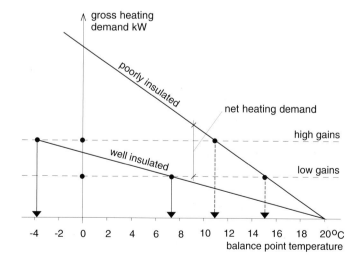

4.2 *Delivered energy use for naturally ventilated and air-conditioned offices in the UK. Source: BRECSU (3).*

4.3 *Primary energy use for naturally ventilated and air-conditioned offices in the UK. Source: BRECSU (3).*

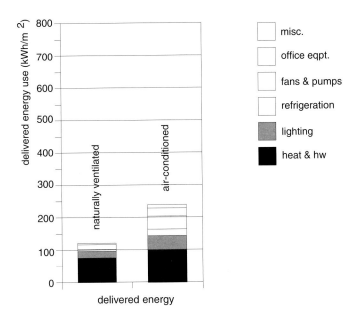

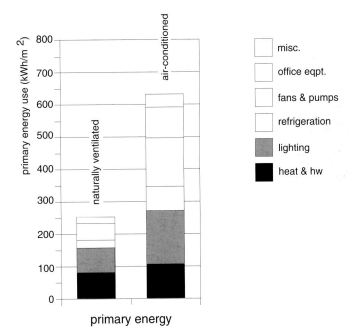

that for the well-insulated building with high internal heat gains, this occurs at –4°C whilst for a poorly insulated low gains building, it is as high as 15°C.

However, a balance point at a low temperature, achieved partly by gains from high levels of artificial lighting and other electrical equipment, will be expensive in energy terms. In addition, if the balance point is comparable with prevailing winter temperatures then in summer the building will overheat, and may have to be mechanically cooled, at the expense of further energy consumption.

For the past three decades there has been an emphasis on reducing heat loads in non-domestic buildings, whilst other energy uses have been somewhat neglected. This stems partly from a simple extension of energy conservation techniques in housing to the non-domestic sector. It must also be due to a consistent lack of attention to the significance of electrical loads for lighting and mechanical ventilation.

This is illustrated in Figure 4.2 which gives the results of an energy audit of office buildings in the UK generally representing good practice. It shows that for delivered energy in naturally ventilated daylit buildings, heating is greater than the rest of the energy inputs. But for air-conditioned buildings the heating energy is about the same as that used for lighting, fans, pumps and refrigeration.

However, a truer picture is given by a breakdown of primary[1] energy use. Primary energy is the value of the energy at source – in the case of electricity it is the energy value of the coal or oil used to raise the steam which powers the turbines. This is shown in Figure 4.3 and it is clear that even for naturally lit and ventilated buildings, heating is not the largest energy user. For air-conditioned buildings, heating is only about one quarter of the primary energy used for lighting, fan power and pumps. A more detailed discussion of primary energy is given in Chapter 10.

---

1 Primary energy relates closely to CO_2 production and other environmental impacts. For electricity production it depends upon the mix of coal, oil, gas, nuclear power and renewable energies such as hydropower and wind power which is also used for generation. Primary energy also relates well to cost.

4.4 *Solar radiation absorbed generates heat which is then redistributed by long-wave radiation, convection and conduction.*

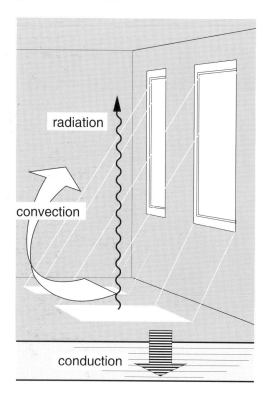

4.5 *Solar Utilisation Factor showing fraction of useful solar gains as a function of solar gains/loss ratio for medium-weight office building. Source: van Dijk and Arkesteijn (4).*

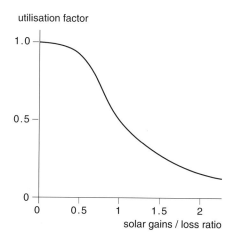

4.1 Useful solar gains and thermal mass

Although the requirement for heating in non-domestic buildings may be modest, there will often be a heating requirement in the early part of the day before the building fabric has warmed up. Also, small non-domestic buildings (of a domestic scale) may have significant heating loads due to fabric losses and infiltration.

Solar gains through glazing (Figure 4.4) can be usefully employed partially to meet these loads, which results in reductions in the heat required from the auxiliary heating system. However, owing to the fact that most non-domestic buildings require pre-heating early in the day, before significant solar gains are available, the potential for useful solar space heating is limited in a relatively mild climate such as that of the UK. Thermal mass, usually forming part of the structure of the building, plays an important role in

storing these gains until required, and reducing the chance of overheating during the period of insolation [5.5].

It follows that buildings with low internal gains are most likely to benefit from solar gains, and orientations to the east of south are more likely to yield useful solar gains. Orientations to the west of south result in solar gains in the afternoon when the building is already heated, and ambient temperatures are at a maximum. South-westerly glazing orientations are most likely to lead to overheating in the summer.

The size of the raw solar gain entering a room can be easily calculated.[2] However, the usefulness of the gain depends on the instantaneous demand for heat; if the heat demand is large in comparison with solar gain, almost all of the solar energy will be useful. On the other hand if the demand for heat is small, then the fraction of useful solar energy will be smaller.

Simplified calculation methods use Utilisation Factors to evaluate the usefulness of solar gain. The curve illustrated in Figure 4.5 shows the monthly utilisation factor for

---

2 The solar gain is given by: $W_s = I . A . sg$

where **W_s** is the solar gain, **I** is the incident solar radiation (W/m²), **A** is the area of glazing (m²), and **sg** is the solar gain factor which is mainly influenced by the transmittance of the glazing.

Giving typical values for a room 6m × 6m with 8m² of glazing on one side:

$$W_s = 600 \times 8 \times 0.75 \quad = 3600 \text{ W or } 3.6 \text{ kW}$$

4.6 *Netley School in Hampshire uses solar gains in the conservatory to pre-heat ventilation air for the classrooms.*

gains made in a medium heavyweight office building. Note that only about 60% of the gains are useful, when the total gain is equal to the loss (GLR=1), and that the utilisation falls off rapidly for higher gains to loss ratios.

The most promising use of solar energy in non-domestic buildings is for ventilation pre-heating. Unless heat recovery systems are employed, buildings require energy to pre-heat ventilation air throughout the occupied period during the heating season. If solar gains can be used to offset this ventilation heat load, a better utilisation of solar energy can be made. This is normally done using a secondary space such as a conservatory or atrium (Figure 4.6), or a specialised element such as a cladding or roof-space collector (Figure 4.7).

4.7 *Cladding and roofspace solar collector used to pre-heat air for ventilation.*

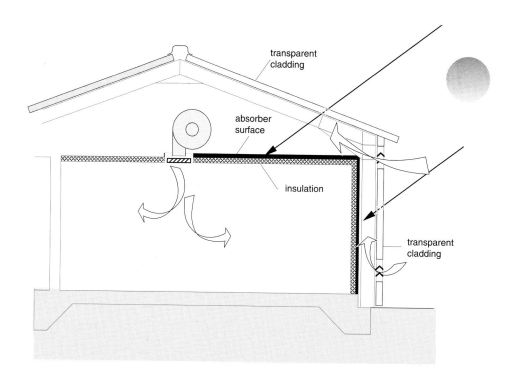

4.2 Thermal balance of glazing

Although glazing can admit useful solar energy it is a poor insulator. For example, double glazing has a thermal conductance about five times that of a moderately insulated opaque wall. As the area of glazing is increased to collect more solar energy, the heat losses through the glazing are increased.

Due to the effect of the solar gain to heat loss ratio (described above), in principle optimum values for glazing areas exist above which the glazing would lose more heat than it gained. However, the optimum is very shallow and in practice the most significant parameter is the insulation value of the glazing system (Figure 4.8). Curves of this type are produced by computer simulations and many factors are found to be significant. For example, for buildings used

mainly during the evening, the heating demand will not coincide with the availability of solar gain. This results in a poorer net energy balance at the glazing. The thermal performance of the glazing can be improved with the use of curtains or shutters or night insulation. The overall energy balance of the glazing can also be improved if the building can store heat gained during the day in the thermal mass of the structure. In the non-domestic sector, small buildings with low internal gains could be expected to show a similar behaviour.

Curves for energy use in typical office buildings (Figure 4.9), derived from the LT Model,[3] actually show a slight increase in heating energy demand, even for south-facing double glazing. The total energy demand for heating and lighting shows almost no increase with glazing area, after a shallow minimum, since the increas-

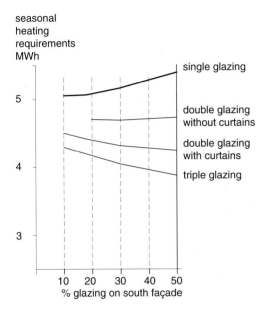

4.8 *Annual heating requirements as a function of glazing ratio of south façade, for houses in the UK. Source: ETSU (5).*

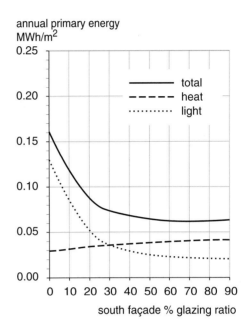

4.9 *LT curves showing relation between heating and lighting energy as a function of glazing ratio for a south-facing office in the UK.*

ing heat loss is partially offset by the decrease in the need for artificial lighting. However, large glazing areas increase the risk of overheating [5.2] and local cold discomfort and are therefore not recommended. The graph for north-facing glazing would show a strong increase in heating energy with glazing area, since the solar gains from the diffuse sky would be insufficient to offset the heat losses.

---

3   The LT Model is a mathematical model representing the main energy flows in a non-domestic building. It quantifies energy use for heating, lighting and cooling, taking account of interactions between them. It was used to generate the curves used for the LT Method described in Part Two and the model is described in more detail in Appendix 2 [pp. 223-24].

4.3 Orientation and overshadowing

It follows that for heating energy conservation the orientation of larger buildings is not highly critical. Although the maximum incident solar radiation in winter on a vertical surface occurs for an orientation which is due south (Figure 4.10), in temperate climates such as the UK, more easterly orientations will result in a greater displacement of auxiliary heating energy, and less risk of overheating than southerly or south-westerly orientations, since the gains will be made earlier in the day when a greater heating demand exists.

Inclined south-facing surfaces receive more radiation than vertical surfaces, and also receive significantly more in the summer, due to the higher sun angle. This can lead to unwanted solar gains. In general, sloping glass should only be used in cool high latitude climates, or for atria and conservatories with shading devices. It should be kept to a minimum in densely occupied areas.

Overshadowing, characterised by the Urban Horizon Angle (that is, the average angle of elevation of the surrounding buildings (Figure 12.8 in Part Two)), has a significant influence on the solar thermal contribution (Figure 4.11). This is because the greatest demand for solar heating occurs in the winter when solar altitudes are low, and hence the obstruction due to neighbouring buildings is likely to be significant. Note that the sensitivity arises because the energy balance is changed – heat is still lost from the glazing without the compensatory solar gain.

However, when considered in relation to total energy consumption, orientation and overshadowing will be seen to have more impact on lighting and cooling energy. This is not surprising when one considers the relative magnitude of these components to the total, as already illustrated by the data from real buildings shown in Figure 4.3. This is also demonstrated by the LT Method Urban Horizon Factors [12.7].

4.4 Insulation and cold bridges

It has already been pointed out that due to the envelope surface area to volume ratio (and hence, floor area to volume ratio) becoming smaller the larger the building, together with the high internal gains due to dense occupation, heating demands for non-domestic buildings are usually small in comparison with other energy uses (Figure 4.3). It follows that the benefits of high levels of insulation are less significant in larger buildings, and it is unlikely that 'super-insulation', i.e. standards well above those demanded by current Building Regulations, will make significant savings in larger buildings.

However, the demand for shallow plan buildings in order to facilitate daylighting and natural ventilation does result in an increase in surface area to volume ratio. Increased insulation standards can compensate for this. Conventional heat loss calculations for a proposed design will enable a simple index of merit – total heat loss through the envelope per square metre of floor area, to be evaluated, and a figure less than 1.0 would be an appropriate target.

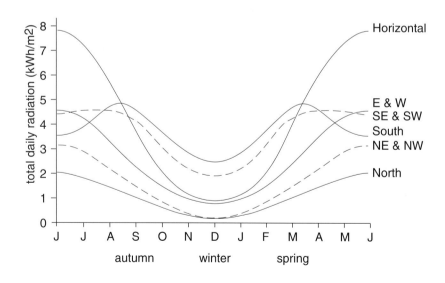

4.10 *Daily solar radiation falling on horizontal and vertical surfaces in southern UK.*

In many constructions, the insulation layer may be breached by structural elements which by necessity are dense and have high thermal conduction. During the heating season this causes areas of low surface temperature within the building which may subsequently cause condensation and mould growth. This is undesirable for both aesthetic and functional reasons, and in some cases can lead to structural damage. A number of design guides exist for the avoidance of cold bridges in new design and refurbishment.

From the point of view of energy consumption, in most common constructions, cold bridges would increase the total heat loss from the envelope by only a few per cent, so this is not the main motivation for their avoidance. In modern structures envelope losses are dominated by losses through the glazing, which are in fact cold bridges, but are not amenable to conventional insulation treatment.

Heating loads in non-domestic buildings tend to be small in relation to other energy uses – energy conservation is not just a matter of minimising heat loss. Solar gains may be used to reduce the requirement for auxiliary heating. The fraction of the solar gain which is useful decreases with the increase in the ratio of solar gain to heat load. Because of the low insulation value of glazing, the energy balance between useful solar gains and conductive losses has to be considered. However, the value of the glazing for admitting daylight also affects the energy balance.

The heating energy of non-domestic buildings is not critically dependent on orientation. During the heating season most solar radiation falls on south-facing surfaces. However, due to the small demand for heating by midday, glazing facing south-east will have a better overall heat balance. Sloping south-facing glazing causes higher gains, but may cause overheating in summer unless shaded and ventilated.

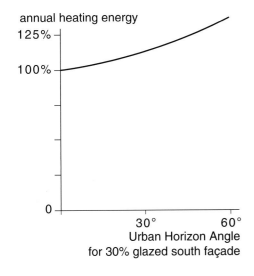

4.11 *Influence of Urban Horizon Angle on annual heating energy for south-facing office (from LT Method).*

5

Prevention of overheating

Non-domestic buildings tend to be densely occupied, and to have heat gains from equipment and lights (Figure 5.1). They generally have lower surface area to volume ratios than smaller domestic buildings, and hence lower fabric losses. They are occupied during the daytime when the air temperature is at its highest and when solar gains are most likely to be present. These factors often result in overheating unless steps are taken to avoid it.

Traditionally most large buildings had shallow plans. Where deeper spaces were essential they were designed with large floor-to-ceiling heights. Overheating was prevented by having large openings for natural ventilation and by relying on natural rather than artificial light. The buildings tended to be thermally massive, acting as heat sinks, providing internal temperatures close to the average 24-hour temperature.

In contrast, many modern buildings have deep plans with low ceilings, are highly glazed and are constructed of lightweight materials and finishes. In these buildings many of the elements of the traditional building which had helped to provide a comfortable thermal environment have been eliminated. This, together with increased gains from equipment and permanent artificial lighting, results in overheated conditions unless mechanical cooling is provided. The latter usually leads to very high energy consumption.

There is now an increased awareness of the benefits of passive approaches to energy conservation. Three alternative strategies are relevant here. The first strategy is the avoidance of mechanical cooling (Figure 5.2). This should be possible for most shallow plan buildings on cooler European sites, except where excessive noise or atmospheric pollution exists. Where this strategy is not possible

5.1 *Densely occupied modern office with gains from lighting and equipment.*

5.2 *The new Low Energy Office at the BRE is naturally ventilated in all occupied spaces.*

5.3 *This office building at No. 1 Bridewell Street in Bristol is air-conditioned but is a low-energy consumer due to the adoption of passive load-reducing strategies.*

the second strategy of reduction has to be adopted (Figure 5.3). Here, passive measures such as shading, insulation and avoidance of unnecessary artificial lighting, for example, are used to reduce the daytime mechanical cooling loads to a minimum.

The third strategy is a combination of the first two. This is referred to as mixed mode (Figure 5.4) and covers two conditions where a building:

1 has its perimeter zone operating in passive mode (with openable windows etc.) and air-conditioning is used only in certain internal spaces or where there are particular environmental requirements, or

2 operates for part of the year in a passive mode, and only adopts air-conditioning during extreme (warm) conditions. This is commonly provided by local packaged or stand-alone units and is often referred to as 'comfort cooling'.

5.4 *The National Farmers' Union building, Stratford-upon-Avon operates under mixed mode - partially naturally ventilated, with mechanical fresh-air supply in winter and comfort cooling in summer.*

This third strategy looks promising as a low-energy solution to large, medium-deep plan buildings, but needs careful engineering design to ensure that the interaction between the passive and air-conditioned zones does not lead to energy wastage. An example of this is shown in Figure 5.5, where solar gains in a south-facing zone could prompt window opening, which in turn could create cross-ventilation taking cooled air from the central air-conditioned zone into the north perimeter zone which would then require heating.

In a building which is not air-conditioned, comfort conditions can be improved if passive methods of avoiding overheating are employed. In an air-conditioned building the benefit is realised in reduced running costs. In most cases the same passive measures can be applied in both strategies, although natural ventilation is not applied in the

5.5 *Simultaneous heating and cooling caused by window opening in a mixed mode building.*

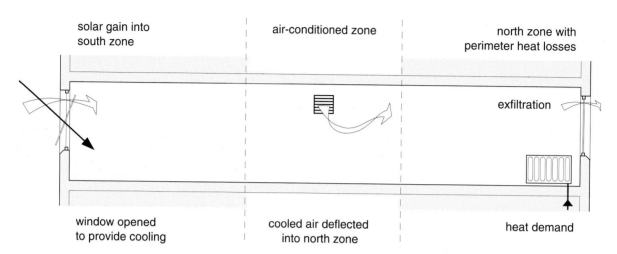

solar gain into south zone

air-conditioned zone

north zone with perimeter heat losses

exfiltration

window opened to provide cooling

cooled air deflected into north zone

heat demand

5.6 *The sources of heat gains likely to cause overheating.*

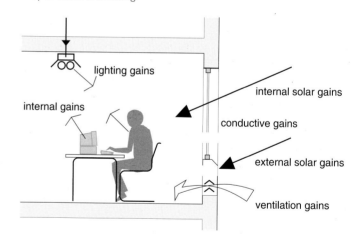

lighting gains

internal gains

internal solar gains

conductive gains

external solar gains

ventilation gains

same way to both passive and air-conditioned buildings [Chapter 7].

5.1 Cooling load reduction

The main gains which create overheating or the need for cooling are shown in Figure 5.6, and can be simply classified as follows:

1 *External solar gains:* the heating effect of solar radiation on external surfaces conducted into the building interior.
2 *Internal solar gains:* solar radiation passing through windows.
3 *Conductive gains:* heat flowing from the hot air outside to the cooler interior through opaque fabric and glazing.
4 *Ventilation gains:* heat carried into the building by warm fresh air introduced to replace stale but cooler air.
5 *Artificial lighting gains.*
6 *Internal gains:* from occupants and equipment.

Reduction at source is always the best strategy. However, residual gains may be rejected by ventilation, provided external air temperature is below internal air temperature [p. 37]. The effect of the gains may also be moderated by the presence of large areas of medium or heavyweight (high admittance) exposed internal surfaces.

5.2 Shading and orientation (reduction of solar gains)

External solar gains

External solar gains are the gains due to solar energy being absorbed on the outside of the building, heating up the surface and then transmitting this heat to the inside through the fabric. Typical UK summer surface temperatures in direct sun are about 35°C for a light-coloured surface and as high as 45°C for a dark surface. For a building with an interior temperature of 25°C and an outdoor air temperature of 30°C, this effect increases the temperature differential by ×2 and ×4 respectively.

In cool climates such as the UK, the insulation value of walls and roofs has been established from considerations of heat retention during the heating season. Values required by current Building Regulations are sufficient to control external solar gains in summer. However, in cases of refurbishment of existing poorly insulated buildings, the benefit of adding insulation may be greater in reducing the cooling load than reducing the heating load. This is particularly true of poorly insulated flat roofs on deep plan buildings.

The following methods to reduce external solar gains are available:

1 Shade external building surfaces, particularly roof and east and west walls. This could be done by other buildings, in which case it may influence the positioning of the new building on the site, or by vegetation. It is unlikely that external shading screens would be worth while for the moderate UK climate, although this technique is appropriate in hotter climates.

2 Use light-coloured external finishes, e.g. paint or chippings, to reflect radiation (Figure 5.7).

3 Ventilate existing cavities; in new build, insulation is more effective than cavities of the same thickness, but if they are incorporated use low-emissivity surfaces (e.g. aluminium foil) facing the cavity (Figure 5.8).

4 Heavyweight envelope construction can delay the ingress of solar gain until the unoccupied period. These gains can subsequently be rejected by ventilation.

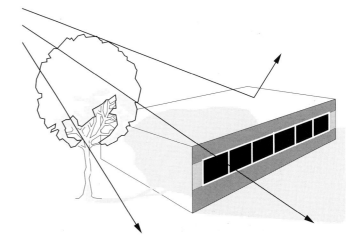

5.7 *Shading by vegetation and the use of light-coloured surfaces to reduce solar gains to the envelope.*

However, the main value of thermal mass is to absorb internal gains [5.5].

5 Insulate surfaces which receive sun. For heavyweight construction external insulation will be more effective than internal insulation since it prevents the build-up of heat and its retention in the massive element. This is particularly relevant to retrofit insulation on flat roofs.

Internal solar gains

Solar gains made through windows are likely to have the greatest impact except in buildings with very poor insulation standards. Typically, direct sunlight falling onto a window can create about 0.5kW/m² of heat gain. A 5m × 5m office with 6m² of glazing would receive 3kW, about 5 times greater than the heat gains from 3 occupants and 3 PCs.

The first line of defence is to consider the orientation of the building, if this is an option. The major glazed façades should face south or north, the former receiving useful gains in winter but relatively little in summer due to the high solar elevation. Rooms facing west and south-west are particularly vulnerable to overheating from solar gains. Even sloping rooflights facing north-east can contribute to overheating in summer.

After orientation, the next line of defence is shading. The purpose of shading is to reduce the amount of radi-

5.8 *Ventilated cavity with low-emissivity foil to provide protection from solar gains.*

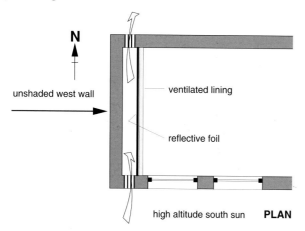

5.10 *The performance of shading by internal and external louvres.*

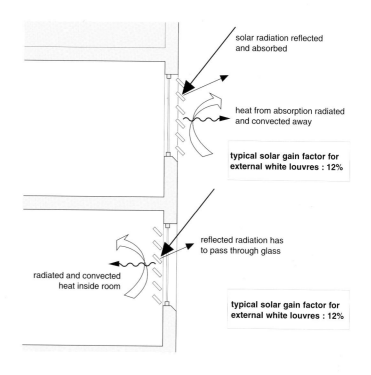

ant energy passing into the room. This reduces the heat gain to the room, when the radiation is absorbed by the room surfaces. Shading may also be important in preventing solar radiation from falling directly onto occupants. This can typically increase the effective temperature experienced by a person by about 6°C (Figure 5.9).

Overheating can take place in the heating season. A south-facing room may require no heat, or even cooling, whilst a north-facing room in the same building requires heat. Local thermostatic control can respond to this.

5.9 *The effect of direct radiation on the effective temperature as experienced by a person.*

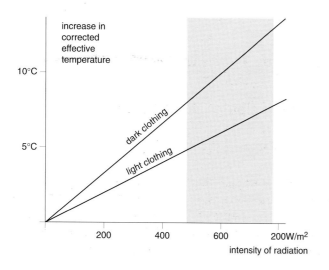

The main measures to minimise the impact of internal solar gain are:

1   Prevent the ingress of direct solar radiation by shading; external shading is more effective than internal shading (Figure 5.10). Louvres between panes of double or triple glazing have a shading performance approaching that of external louvres, but at lower cost.

2   Movable shades give better response to varying sky conditions than fixed overhangs, which respond to seasonal solar elevation only (Figure 5.11). Fixed shades often compromise daylighting during times of lower sky luminance [Chapter 6].

3   Gains from west-facing glazing are more likely to cause overheating than gains from south-facing glazing. Gains from east-facing glazing can sometimes cause overheating in lightweight buildings or buildings with lightweight finishes.

4   Types of shading devices (Figure 5.12) perform differ-

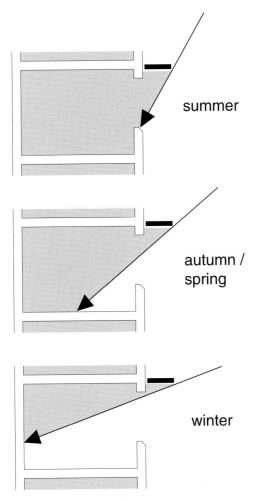

5.11 *The transmission of solar radiation beneath fixed overhangs responds to solar elevation but does not synchronise well with seasonal heat demand and the need for daylight.*

summer

autumn / spring

winter

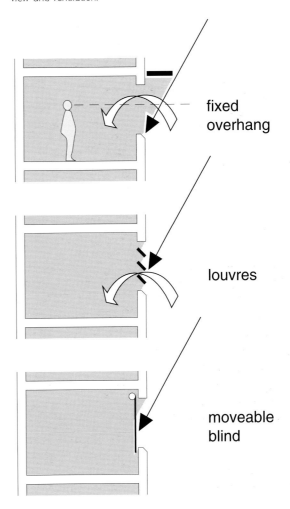

5.12 *Three classes of shading devices having different effects on view and ventilation.*

fixed overhang

louvres

moveable blind

ently with respect to ventilation and view. Blinds are obviously a poor choice for openable windows which provide summer ventilation, or where view is important.

5   The use of tinted and reflective glass is not recommended as a shading strategy. Most of these materials reduce the daylight by a similar or greater factor than their thermal shading coefficient, and thus offer no advantage over using smaller glazing areas. Recently developed high-performance types do reduce the thermal gain by a greater factor than the light transmittance, but this does not affect their heat loss in winter which is higher than insulated opaque wall.

6   Install local thermostats, especially in zones of different orientation.

5.3 Reduction of other heat gains

Conductive gains

This is the conductive heat flow through opaque fabric and windows, when the external temperature is higher than the internal temperature. These gains are likely to be relatively small, except in very hot climates. In the UK the proportion of time that the air temperature is above an appropriate cooling set point is very small. External solar gains are likely to be considerably greater; the surface temperature due to solar radiation will always be higher than the air temperature. Conductive gains will be reduced by:

1 Insulation of the opaque envelope.
2 Double glazing or low-e glazing.

Ventilation gains

As above, these occur when the outside air temperature is above internal temperature. Although this occurs relatively rarely, significant gains could be made in a mixed mode building. To minimise ventilation gains:

1 Minimise the fresh-air ventilation rate when the external air temperature is above the internal temperature.
2 Use desk or ceiling fans to provide air movement, rather than open windows, when external temperatures are above internal comfort target temperatures.
3 Maximise the fresh-air ventilation rate when the ambient air temperature is below the internal temperature (for a building with a cooling load). Use night ventilation to cool down heavyweight buildings. This is dealt with in more detail later [5.4].

Artificial lighting gains

Many buildings overheat due to heat gains from lighting. This may be largely due to the adoption of unnecessarily high lighting levels, or of inefficient lighting systems. Even when daylight is available, artificial lighting is still used due to poor switching layout and controls [10.7]. To reduce heat gains from artificial lighting:

1 Optimise the availability of daylight (but see comments in Chapter 6).
2 Provide good daylight distribution; freedom from contrast and glare will delay artificial lighting switch-on.
3 Install occupant-detecting switches or time switches to ensure that spaces are not lit unnecessarily.
4 Install light-sensitive switching controls to ensure that artificial light is not used when there is sufficient daylight.

5 Avoid unnecessarily high artificial lighting levels. Consider using task lighting with low background illumination levels.
6 Use high luminous efficacy light sources [6.1]. Incandescent tungsten or halogen lamps should be avoided except for specialised and limited applications.
7 Use high light-output ratio, low-glare luminaires. For the specification of low-energy sources and luminaires, consult manufacturers' data.
   (Note that all the above measures carry the double benefit of reducing internal gains as well as the energy needed for lighting.)
8 Reduce the heat gains to the space by using extract ventilation through the luminaire.

Occupant and equipment gains

The growth of business machines and information technology (IT) has led to a significant increase in heat gain produced in office, educational and institutional buildings. This heat gain may be partially beneficial in winter to offset heating loads, but also contributes to overheating in summer.

Surveys, as described in *Energy Consumption Guide* 35 (6) show that actual internal gains are usually much smaller than claimed, even for buildings such as dealer rooms, with very high IT content. This is partly due to the equipment being used more intermittently than assumed, and partly the variability of the manufacturers' nameplate rating compared with actual power consumed. Typical values for offices for equipment and occupants (but excluding lighting) are in the range $15-30$ W/m^2. For a classroom, the high density of occupation could result in gains up to 35W/m^2. To reduce the effect of internal gains:

1 Heat-producing equipment should be located in areas of high ventilation away from occupants.
2 Local mechanical extract ventilation may be appropriate for specific items of equipment.
3 Where possible, low-energy equipment should be specified, e.g. photocopiers with low power stand-by mode, highly insulated cookers and refrigerators.
4 Avoid high occupant density.

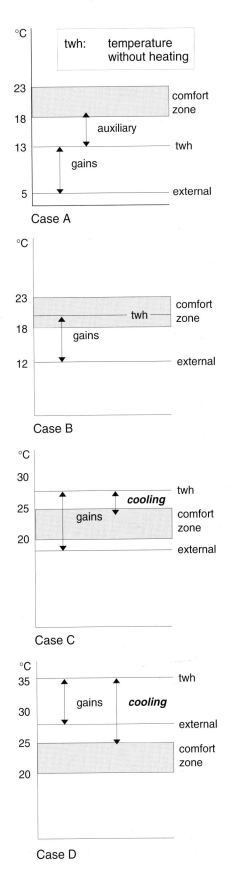

5.4 Ventilation cooling

Ventilation is the most obvious measure to provide cooling, and is the most likely to result from occupant action. However it is not well understood, and confusion about the principles and practice often results in energy waste or poor comfort performance. Here we describe the principles of the cooling function of ventilation; design aspects are covered in Chapter 7.

For ventilation to result in useful heat loss, the ambient temperature must be lower than the maximum comfort temperature indoors. To illustrate the usefulness of ventilation cooling consider a building in four conditions, as illustrated in Figure 5.13.

In Case A the building is experiencing an ambient temperature which is well below the comfort temperature, typical of winter conditions. Some of this difference will be made up by the internal and solar gains. The temperature attained by this is referred to as the temperature without heating (twh). The remainder of the temperature difference must be made up by the auxiliary heating system. In these circumstances the ventilation rate should be the minimum to maintain adequate air quality. This will depend on the density of occupation or rate of production of a pollution source such as smoke, dust or water vapour. Increasing the ventilation rate above the necessary minimum will increase the heating load.

In less cold conditions, Case B, the ambient temperature is still below the comfort temperature, but the internal gains and solar gains may now be sufficient to raise the building temperature to within the comfort zone without the use of an auxiliary heating system. This is now a condition of thermal balance. Higher rates of ventilation could result in the internal temperature without heating (twh) dropping below the comfort zone, thereby creating a heating demand. Lowering the ventilation rate could cause the temperature to rise above the comfort zone.

In warmer conditions, Case C, the ambient temperature may still be below the upper comfort limit or even the lower comfort limit, but now the gains increase the building temperature to a level above the comfort zone. This is a situation in which increased ventilation will reject heat and be a useful cooling measure. Ventilation may be passively introduced by opening windows or it may be necessary to provide it mechanically. Cooling of this type is often referred to as 'free cooling', but if provided mechanically it cannot be considered totally 'free' since the fans require energy.

The greater the gains, the greater the ventilation rate needed, and thus it is best where possible to reduce the gains to a minimum. This is also the condition when high fabric insulation levels actually work against us, reducing useful heat loss to the outside. However, heat loss through the fabric is much smaller than by ventilation, and there is no case in the UK climate for lowering the insulation standards for this function.

Cases B and C are typical of many modern non-domestic buildings in spring, summer and autumn in the UK.

In hot conditions, Case D, where the ambient temperature is above the upper limit of comfort, ventilation will cause heat gain and it should be reduced to the minimum needed for fresh-air requirements. In this situation the only alternative to mechanical cooling is to build with exposed heavyweight (high admittance) surfaces and to cool by night ventilation. This is described in the next two sections, [5.5] and [5.6].

In practice, buildings could go through this range of conditions even in one day; certainly over the year. Thus it is easy to see that for a partially air-conditioned building to be energy efficient, a fairly sophisticated and intelligent system of control is necessary. In naturally ventilated buildings this is further complicated by the fact that air movement causes a physiological cooling effect even when the temperature of the air is slightly above the top end of the comfort zone (up to 3°C). It would probably be better in this situation to minimise the fresh-air ventilation rate and provide air movement by desk or ceiling fans. An air velocity of 1 m/s, easily achievable with a fan, causes an effective temperature reduction of about 3°C (Figure 5.14).

A technological development which would facilitate intelligent optimised control of natural ventilation would be mechanical closers to windows or ventilator grilles. If these were electrically driven, they could be under central control. This could be achieved for grilles using existing air-conditioning equipment, but equipment for windows compatible with manual opening and closing is not in general

5.14 *Ceiling fans with automatic temperature-sensitive switch-on and manual switch-off in an architect's office in Athens.*

use, although low-cost electrical window actuators are already available for rooflights.

5.5 Thermal mass

Thermal mass can be defined as the material of the building which absorbs or releases heat from or to the interior space. The material concerned is usually part of the structure or envelope and is typically dense material such as concrete, brick or stone. The physical property which describes the ability of a material to store heat is the specific heat; that is, the heat energy required to raise a kilogram of the material 1°C. For buildings it is more relevant to consider the volumetric specific heat; that is, the heat required to raise 1m³ of the material 1°C. Table 5.1 gives values for common building materials.

The way in which thermal mass influences the thermal behaviour of a building is often misunderstood. A vital parameter is the degree of coupling with the thermal mass. For example, the same amount of mass in Figure 5.15(a) distributed as in Figure 5.15(b) will have far more effect in case (b) because the conductance between the space and the mass is so much greater. It has been found from both experimental observation and mathematical modelling

Table 5.1 Typical values of specific heat of building materials

Material	Heat capacity kJ/m³°C	Specific heat kJ/kg°C
Exp. polystyrene	25	1.00
Fibreboard	300	1.00
Softwood	730	1.20
Hardwood	900	1.23
Gypsum plaster	1050	1.10
Lightwt. conc.	1000	1.00
Brick	1360	0.80
Dense conc.	1760	0.84
Water	4200	4.20

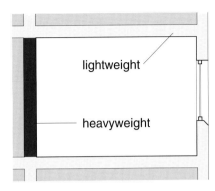

(a) *Concentrated thermal mass*

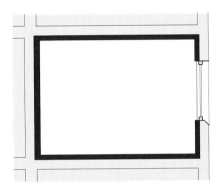

(b) *Most effective thermal mass*

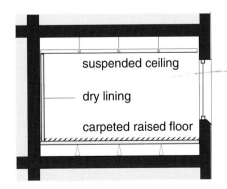

(c) *Least effective thermal mass*

that thicknesses of concrete greater than about 50mm have very little effect for diurnal temperature cycles; that is, temperature varying over a 24-hour period. Furthermore, buildings may contain massive material, but if it is isolated by lightweight finishes, as in Figure 5.15(c), it will play little part in the thermal behaviour of the building. Unfortunately, this is currently the favoured solution for many non-domestic buildings in the UK, incorporating raised floors and suspended ceilings. The only exception to this is where the voids are coupled by ventilation to the interior by day and to the exterior by night [5.6].

However, it also follows from this that all the material contents of a room contribute to the effective thermal mass of a building, and even relatively lightweight structures such as furnishings make a significant contribution due to their large surface area and hence large thermal coupling between the space and the mass.

In a building with direct solar gains, the position of the thermal mass is important in relation to its effectiveness (Figure 5.16). Figure 5.17 shows that we can identify three classes of thermal mass in relation to the absorption of energy from the sun-patch. Figure 5.18 shows the relative effectiveness of these three classes. It is clear that the common practice in many non-domestic buildings of lightweight

5.16 *Exposed concrete floor slabs in the Inland Revenue Building at Nottingham provide thermal mass, coupled to the occupied zone, to stabilise temperature.*

5.17 *Classification of thermal mass: primary (direct radiation), secondary (reflected, re-radiated and convective) and tertiary (convective only).*

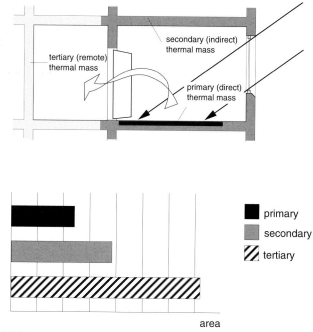

5.18 *Relative areas of exposed thermal mass for equivalent effect.*

carpeted floor and lightweight suspended ceiling results in minimising both primary and secondary thermal mass.

It is often held that thermal mass is universally 'a good thing'. This probably stems from experience in many traditional buildings which are comfortably warm in winter and cool in summer. However, set against the constraint of energy conservation, it is not quite so simple; there may be cases where thermal mass is not beneficial.

The effect of thermal mass on intermittent heating

Figure 5.19 shows the heating curves for a lightweight and a heavyweight office building heated for normal daily occupancy. Note that the 24-hour average temperature is higher for the heavy than for the light building. This has to be paid for. Note that the area under the curve during the warming-up period is greater for the heavy building than the light building and this represents a greater heat input from the heating plant. Bearing in mind that as soon as the building is occupied casual gains may provide the majority of the heating load, the heavy option may use considerably more energy due to the increased load at warm-up.

This difference increases for buildings with very short occupancy periods such as schools, but becomes negligible for continuously occupied buildings such as hospitals. However, in order to illustrate the effect, these theoretical curves are rather exaggerated, corresponding to poorly insulated buildings. New buildings with better insulation standards will cool down more slowly, and the difference between heavy and lightweight buildings will be smaller.

However, thermal mass brings an energy benefit in its effect on the usefulness of solar and casual gains. Figure 5.20 shows the effect of the input of solar gain to a lightweight and a heavyweight building. In the lightweight case it quickly leads to overheating, and the maintenance of

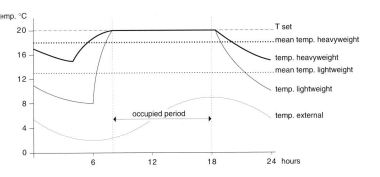

5.19 *Temperature curves for intermittent heating of heavy and lightweight buildings.*

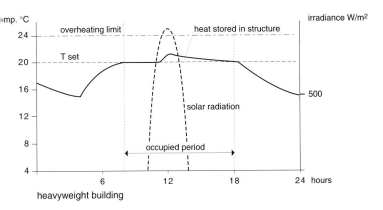

5.20 *The effect of solar gains on heavy and lightweight buildings.*

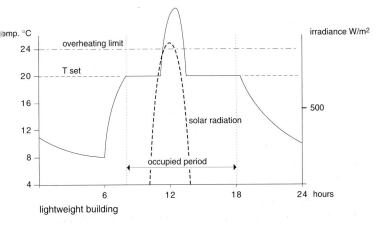

comfort requires rejection by either shading or ventilation, or, even worse, by mechanical cooling. The heavyweight building is able to absorb the sudden input of solar gain, and this stored energy helps delay a demand for heating as the outside temperature drops. It maintains a higher internal temperature overnight, thereby reducing the pre-heating energy required the next morning.

The net result of these two conflicting effects on energy consumption is difficult to generalise. Bearing in mind the relatively small heating loads of well-insulated, non-domestic buildings, if we could assume an ideal heating control system it is probable that for an intermittently operated building the lightweight solution would consume less energy. However, in reality control systems are not perfect, and the difference would probably be insignificant. However, the heavyweight building is a far more robust solution in terms of occupant comfort. The non-ideal behaviour of a real control system is far more likely to cause comfort problems in a lightweight building – subsequent efforts to overcome this may lead to non-optimal use of plant and hence poor energy performance [10.7]. On balance, the adoption of medium to heavyweight buildings is recommended in all cases except for highly intermittently occupied buildings, provided there is little chance of wide swings in internal gains.

Thermal mass has an important role to play by minimising temperature swings in unheated spaces such as conservatories and atria. This is dealt with in Chapter 9. Very massive buildings do have advantages during exceptional heat waves since their time constant of several days (maybe weeks) will delay the build-up of heat. This is noticeable in historic buildings such churches and castles. However, they may carry disadvantages, having a very long warm-up period in winter after periods of unoccupation.

5.6 Night ventilation

The beneficial effect of thermal mass in its prevention of overheating is simply that a heavy building more nearly follows the 24-hour average ambient temperature than the instantaneous ambient temperature. Furthermore, as illustrated in Figure 5.20, a lightweight building responds rapid-

5.21 *Increased thermal coupling by incorporating hollow floor elements connected to the interior by ducts (the Termodeck system).*

5.22 *Options for air-flow paths for night-time and daytime ventilation.*

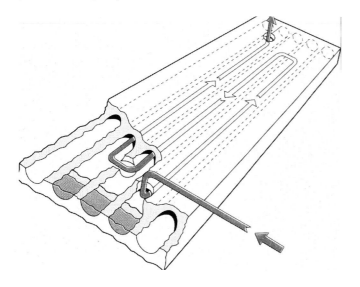

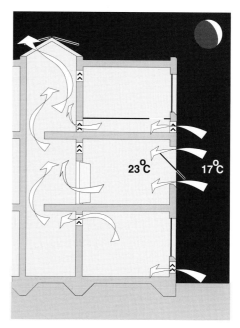

Maximum ventilation

ly to solar gains taking room temperature above the upper comfort limit.

However, for the average temperature of the building to be *below* the average ambient temperature, the building interior must be coupled to the outside selectively; that is, only when the ambient temperature is well below the temperature inside the building. This is done by providing high rates of ventilation at night.

Night ventilation is appropriate in hot weather when the daytime temperature is expected to be above comfort temperature. It is also appropriate in buildings with a cooling load due to high internal gains, but there is a need for caution here because night ventilation could result in too low temperatures at the beginning of the occupied period.

It is important that at night the ventilation cools the structure and that the structure is massive enough to store the cooling effect until the building is occupied during the next day. It is also important that the occupants are not isolated from the cooled mass. This may conflict with modern open plan office layout where, for acoustic reasons, finishes include carpet and lightweight suspended ceilings. Compromises must be reached as previously described [3.4].

It may be advantageous to direct the night ventilation air-flow paths differently from daytime paths, to ensure maximum cooling of the mass. Some designers direct night

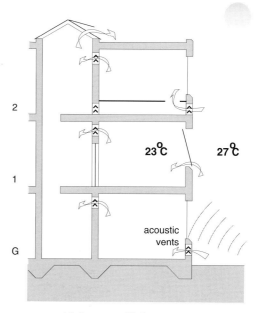

Minimum ventilation

5.23 *The response of lightweight and heavyweight buildings to night ventilation. From computer simulations. Source: Szokolay (7).*

5.24 *The new BRE Low Energy Office uses stack-induced night ventilation to lower daytime temperatures.*

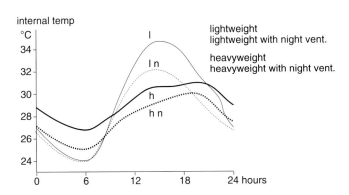

ventilation through voids actually within the structure, such as hollow floors (Figure 5.21). Considerations have to be made for security of the building. Figure 5.22 illustrates several ventilation options. More information concerning natural ventilation mechanisms is given later [7.2].

Figure 5.23 has been derived from computer simulations. It shows that for a diurnal temperature variation of as little as 8°C, night ventilation combined with a heavyweight building [5.5] can be beneficial to daytime conditions. Larger variations between day and night temperatures will improve the potential for night cooling. Typical diurnal variation in sunny weather in the UK is 10-14°C and daytime temperature depressions of 3-5°C (depend-ing on occupation density) are easily achievable.

Ideally night-time ventilation would be driven by natural forces. Wind pressure would require a reliable night-time breeze whereas thermal buoyancy or 'stack effect' would require generous temperature differences, considerable stack heights and large areas of opening to get significant volumes of air through the building (Figure 5.24).

Where neither of the above natural conditions prevail, mechanical ventilation must be used. If the daytime mechanical ventilation equipment can be used at night this may still prove to be an economical solution. However, the energy cost of the fan power must be considered in relation to the cooling achieved.

Heat gains should always be reduced at source if possible. Reduction of unwanted solar gains by shading is of high priority. Insulation and reflective finishes also reduce gains through fabric. Internal gains from lighting and equipment should be reduced as much as possible by the use of energy-efficient lighting and equipment.

Ventilation may be used to remove heat when external temperatures are lower than internal ones. Local extraction ventilation in places of high heat production increases ventilation efficiency.

Thermal mass, when coupled with the interior space, reduces daytime temperatures. Night ventilation can lower daytime temperatures in heavyweight buildings by about 3°C. For diurnal moderation, most effect is provided by the first 50mm of heavyweight material. Very massive buildings may show advantages during exceptional heat waves.

Chapter 6

Daylighting

The provision of daylight in a building is strongly linked to the spatial and architectural design. Unlike other environmental services, the elements of daylighting – windows and surfaces – are surely the most visual and expressive. For this reason windows have a long history of attention from architects; indeed, architectural style has been defined by patterns of fenestration probably more than by any other single characteristic. It should be of interest then, to the architect, that daylighting design also has a strong influence on both the energy use of a building and the general comfort and well-being of the occupants (Figure 6.1).

6.1 Daylight as energy

Daylighting can save energy by displacing the electrical energy that would otherwise be used to provide artificial lighting. In most non-domestic buildings this is potentially the most significant energy-saving measure. Reference to Figure 4.3 shows that for air-conditioned and predominantly artificially lit buildings, lighting is the single largest user of energy, but can be reduced by more than half in daylit, shallow-plan buildings. In fact a typical shallow-plan office building, with a plan depth not greater than 15m, occupied for normal working hours, can obtain 70% of the working illumination by daylight.

In addition to this benefit of saving lighting energy, the heat generated for a given amount of light is less for daylight than for artificial light. Typical luminous efficacies are given in Table 6.1.

Thus in principle, for a given level of illumination tungsten lighting would produce between 5 and 14 times more heat than daylight.

6.1 *A well-daylit working environment not only saves energy but is also preferred by the occupants. (Housing 21 Beaconsfield, Architects Jestico and Whiles.)*

Table 6.1 Luminous efficacies of common light sources

Lamp	Luminous efficacy lm/W
Tungsten GLS	8-20
Tungsten halogen	12-25
High-pressure mercury	40-60
Compact fluorescent	50-60
Tubular fluorescent	60-90
Metal halide	70-80
High-pressure sodium	60-120
Daylight	115

If daylight were evenly distributed throughout the room and held at constant intensity by controls, the full benefit of the increased thermal efficiency would be realised. However, in reality the variation of daylight level within a space and the variation with time will lead to over-illumination in some parts of the room and at some times of the day. The resulting increase in thermal gain will probably nullify the benefit of the higher luminous efficiency. Thus in practice, without resorting to a sophisticated variable transmission control and distribution system, the use of daylight cannot be expected to lower thermal gains.

Although this over-illumination carries the penalty of creating a cooling load in summer, it is not in other respects a disadvantage. It is the variation of lighting levels in time

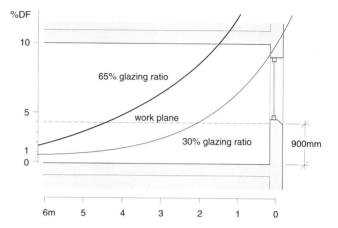

6.2 *Variation of Daylight Factor (DF) in a side-lit room for glazing ratios (glazing to external wall area) of 30% and 65%. DF averaged across breadth of room.*

and space which gives daylight its essential quality. Too great a spatial variation, however, can lead to glare and inefficient use of artificial lighting. Furthermore, in special buildings such as art galleries and museums, over-illumination must be prevented for the protection of the contents. For other buildings in the UK climate, by simply restricting shading controls to the function of cutting out direct radiation and allowing only diffuse light to enter a room at ambient level, cooling loads and glare can be reduced sufficiently.

6.2 Daylight factor

The effect of daylight in a room reduces as one moves farther away from the daylight source. This variation of light intensity is not linear and shows a wide range across the occupied part of a room. The daylight intensity at a given point is related directly to the size of the windows or rooflights. The reflectance of the ground and room surfaces, the shape of the room and the detailed design of the window opening are all factors which influence the intensity and distribution of daylight.

This important topic of daylighting design is outside the scope of this volume and the reader is referred to other sources listed in the Select Bibliography [p. 227]. Here we are concerned with how the initial design decisions on building shape and façade design affect the potential for energy saving by daylighting.

Due to the variation of the illumination from the sky, it is not useful to describe the daylighting in a building in units of illuminance. Rather, the daylighting performance of a building is described using a ratio of the illuminance inside the room to that from the unobstructed sky outside. This is called the Daylight Factor.[1]

Figure 6.2 shows the variation of Daylight Factor (DF) for a side-lit room. In a room 3m high, at a distance greater

than 6m from the window, the DF on the work plane will fall to typically less than 1%, which will be a lower limit for most uses. Increasing the glazing area above 40% of wall area will increase the minimum DF, but will also lead to an unacceptably low uniformity ratio. Thus if a building is greater than 12m deep the inner central zones, i.e. beyond 6m from either side, will need to be permanently artificially lit. Furthermore, the intermediate zone between 3m and 6m will be daylit for fewer hours than the outer zone. A double height space will allow useful penetration up to 12m (assuming the window height is close to that of the wall), indicating that the penetration of daylight is dependent upon the ratio of room height to depth. If it is possible to use rooflights then there is no constraint on plan depth, although clearly this can only be adopted for top floors or single-storey buildings.

The Daylight Factor is predictable from design parameters by various procedures. Physical scale models may be used under real or artificial skies. It may be evaluated from tables or graphical tools such as the BRE Daylight Factor Protractors, or from computer-based mathematical models, which are becoming increasingly available.

6.3 The sky as a light source

The illuminance from the sky varies over a wide range on an hourly and seasonal basis. There is a large difference, up

---

1 The daylight in a room is described using a relative value, the Daylight Factor (DF). The daylight factor is defined as:

$$DF = I_i/I_o \times 100\%$$

where I_i is the illuminance in the room at the point of interest and I_o is the illuminance from the unobstructed sky, i.e. nominally the outdoor ambient illuminance.

to tenfold, between direct sunlight and light from the diffuse or clear sky. A typical overall variation might be from 2000 lux at midday on a gloomy day in December to 100,000 lux in full sun in June. In the British climate, unfortunately, cloudy skies prevail and daylighting design is generally based on this assumption. Daylighting from direct sunlight is rarely considered and generally presents problems due to its strongly directional nature.

Sky illuminances – that is, the intensity of light falling on a horizontal surface from the unobstructed sky – have been measured at various sites. A useful way of recording this data is in the form of cumulative frequency curves. Figure 6.3 shows the percentage of working hours that the sky illuminance is above specified illuminance values. Working back from a required internal illuminance it is possible to predict the fraction of time that this level could be met by daylight, and thus the duration for which artificial light would be needed.

This is the principle of the evaluation of lighting energy in the LT Method described in Part Two.

6.4 Interaction of shading with daylighting

Shading is an almost essential part of passive building design. Its use has three purposes:

1   to reduce the solar heat gain to the room;
2   to prevent sunlight from falling onto occupants;
3   to reduce glare.

However, the presence of most shading devices will also reduce the useful daylight. All too often the 'blinds down lights on' strategy will be adopted and ironically, extra lighting energy will be used when in fact there is a surplus of luminous energy. In other cases, where poorly designed fixed shading devices are used, their obstruction to the diffuse sky is such that artificial lighting is needed at all times except perhaps when there is bright sunshine.

How can this conflict be resolved? First let us consider movable shading devices. Figure 6.4 indicates that in sunny conditions the critical illuminance level is easily achieved at the back of the room, whilst in overcast conditions the shading device is removed from the win-

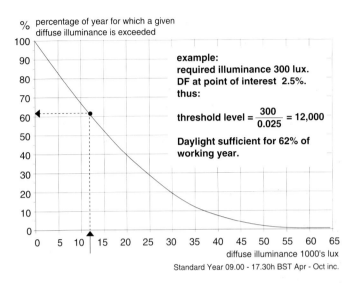

6.3 *Availability of daylight for southern UK. Example shows how from a required minimum illuminance and DF, the fraction of daylight sufficiency over the working year can be evaluated.*

dow aperture. Since the shading device does not affect the illuminance at critical positions and times, i.e. when artificial light has to be switched on, a shading device such as this, provided it is operated correctly, carries no energy penalty. This also presumes that its transmission can be adjusted to allow sufficient daylight when it is deployed. Louvre blinds can be adjusted to do this.

Figure 6.5 shows a light shelf, which partly performs a shading function and partly a redistribution function. Although it completely shades the lower part of the window (greatly reducing the illuminance gradient in the room), reflections from the upper surface redirect light to the back of the room compensating for the obstructing effect of the shelf, even in overcast conditions. Thus, due to its redistribution function, this type of device also has no negative effect on energy consumption. Even a simple overhang can perform nearly as well as this provided there is good reflection from the ground outside to redirect light to the back of the room.

We will call these shading types A1 and A2 respectively – neither increase the use of artificial light.

Now consider a fixed shading device as in Figure 6.6. This reduces daylight by the same amount as it reduces solar gain, and because it is not geometrically selective, it reduces diffuse light by the same amount as direct sunlight. Thus the room is now under-illuminated on diffuse days,

6.4 *A movable shading device is only deployed when there is a surplus of light and thus does not have a detrimental effect on the daylighting at times of poor daylight availability. These devices are classified type A1.*

6.5 *A fixed light shelf has a dual function, to shade and reject direct radiation from the front of the room and to redirect light to the back of the room. In spite of being a fixed device, its redistribution function ensures that the illuminance at the back of the room (i.e. the limiting condition) is not affected. These devices are classified type A2.*

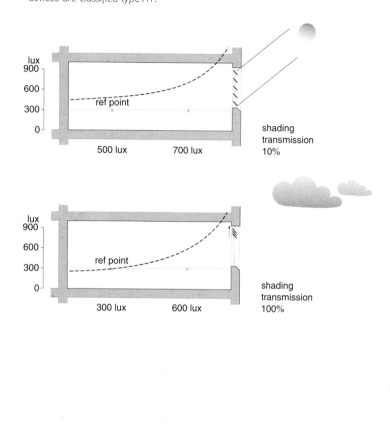

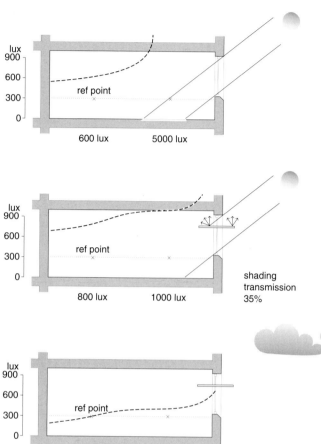

demanding more artificial light and hence leading to extra energy demand. If the shading effect is compensated by extra glazing area, this is self-defeating since the window will now allow more solar gain from direct sunlight. We will call this type B shading.

A summary classification of shading elements is given in Table 6.2.

In practice, many shading devices do not fall exactly into these two categories. But the list below indicates broad categories. Furthermore, some devices, often referred to as advanced daylighting elements, primarily function as redirecting devices rather than shading devices (Figure 6.7). These may increase the daylight level at the back of the room in both direct and diffuse conditions.

It is beyond the scope of this volume to give detailed information on shading design. However, the important message is that not all shading devices are equal and they have a widely differing impact on lighting energy use, as well as ventilation and view. This classification of shading type is used in the LT Method.

6.5 Lighting control systems

It is obvious that the energy saving of daylight will only be realised if the artificial lighting is turned off when there is sufficient daylight. Because artificial lighting rarely contributes significantly to over-illumination, i.e. a level which threatens visual comfort, there is not a comfort incentive

6.6 *A fixed type B device reduces the diffuse light by the same fraction as the direct sunlight, i.e. it is not geometrically selective. This will create an increased demand for artificial lighting.*

6.7 *Advanced daylighting devices, such as reflecting louvres and prismatic glass, redirect light to the back of the room, thereby reducing the demand for supplementary artificial lighting.*

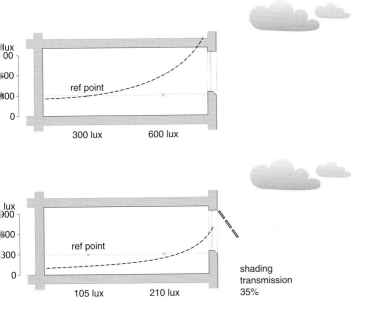

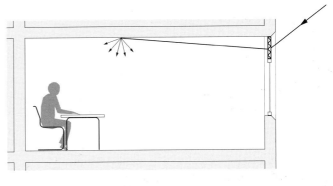

Table 6.2 Classification of shading elements

Type A1	Type A2	Type B
Movable blinds and louvres with variable transmission	Light shelves, fixed reflective louvres, overhangs (with ground reflection), prismatic glass, holographic film	Fixed grids and fixed non-reflective louvres, fritted, tinted and reflective glass

to turn lights off. The incentive has to be an 'intellectual' one, i.e. a moral attitude to energy use or at least a reasoned concern for energy cost.

This results in light-switching performance in non-domestic buildings being very poor. This is often further exacerbated by light switches not being easily accessible, or luminaires wired in large groups not corresponding to daylight distribution. For example, if a deep room has one lighting circuit, the lights will be switched on, or left on, to provide artificial light to the back of the room, although the front half of the room may be adequately daylit.

Automatic lighting systems which detect daylight illuminance levels can replace the need for switching by the occupants. Field studies have shown that annual lighting energy is typically reduced by 30–40%. However, fully automatic systems are unsatisfactory, causing annoyance to the occupants mainly due to the frequency and apparent randomness of their operation, often responding to short-term changes in the sky. Modern systems now adopt a compromise approach:

1   the lights are switched off at pre-set times, e.g. on the hour, if the daylight illuminance is above the critical datum;
2   lights may be manually switched on again at any time;
3   no automatic switch-on is provided;
4   lights may also be switched off by a null occupancy detection from an occupancy detector leading to further savings.

6.8 *Decision chart for choosing a lighting control strategy for the most cost-effective energy savings. Source: Littlefair, BRE.*

Decision chart for choosing a lighting control strategy

	Pattern of occupancy		Lighting control strategy			
	Number of people	Time	Time switching	Localised switching	Occupancy linking	Photoelectric daylight linking
If daylight is available	Many people	Variable	●●●	●●	●	●
		Intermittent but scheduled	●●●	●	●	●
		Continuous	●●●	●●	—	●●●
	One or two people	Variable	●	●●●	●●	●
		Continuous	●	●●●	—	●●
	Rarely occupied	Intermittent	●	●●	●●●	●
If no daylight	All types of occupancy		●●●	—	●●●	—

Further improvements can be made by top-up or dimming controls. Suppose the daylight illuminance is 200 lux in a space requiring 300 lux. Instead of the artificial lights being switched fully on, which would then provide an illuminance of 500 lux, the artificial lights are dimmed to provide only a further 100 lux, saving power and making the control less obtrusive. Dimming controls save more energy than on/off controls since they make use of daylight even when there is insufficient to meet the illuminance datum, and can reduce annual lighting energy by as much as 60%.

Recent advances in control systems by lighting manufacturers have been to provide 'local intelligence' not linked to a central control system. This has reduced costs, and provided the occupant with much more personal control. In some systems operation can be carried out by TV-style infra-red controllers, greatly simplifying switching layout and reducing hard wiring. Details of these systems can be obtained from the leading lighting manufacturers.

A decision chart for choosing a lighting control strategy, developed by P. Littlefair, is reproduced in Figure 6.8 by kind permission of the BRE.

6.6 Daylighting and thermal function of glazing

The parameters of the glazing of a building envelope cause a complex energy balance to occur, as illustrated in Figure 6.9. Radiation passes through the glazing where the visible part may displace the need for artificial lighting. When absorbed, this same radiation will create heat, and possibly displace auxiliary heating. Both of these functions represent an energy gain. In the summer, however, the heat gain may not be useful and may lead to a cooling load. Also, since glazing usually has a much poorer insulation value than an opaque wall, the inclusion of glazing in the envelope to provide light and useful thermal gain is at the cost of increased conductive losses.

This building energy balance varies hour by hour, month by month, throughout the year. Figure 6.10(a) shows the total monthly primary energy consumed by a double-glazed south-facing office room of 54m² with 40% glazed external wall in the southern UK. These figures were

6.9 *The energy balance at the glazed envelope of a building.*

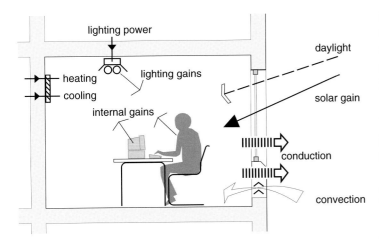

derived from the LT Model, which has been used to produce the curves in the LT Method. It clearly shows how the demand shifts from energy for heating and lighting in winter to cooling in summer. In reality, both heating and cooling requirements can occur in one month or even one day. Because the model is based upon a monthly energy budget, the results do not show this. However, this limitation is of little significance to the predicted annual energy.

For comparison, Figures 6.10(b) and 6.10(c) show a similar analysis for two rather different European climates. Figure 6.10(b) shows the monthly consumption by a similar south-facing office in Athens. Here, there is a much smaller heating load and a smaller lighting load. The cooling load forms 56% of the total energy demand compared with 15% for the UK. The lighting load is actually larger in the summer for Athens compared with London due to the need for shading devices and the shorter day.

Figure 6.10(c) shows the results for a similar office in Copenhagen. Cooling energy is now reduced to only 10% of the total. Heating is the main component of the primary energy demand. Note that in all cases it is assumed that full

use is made of daylight, i.e. the lights are not on when the daylight is above a datum value of 300 lux. Note too that for the sake of comparison the same U-value for walls is assumed, whereas in practice the insulation standards for Denmark would be much higher than those for Greece.

Figure 6.11 shows two sets of curves generated by the LT Model, giving the annual primary energy demand per m² for a south-facing office in the UK, as a function of glazing ratio, for single and double glazing. Energy units are primary energy. The glazing ratio is the area of unobstructed glass as a fraction of the total wall area (including glass). The LT Model assumes that full use is made of the available daylight by automatic controls or good occupant control.

In both cases, as glazing is introduced from zero there is a rapid initial reduction in lighting energy demand due to the sudden benefit of quite modest glazing areas replacing the need for artificial lighting. For a glazing ratio of 20% the double-glazed office consumes slightly more lighting energy than the office with single glazing. This is because double glazing transmits about 15% less light than single glazing. As the glazed area increases, the rate of increase of useful lighting reduces and the thermal benefit of the double glazing becomes more significant. By 80% glazing ratio the single-glazed building consumes nearly twice the heating energy of the double-glazed building, but the same amount of lighting energy.

For single glazing there is an optimum area of 35% glazing for heating and lighting, but rather less than that in buildings with mechanical cooling. For double glazing, energy consumption for heating and lighting is still reducing at 70% glazing ratio and is 17% less than the energy demand for the optimum single-glazing value. However, the risk of overheating is greatly increased for large glazing areas on east, south and particularly west façades.

This increased overheating risk is rather under-represented by the LT curves because the cooling load is shared over a year. This issue is discussed in more detail later [12.6].

The cooling energy shown here is mainly the energy needed for heat rejection (refrigeration) and the extra fan power needed for cooling at higher air-change rates. This assumes a Variable Air Volume (VAV) system where the

6.10 *Monthly primary energy consumption (kWh) for south-facing offices in London, Athens and Copenhagen (from LT Model).*

LONDON

	heat	cooling	lights	total
JAN	969	0	650	1620
FEB	665	0	296	961
MAR	390	0	232	622
APR	232	0	90	497
MAY	17	0	46	322
JUN	0	251	45	296
JUL	0	467	46	513
AUG	0	354	46	400
SEP	0	73	135	208
OCT	132	0	279	411
NOV	458	0	405	863
DEC	819	0	697	1515
ANNUAL	3681	1145	2968	7795

Table 6.10a: Monthly primary energy consumption (kilo-Watt hours) for a south-facing office room in London (from LT Model)

ATHENS

	heat	cooling	lights	total
JAN	240	0	325	565
FEB	164	0	212	375
MAR	193	0	239	332
APR	0	185	93	721
MAY	0	628	46	63
JUN	0	586	90	676
JUL	0	609	93	702
AUG	0	579	139	719
SEP	0	527	135	662
OCT	0	483	232	716
NOV	0	38	270	307
DEC	63	0	325	388
ANNUAL	660	3634	2188	6482

Table 6.10b: Monthly primary energy consumption (kilo-Watt hours) for a south-facing office room in Athens (from LT Model)

COPENHAGEN

	heat	cooling	lights	total
JAN	1589	0	697	2286
FEB	1080	0	381	1461
MAR	640	0	232	872
APR	407	0	90	497
MAY	119	0	46	165
JUN	0	153	45	198
JUL	0	505	46	551
AUG	0	399	46	445
SEP	4	0	180	184
OCT	221	0	279	499
NOV	678	0	674	1352
DEC	1216	0	697	1913
ANNUAL	5953	1056	3414	10423

Table 6.10c: Monthly primary energy consumption (kilo-Watt hours) for a south-facing office room in Copenhagen (from LT Model)

6.11 *LT curves showing annual primary energy consumption (megawatt hours per square metre) for heating, lighting and cooling, for south-facing office in southern UK.*

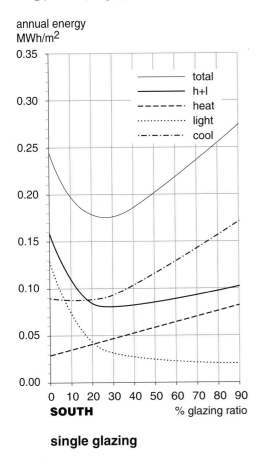

single glazing

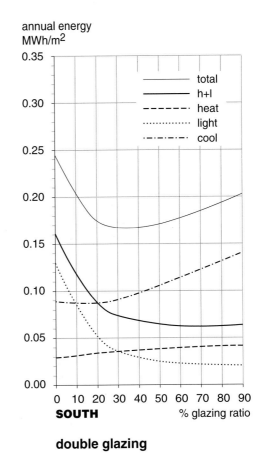

double glazing

flow rate responds to the cooling (or heating) demand. In buildings where the fans operate at a constant rate, unnecessarily high recirculation occurs continually and leads to wasteful energy use.

For a successful passive building, the perimeter zones will not need mechanical ventilation nor cooling, and will make maximum use of daylight. This is the basic concept of the passive zone which is discussed in more detail in Chapter 8.

(Note that energy is given in Primary Energy units. The reason for this has been discussed in Chapter 4. All of the values in this chapter are given as examples only and should not be used for calculation.)

The fraction of glazing, the glazing type of the façade, and the depth of plan and section, all influence the proportion of the floor area to which daylight is available. For typical ceiling heights the depth over which daylight is useful is no more than 6m, but a rooflit space will place no such restrictions on plan depth. Strong variations of daylight factor lead to the use of more supplementary artificial lighting.

The energy balance of the glazed envelope leads to a shallow optimum for glazing ratios from 25% upwards according to glazing type and orientation. However, glazing ratios in excess of 50% should generally be avoided due to increased risk of overheating.

7

Ventilation

Ventilation is the exchange of air between inside and outside the building and is a fundamental requirement resulting from occupancy. It is as important as the provision of daylight, and historically it has had almost as much influence on the development of plan, section and envelope. In contemporary buildings in temperate climates, natural ventilation is usually provided by openable windows, rather than specialised elements. This has not always been so, as typified by the Victorian fascination with ventilation, and the expression of these functional elements in schools, agricultural and factory buildings (Figure 7.1).

In the 1930s, the developing technology of electric motors, fans and ductwork gradually freed the designer from considering the envelope as the main source of ventilation, in much the same way that developments in artificial lighting removed the form-giving influence of daylighting. Not only were the plan and section freed from constraint, but the ability to control ventilation with engineered precision was seen as a good thing. As our urban environments became more noisy and polluted, mechanical ventilation and finally full air-conditioning seemed to be indisputably appropriate.

Quite recently, however, we are beginning to have second thoughts. Firstly, from an energy point of view mechanical ventilation is costly, as illustrated by the energy breakdown for offices already shown in Figure 4.3. Secondly, it appears that in many cases occupants are much happier and healthier in naturally ventilated buildings, in spite of the variability of environmental conditions which results. Sick-building syndrome is almost exclusively observed in mechanically ventilated buildings.

However, natural ventilation is not a soft option for designers and, like other aspects of passive environmental

7.1 *The Maltings at Snape in Suffolk. These giant ventilators or 'tofts' extracted the moisture laden fumes from the malting process. Built in 1846, the Maltings was converted into a concert hall in 1967, the ventilators maintaining their original function.*

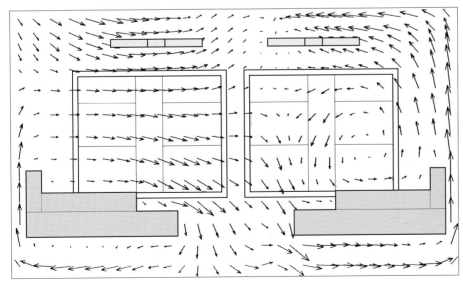

7.2 *Computational Fluid Dynamics (CFD) is a computer-based technique for predicting air flows between rooms and within rooms. Here it is being used to investigate the flow of air from ceiling fans around hospital beds. Temperature profiles can also be predicted.*

design, has much more impact on the architecture of the building. In small buildings such as houses, ventilation has in the past been left to chance. Even this has begun to present problems as the standard of air-tightness has increased. In larger buildings, natural ventilation must be designed with some understanding of the principles upon which it operates. Buildings will not necessarily be satisfactorily ventilated by simply providing openable windows. New analytical techniques are now being developed to assist in natural ventilation design, but they are complicated and their use is generally restricted to specialist consultants (Figures 7.2 and 7.3).

7.1 Ventilation regimes

Three regimes of ventilation can be identified. These are *minimum ventilation*, *space cooling* and *air movement*.

Minimum ventilation

This is the introduction of fresh air to replace stale air. Typical rates are about 0.5 to 3 air changes/hour depending upon density of occupation. Typical recommended values per occupant range from about 5 to 25 litres/sec/person.

Indoor air has to be replaced due to contamination with pollutants. These can be from the occupants – CO_2, water vapour, body odour or tobacco smoke for example. Or the contaminants may come from the building itself or equipment or processes being carried out in the building. There is growing concern about the health implications of air quality. In particular there is concern for the possible effects of pollutants such as formaldehyde and other organic substances emanating from modern building materials and finishes.

In cool-climate situations, ventilation creates a heat loss[1] during the heating season. This results in the interests of energy conservation and air quality being in conflict. However, in most non-domestic buildings, heating energy is quite a small fraction of the total consumption [Chapter 4]

---

1 The ventilation heat load **Wv** is given by: **Wv** = 0.33 × N × V × Δt where **N** is the number of air changes per hour, **V** is the room volume, and **Δt** is the temperature difference between inside and outside.

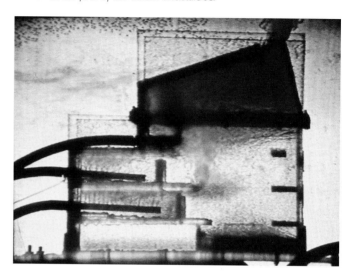

7.3 *In salt tank modelling, physical models are used and convective air flows are modelled by changes in salt-solution density, rather than the changes in air density in the real case. Here the technique is assessing the use of an atrium to draw fresh air through the adjacent rooms, whilst leaving the cool air at the floor of the atrium undisturbed.*

and thus the indoor air quality should not be compromised. For buildings with locally high ventilation requirements such as school classrooms or lecture theatres, solar ventilation pre-heating [9.2] or heat recovery [10.6] may be appropriate since they allow high ventilation rates without high energy cost.

Space cooling

When a space is too warm and the external temperature is below the comfort temperature level, air can be introduced to the building for 'free' cooling. Typical rates are 5 to 25 air changes/hour depending upon the intensity of heat gains and the prevailing temperature difference. In this case, heat can be regarded as the 'pollutant' and the ventilation rate can be as high as is required to bring the internal temperature down to the comfort zone, since there is, of course, no heating load. This is one of the methods of cooling which has already been discussed in more detail [5.4].

Air movement

This is the generation of direct physiological cooling of the occupants by air speeds of between 0.5 and 3m/s. The main mechanisms of thermal comfort have been discussed

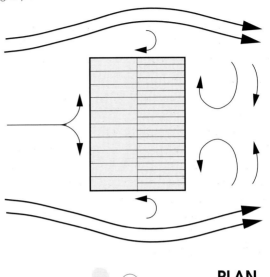

7.4 *Distribution of wind-induced pressure over the surface of a building, in plan.*

in Chapter 3 and it was stated that air movement increases heat loss by both convection and evaporation. For example, air movement of 1m/s (a walking pace) will reduce an air temperature of 30°C to an effective temperature of 27°C – i.e. the same thermal sensation will exist in both cases. In practice, there is an upper limit to air movement on practical grounds; papers will be displaced, clothing and hair will be moved at velocities above about 1.5m/s.

Air movement as a cooling method is applicable during the hottest conditions likely to be found in the UK. It is important to provide both enough air movement, and a good spatial distribution in the room relative to room layout and the position of occupants.

If naturally induced, that is through open windows, it will result in high air-change rates, typically greater than 50 air changes/hour.[2] However, in order to obtain enhanced physiological cooling, it is not necessary to exchange this large quantity of air with the outside. This would cause unwanted heat gains at times when the air temperature outside is higher than that of the interior [5.4].

Air movement can be produced by air recirculation in a ducted system, or more commonly by a ceiling-mounted or desk-mounted fan. An effective temperature reduction of about 3°C can be obtained. Ceiling fans can be very energy-efficient and studies have shown that the equivalent cooling effect by a typical air-conditioning system would use at least six times more energy.

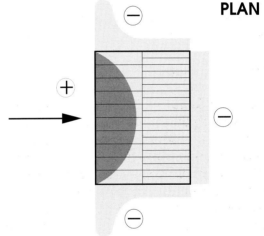

PLAN

7.2 Natural ventilation

Natural ventilation can be generated by *wind pressure* or *thermal buoyancy* (stack effect). Both operate on a building in varying proportions according to the prevailing wind strength and temperature conditions.

Wind pressure

Wind pressure is caused by wind blowing against and/or past a building. This generates pressures on the building

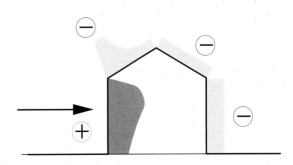

2 For example, an air velocity of 1m/s from an open window of 2m² corresponds to a volume flow of 7200m³/hr. For a room measuring 6m × 6m × 3m this is an air change rate of 67ac/h.

7.5 *Distribution of wind-induced pressure over the surface of a building, in section.*

surfaces due to the change in momentum when the air is deflected or its speed is reduced. The broad pattern of pressures is readily understood by common sense; that is, positive pressures on the windward side and negative pressures on the leeward side (Figure 7.4).

Unless the envelope is completely impervious, this will result in a flow of air into the windward side, across the building and out the leeward side. This simple analysis already underlines the importance of providing for cross-ventilation, when higher rates of ventilation are required. By this is meant the provision of openings on both windward and leeward sides and the existence of an air-flow route within the building.

The fine structure of the pressure distribution is much more complex. For example, the pressure distribution over a simple house form is shown in section in Figure 7.5. Note the non-uniform pressure distribution across the windward façade and the windward roof plane. Also shown is that the windward roof plane is at negative pressure for shallow pitch roofs. Air flows do not only take place between negative and positive pressures, but could take place between an area of slight negative pressure and one of greater negative pressure, provided there is a flow path existing between the two areas.[3]

The situation is further complicated by the variance of wind direction and speed, and turbulence. To some extent these parameters are influenced by site conditions such as other buildings, vegetation and landscape features.[4] These may or may not be in the architect's control. In some locations, particularly in coastal areas, the prevailing wind patterns are variable but predictable and can be relied upon for natural ventilation.

It is fair to say that as a result of the complexity of the problem, we still have to rely heavily upon empirical rules for the design of natural ventilation. One simple rule is that:

Openings should be widely distributed over individual surfaces and different façades of the building envelope. This ensures that the openings will be at different pressures, and that the subsequent air flows will be well distributed in the building.

More detailed configurations of openings are illustrated in Figures 7.8–7.14.

Thermal buoyancy

Thermal buoyancy generates a vertical pressure difference which is dependent upon the average temperature difference between the column of warm air and the external temperature, and the height of the column of warm air.[5] A building containing air that is warmer than the surroundings can be likened to an inverted teacup in a bowl of water which has trapped a volume of air. If there were a hole in the top of the teacup, air would be forced out, driven by the pressure which is dependent upon the difference in density between the water and the air, and the height of the trapped air bubble. In the case of a building, warm air will tend to flow out of openings at the top, and cool air will flow in at ground level (Figure 7.6).

The problem with thermal buoyancy for driving natural ventilation is that it is at a maximum in the winter when the greatest temperature differences exist. This is

---

3 The pressure induced by wind is given by: $P = 0.5\ C_P\ \rho\ u^2$, where P is the pressure in Pascals, C_P is the pressure coefficient, ρ is the density of air and u is the undisturbed upstream air velocity.

   The airflow through an opening is given by: $V = A\ C\ \Delta P^n$, where V is the volume flow rate in m^3/s, A is the area of the opening, C is the discharge coefficient ranging from about 0.3 to 0.8, ΔP is the pressure difference, and n is the flow exponent ranging from 0.5 for wide openings to 1 for long narrow cracks.

4 The windspeed, as experienced by the building, is strongly influenced by the surrounding terrain. For example, when for a region in the country the meteorological windspeed is 4.5m/s, in a dense urban situation at 2m above ground the windspeed would be reduced to about 1.7m/s.

5 The pressure difference due to thermal buoyancy is given by: $\Delta p = 0.043\ h.\Delta t$, where p is the pressure in Pascals, h is the height of the column at mean temperature difference of Δt from the surrounding air.

   The resulting air flow is approximately given by: $V = 0.121\ A\ (h\ \Delta t)^{0.5}$, where V is the volume flow rate (m^3/s) and A is the area of each opening (top and bottom of equal area).

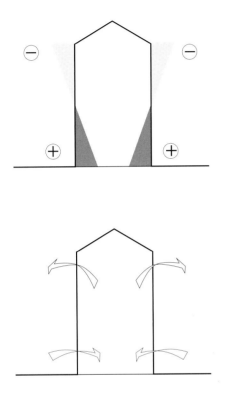

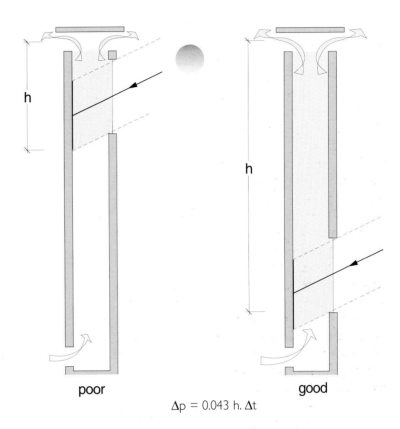

poor   good

$$\Delta p = 0.043 \, h. \, \Delta t$$

usually when only minimal ventilation is required. In tall buildings in cold climates very large pressure differences can be set up.

In warm conditions, temperatures can be deliberately elevated above comfort temperatures to induce greater pressure differences, but only in unoccupied areas such as roof spaces or 'solar chimneys'. It is important to realise that the temperature difference upon which the pressure difference, and hence air flow, depends is the average temperature of the column of air, not the temperature of the air as it leaves the stack. Thus it is no use heating up the air just as it leaves the stack; this is a mistake often made in the design of solar chimneys (Figure 7.7).

7.3 Ventilation configurations

For natural ventilation there are a number of basic configurations of openings. Some examples are given here.

Single-sided single opening (Figure 7.8) will give ventilation with shallow penetration, typically 3–6m, or about twice the floor to ceiling height. In summer it relies upon wind turbulence to generate reversing flows in and out of the room. Buoyancy or stack flow is only significant in the winter when greater temperature differences exist.

For single-sided double opening (Figure 7.9), the height between the openings will define the thermal stack height and this can be maximised by separating them from the

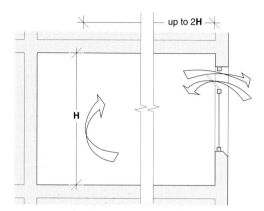

7.8 *Useful depth of single-sided ventilation from single opening.*

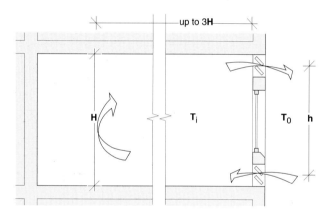

7.9 *Useful depth of single-sided ventilation from double openings for h > = 0.5H.*

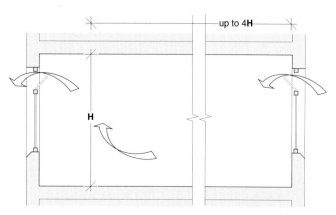

7.10 *Useful depth of cross-ventilation.*

window as illustrated. Wind also generates ventilation as for single-sided single opening, and it is slightly improved due to the increased probability of pressure differences occurring between the two apertures. Effective ventilation depth could be up to 9m, or three times floor to ceiling height.

Cross-ventilation (Figure 7.10) is very effective for wind-generated pressure differences with useful depth up to 9m, or at least three times floor to ceiling height. If back-to-back, 18m zones can be cross-ventilated. But bear in mind that heat (or other pollutants) will build up as the air moves from inlet to outlet.

7.4 Use of stacks and ducts

Stack extract (Figure 7.11) is driven by thermal buoyancy and negative pressure generated by wind over the roof (see Figure 7.5); it can increase the effective depth of natural ventilation for deep-plan buildings (Figure 7.12). However, the performance of this configuration is dependent upon several detailed parameters and cannot be predicted by simple rules. Proposed designs should be tested by mathematical or physical modelling.

Duct or underfloor supply (Figure 7.13) is mainly wind driven and provides cross-ventilation for double-banked rooms. The configuration shown is optimised for a prevailing wind direction.

Stack supply and extract (Figure 7.14) is wind driven but reverts to stack extract in the absence of wind. It is a traditional form in some tropical urban buildings (Figure 7.15). Proprietary components have recently become available from ventilation component manufacturers.

In designing for natural ventilation, the flow paths through the building must be considered. To avoid 'second-hand' air, circulation areas such as stairwells or corridors can be used as plenums or supply ducts to rooms which do not have access to the windward side of the building,[6] as in Figure 7.16. However, care must be taken that a circulation route does not act as a 'short circuit' by providing

---

6 A corridor of 2m × 2.5m cross-section with an air velocity of only 0.05m/s could provide an air change rate of 1.5ac/h for 250m² of office space.

7.11 *Extract ventilation via a stack driven by wind suction and/or thermal buoyancy.*

7.13 *Duct or underfloor fresh-air supply to avoid double-banking.*

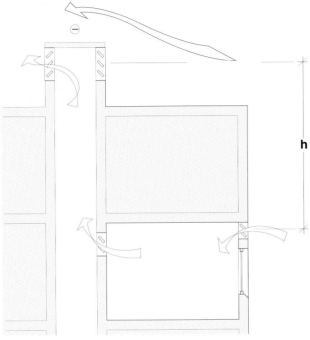

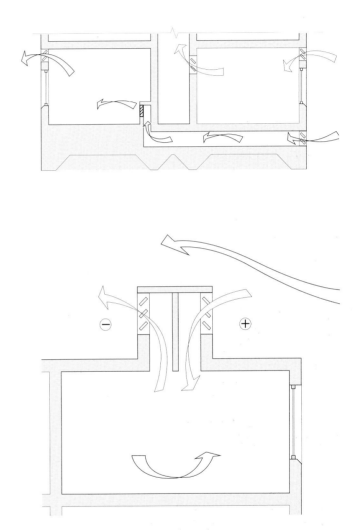

7.14 *Supply and extract via single stack.*

7.12 *The Ionica building in Cambridge uses large ventilator elements located on the roof to ventilate internal spaces via an atrium acting as an extract plenum or chimney.*

7.15 *Traditional ventilation tower or badgir in Iran.*

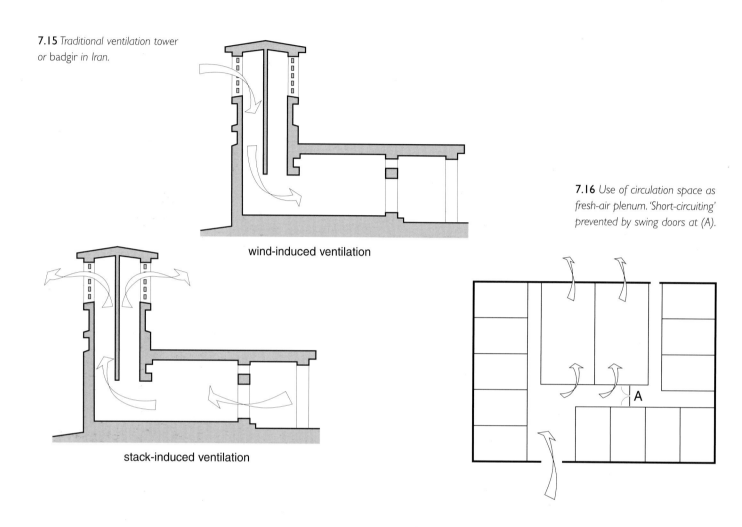

wind-induced ventilation

stack-induced ventilation

7.16 *Use of circulation space as fresh-air plenum. 'Short-circuiting' prevented by swing doors at (A).*

a path of lower resistance and preventing the fresh air from entering the occupied space.

Closely related to this are criteria for fire safety. Requirements for compartmentation often inhibit the use of natural ventilation between zones, especially involving circulation zones. However, electrically operated fire dampers, swing-door and window releasers, may be able to provide a solution in many cases.

Security also often conflicts with good ventilation practice, but this can be solved by design. Clearly, large open windows represent a security risk, especially on the ground floor. However, by adopting particular window-opening designs, or by separating the ventilation element from the window and adopting louvred grilles, natural ventilation can be provided without compromising security. This is particularly relevant for night ventilation.

7.5 Mechanical ventilation

Where a mechanical system is required, the system and its controls will have considerable bearing on energy consumption. There is a spectrum of complexity in mechanical air handling, ranging from simple mechanical extract to full air-conditioning from a centralised plant.

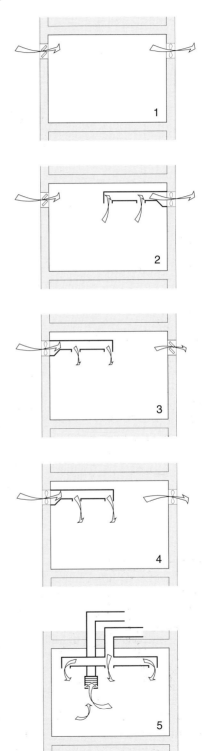

In the cases considered here, the mechanical ventilation is to ensure the provision of fresh air and the removal or dilution of pollutants. In the case of air-conditioning, however, the system will provide heating, cooling, humidity control, and filtration, as well as fresh air. This requires far more mechanical energy to overcome the resistance to air flow by heat exchangers, filters, dampers, grilles and long runs of ducting. Furthermore, fresh-air-only rates are typically around 2ac/h, whereas full air-conditioning will often require around 6ac/h, most of which is recirculated air.

The systems below, illustrated schematically in Figure 7.17, would be compatible with a wet (conventional panel emitter or 'radiator') system.

System 1 shows mechanical extract and passive infiltration. This is appropriate where there exists a local and concentrated source of the pollutant (or unwanted heat gain), e.g. kitchens and machine rooms. Note that control over the make-up air will be governed by the relative resistance of flow paths to the outside. This needs consideration to avoid drawing air from an already polluted region.

System 2 differs from the above only in that air from multiple extract grilles is collected by one fan. This would be appropriate where pollution sources are numerous and some distance from an external wall. The ducting would offer some opportunity for noise attenuation.

System 3 is a mechanical ducted supply, with passive exfiltration. This is appropriate for background fresh air supply for winter, when the air can be pre-heated, possibly from waste or solar heat sources. It carries a further advantage that uncontrolled draughts from incoming air are almost eliminated due to the over-pressure of the interior. It is not appropriate for buildings with highly concentrated pollution sources, since these will be distributed before being expelled by exfiltration.

System 4 illustrates mechanical extract and supply which gives the opportunity of controlling the internal pressure and combines the advantages of both. The extract may also be ducted. If the supply and extract duct can pass physically close to one another, then there is the opportunity for heat recovery [10.6].

System 5 shows supply and extract from a central source or plant room. This configuration is usually adopted to provide full air-conditioning, permitting recirculation and heat recovery, but at the cost of a significant increase in fan power.

Fan coil units are a common solution which combine some of the advantages of air-conditioning, with non-centralised perimeter heating systems. Figure 7.18 shows the small local air-handling unit recirculating room air to provide heating or cooling, and a fraction of fresh air. Hot and chilled water is piped to the unit from a central source. This system involves virtually no ductwork, and is a relatively low-cost option, but it does not provide the opportunity for heat reclamation from exfiltrated air. However, some systems can reclaim heat from the cooling water to balance uneven heating and cooling loads in the building. Fan coils are often adopted where the building is naturally ventilated outside the heating season, or where part of the building has to remain sealed due to the presence of external noise or other sources of pollution.

Note that horizontal discharge as shown often causes discomfort, whilst vertical discharge at the perimeter increases heat flow through the glass and leads to poor heat distribution.

Table 7.1 gives typical annual primary energy use per square metre for three cases.

Table 7.1 Annual primary energy use for fans

System	ac/h	Fan energy kWh/m²y primary
Fresh air only	2	30
Fan coil units	2	60
Full air-conditioning	7	240

7.6 Air-conditioning

The energy performance of centralised air-conditioning systems is dependent upon system design, on commissioning, control and maintenance. The topic in detail is beyond the scope of this volume. Brief guidelines to avoid the worst pitfalls are offered here:

1 Avoid dual duct systems or fixed volume terminal reheat systems as they involve cooling air and then heating it again at the point of use.

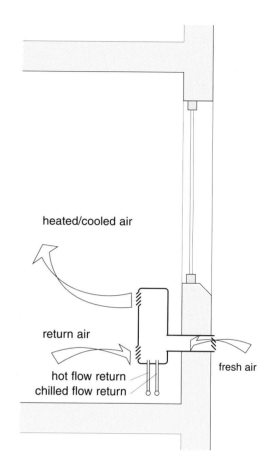

7.18 *Fan-coil units for heating, cooling and fresh-air supply.*

heated/cooled air

return air

hot flow return
chilled flow return

fresh air

2 Avoid high velocity systems – these use more fan power and create more noise.
3 Give local control in the most economical way by employing variable volume systems.
4 Reclaim heat from parts of the building with a heat surplus and consider heat storage to contribute to morning warm-up demand.
5 Consider the amount of space that the air-conditioning plant will take up. Figure 7.19 shows two actual buildings, one is air-conditioned, the other is not. In the same height, the air-conditioned building has four floors, the naturally ventilated building has five floors.

Further information can be found in Good Practice Guide 71, *Selecting Air-Conditioning Systems* (11).

7.19 *Gateway 2 (left) and the earlier Gateway 1, showing extra storey height required for air- conditioning in Gateway 1 (Architects: Arup Associates).*

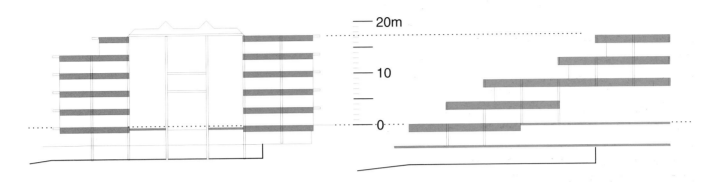

The three main purposes of ventilation are (1) fresh air supply, (2) heat rejection and (3) air movement for physiological cooling. Natural ventilation is driven by (a) wind pressure and (b) thermal buoyancy or 'stack effect'.

The configuration of openings influences the depth of effective natural ventilation. Less conventional options such as underfloor voids, ducts and towers may be applicable in non-domestic buildings to achieve ventilation in deeper plans.

Mechanical ventilation for fresh air supply or local extract can be an effective strategy in a partially passive building and consumes much less energy than full air-conditioning. Centralised air-conditioning requires significant space both on plan and section.

The passive zone concept

Interior spaces in large buildings must rely on artificial lighting and mechanical ventilation or even air-conditioning. Spaces which are on the perimeter of the building and which can benefit from daylight, solar gains and natural ventilation are said to be in the passive zone. For typical ceiling heights the potential passive zone will be about 5.5m deep, or twice the floor to ceiling height. This is a theoretical maximum and in real cases may be reduced by the presence of furniture or obstructions caused, for example, by an atrium. Figure 8.1 indicates on the plan the passive and the non-passive zones of a building with an atrium.

The proportion of the area of the passive zone of the building to the total floor area will give an indication of the building's potential for employing passive energy-saving techniques. Note that it is only potential. In practice many

8.1 *The passive zone depth is twice the floor to ceiling height for an unobstructed façade, but is reduced by an atrium.*

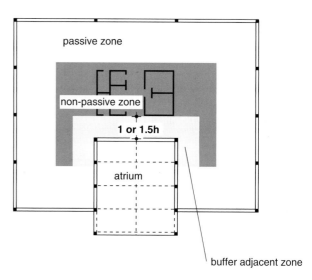

passive zone

non-passive zone

1 or 1.5h

atrium

buffer adjacent zone

h = floor to ceiling height

8.2 *The NMB bank in Amsterdam is planned to ensure all workstations are within 6m of a window. This in effect makes the whole of the building a passive zone. Architect: Ton Alberts.*

buildings have perimeter zones which are wastefully air-conditioned and artificially lit.

The passive zone may also give an indication of the subjective pleasantness of the building for it is now generally agreed that it is more difficult to make a deep-plan, highly serviced building as pleasant to the occupant as a shallow-plan building. Occupant well-being was a high pri-

ority in the design of the NMB bank in Amsterdam, where all workstations are within 6m of a window, which in effect makes the whole of the building a passive zone (Figure 8.2).

The concept of passive zone is used in the LT Method, in order to estimate the total energy consumption of a proposed building at initial design stage.

Atria and sunspaces

Chapter 9

The incorporation of an atrium into a building will not automatically lead to energy savings.

The energy consumption of a parent building may be increased if compared with a similar-shaped building without an atrium. This is due to the increased need for artificial lighting, mechanical ventilation, and possibly cooling. The atrium itself can consume energy if it is artificially lit and air-conditioned, often for the health of the planting rather than the comfort of the occupants.

In practice, atria are rarely incorporated in designs for the main purpose of energy saving. The motivation is more likely to be architectural. Accepting that the atrium is now a very common feature in large public and commercial buildings, it becomes all the more important to ensure that it does not commit the building to a lifetime of high energy consumption.

It is helpful to consider the evolution of an atrium or sunspace from an open space. The open space would provide the parent building with daylight, natural ventilation and, if south-facing, useful passive solar gains. All of these functions are potentially energy saving. If the open space is now glazed over to form an atrium, these original functions must not be jeopardised.

However, the glazing-over could bring new environmental benefits. These are illustrated in Figure 9.1; the presence of the atrium allows solar control by shading, preheated ventilation air, reduced conductive heat loss, and weather-protected useful space.

To ensure that the presence of an atrium space does not increase the energy consumption of the parent building, and that the original benefits of the open court are preserved, the following points must be observed:

9.1 *The environmental benefits of an atrium compared with an open court.*

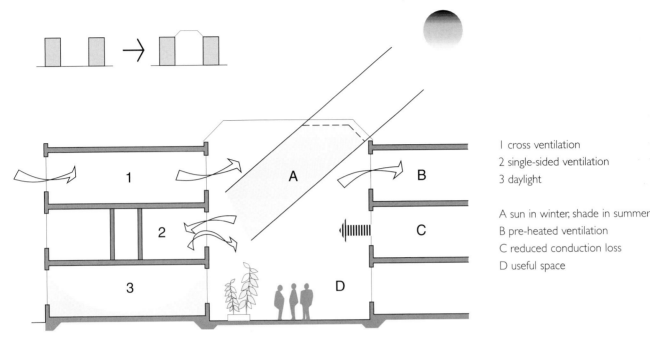

1 cross ventilation
2 single-sided ventilation
3 daylight

A sun in winter, shade in summer
B pre-heated ventilation
C reduced conduction loss
D useful space

1   The daylighting levels in the glazed space must be maximised by the use of reflective finishes and clear glazing. This will allow the surrounding rooms to be daylit and obviate the need for daytime artificial lighting in the atrium.
2   The atrium must have a supply of fresh air which will permit natural ventilation of the surrounding rooms (if fire regulations permit).
3   Shading and high rates of ventilation must be provided in summer to prevent overheating of the atrium and subsequent overheating of the surrounding spaces.

9.1 Daylighting and atria

In many cases requirements for daylight and shading are in conflict. All too often tinted or reflective glass or fixed shading devices are installed in order to prevent summer overheating. This results in reduced daylighting levels in the winter, necessitating permanent artificial lighting in adjacent rooms, and even in the atrium itself (Figure 9.2). In order to overcome this conflict, solar gain control must be variable, i.e. movable shading, and ventilation must also be variable over a wide range to respond to winter and summer conditions. This seasonal response is shown in Figure 9.3 where the Daylight Factor changes from 20% to 4% by variable transmission shading. An example of automatic atrium shading responding to heat and light is shown in Figure 9.4.

Designers are often optimistic about the use of an atrium to provide daylight into surrounding rooms. Figure 9.5 shows how rapidly the depth of the zone with a sky view becomes reduced with atrium height (or rather height above the room in question). The extension of daylighting deeper than the sky-view limit places high demands on the component reflected from the atrium walls.

These comments apply principally to top-lit atria. The critical parameters are shown in Figure 9.6. In deep atria, due to the obliquity of the sky component, even quite shallow projections can cause significant obstruction. The detailed design of the glazing of the surrounding rooms should take this into account. It may be appropriate to respond to the

9.2 *Green-tinted glass and heavily obstructed glazing combine to reduce the daylight to such an extent that permanent artificial lighting is required, mainly for the health of the vegetation.*

9.4 *Automatically operating sunblinds shade the SE and SW surfaces of the pyramidal rooflights at the atrium of Cambridge Consultants Ltd.*

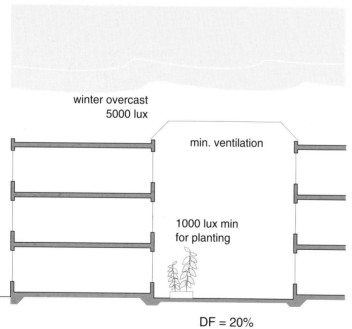

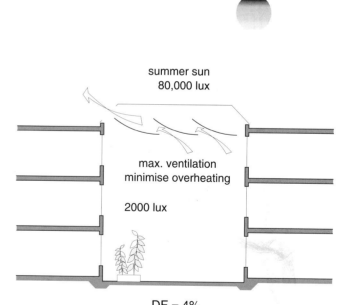

winter overcast
5000 lux

min. ventilation

1000 lux min
for planting

DF = 20%

summer sun
80,000 lux

max. ventilation
minimise overheating

2000 lux

DF = 4%

9.3 *Seasonal variation of shading and ventilation of an atrium. A change of DF from 20% to 4% allows sufficient light in winter and reduces solar gain significantly in summer.*

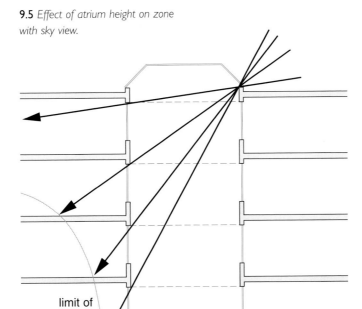

9.5 *Effect of atrium height on zone with sky view.*

limit of
sky view

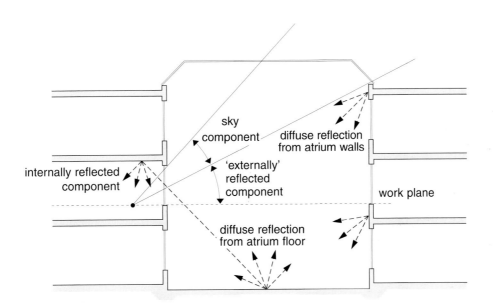

sky
component

diffuse reflection
from atrium walls

internally reflected
component

'externally'
reflected
component

work plane

diffuse reflection
from atrium floor

9.6 *Reflected light plays a vital role as well as direct sky light when the atrium is intended to be a source of daylight.*

9.7 *The glazing of the separating wall on the ground floor is tilted to increase light transmission to the adjacent rooms (School at Modane, France).*

rapid reduction in daylight availability with vertical distance from the atrium roof by increasing the glazing area, tilting the glazing (Figure 9.7) or adopting special components such as light shelves or prismatic glass. For further detail refer to specialist sources listed in the bibliography.

As a rule of thumb, the daylit zone should be considered to be limited to the sky-view zone. In more practical terms, this means a maximum height to width ratio of 3:1 for any significant daylighting to adjacent offices.

In spite of the importance of sky view, reflected light can make a vital contribution. There is much benefit in using finishes of high reflectivity on the opaque part of the atrium walls and the floor (Figure 9.8).

9.2 Winter performance

Atrium temperatures

First consider the unheated atrium. Even if the atrium is without auxiliary heating, the temperature in the atrium will be above the ambient temperature. The increment in temperature will depend on a number of factors:

1   The ratio of external glazing area of the atrium to the wall area of the parent building which is protected by the atrium (Figure 9.9).
2   The thermal transmittance of the separating wall

9.8 *A white atrium. Highly reflective finishes ensure useful daylight contributions to the surrounding rooms. However, the horizontal glazing without shading could lead to overheating in the summer (Innovation centre in Nantes, France).*

between atrium and parent building. This will normally be dominated by the amount of glazing in the wall.

3 The thermal transmittance of the external glazing of the atrium or sunspace.

4 The orientation, inclination and solar radiation transmittance of the external glazing of the atrium or sunspace.

The first three factors can be combined to form a simple calculator (Figure 9.10) which can be used to estimate average temperatures in an unheated atrium in the absence of solar gain. Due to the low thermal capacitance and high thermal transmittance of glass, temperatures in the atrium respond quite quickly to the ambient conditions, resulting in a steady state calculation such as this being useful. The calculator can be used to indicate typical daytime conditions, by using indoor daytime set-point temperature and average daytime outdoor temperature.[1]

---

1 Short-term averages may be calculated as follows:

$$\text{Daytime average } T_{day} = (1.7 T_{max} + 0.3 T_{min}) / 2$$

$$\text{Night-time average } T_{night} = (0.3 T_{max} + 1.7 T_{min}) / 2$$

where T_{max} and T_{min} are the average daily maximum and minimum temperatures respectively.

9.9 *The ratio of external glazing to the protected area (or separating wall) has a strong influence on the thermal performance of the atrium.*

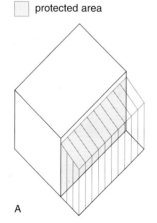 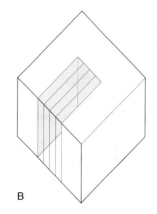 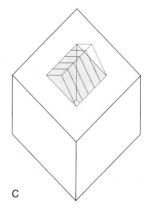

protected area

A

B

C

9.10 *Nomogram for estimating average temperature in an unheated atrium. The dotted lines show typical examples for atrium types A and C, from Figure 9.9, for a 50% glazed separating wall.*

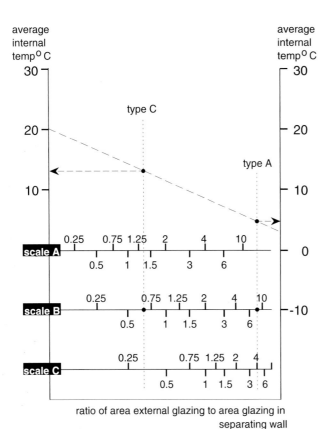

- Draw a straight line between appropriate points on the internal and external temperature scales.

- Choose scale according to glazing type.

- Draw vertical line from ratio of glazing areas.

- From intersection move horizontally to either temperature scale for atrium temperature.

scale A: double external / single separating
scale B: double / double or single / single
scale C: single external / double separating

A more detailed model, which takes account of solar gains and the exchange of air between the atrium and the parent building, has been used to generate the graphs shown in Figure 9.11. They are drawn for an unheated atrium in the UK, roughly of the form shown in Figure 9.9 (case C).

Figure 9.11(a) shows the effect of the glazing ratio of the separating wall. The 'seasonal shift' indicates the climatic equivalent inside the atrium; in this example the temperature in the atrium in January is equivalent to the temperature outside in late April. It is a useful concept rein-forcing the idea that the atrium has a climate, rather than rigid environmental standards. Note that during the winter the atrium temperature is higher where the glazing ratio of the separating wall is 75%.

Figure 9.11(b) shows the contribution made by solar gain and compares this with the effect of an opaque insulated roof. Note that the opaque roof performs better (thermally) than the glazed atrium in the mid-winter months due to the poor solar radiation. However, the precise performance in this respect will depend on the relative amounts of south-facing and non-south-facing atrium glazing.

9.11 *Predicted monthly temperatures for a typical atrium of type C.*

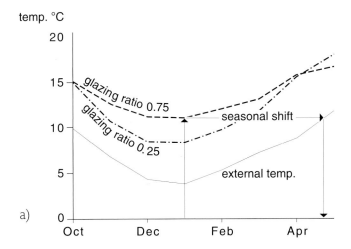

temp. °C

a)

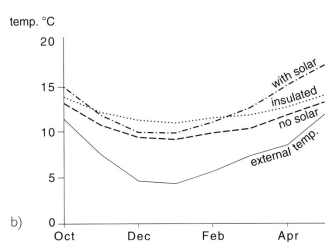

temp. °C

b)

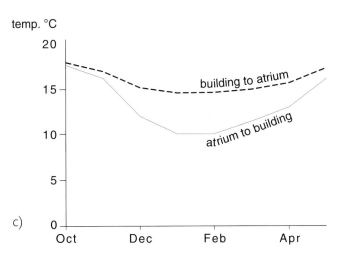

temp. °C

c)

Figure 9.11(c) shows the effect of ventilation air flowing from the heated building to the atrium, or into the building via the atrium. In the first case, a useful enhancement to the atrium temperature is gained. In the second case, there is the energy-saving potential of ventilation pre-heating. The temperature increments, together with the protection from rain and wind, will greatly increase the amenity value of the atrium space when compared with an open space.

The temperatures shown in Figure 9.11 are daily averages. Temperatures on an hourly basis have been simulated and results for a typical day in February are shown in Figure 9.12. It can be seen that the daytime average during occupancy is quite close to a comfort temperature – quite adequate for a circulation area, or even a seating area with minimal local radiant heating [9.4]. Figure 9.13 is also derived from the results of hourly simulations, showing mean atrium temperatures during occupied hours on sunny days and cloudy days.

Minimum temperatures at night are often important for the survival of plants. Most buildings will have a night set-back temperature of about 12–14°C, and heat flow from the building, together with stored heat in walls and floor, will maintain a temperature well above ambient for all but an atrium with a very large ratio of external glazing area to protected area. Figure 9.15 shows the monitored results from the unheated atrium shown in Figure 9.14, where during a very cold period with minimum outdoor temperatures of –10°C, the atrium minimum was around 7°C.

Two useful concepts when considering the performance of an atrium are the *protectivity* and the *solarity*. The protectivity is defined as the ratio of the separating wall area to the atrium external envelope area. In the examples shown in Figure 9.9, the protectivity varies from about 0.25 (case A) to about 3 (case C). The solarity is defined as the ratio of south-facing glazing (or inclined greater than 45°) to the total area of glazing in the external atrium envelope. In the examples in Figure 9.10 this has approximate values of 0.33 (A), 0.66 (B), 0.2 (C).

Thermal energy saving

The temperature increment in an atrium reduces the heat losses from the parent building and can provide tempered

9.12 *Computer simulation of hourly temperatures in an unheated atrium in winter.*

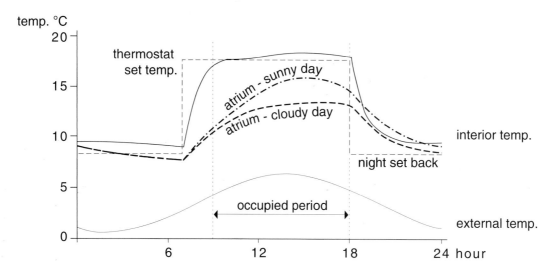

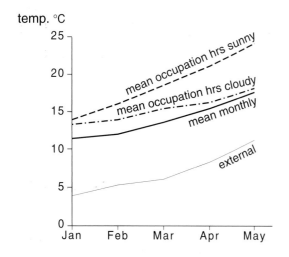

9.13 *Mean daytime temperature increment over monthly average for unheated atrium.*

9.14 *Unheated atrium at Cambridge Consultants Ltd maintains a minimum temperature sufficient for the tender but not tropical plants.*

fresh air to reduce the ventilation heating load. Even when air is being dumped from the parent building, the increase in atrium temperature reduces heat loss compared with the case where the air is dumped direct to the outside – i.e. there is a kind of heat-recovery effect. As with atrium temperatures, the energy saving is strongly dependent upon the critical parameters of the atrium, the protectivity and the solarity, and the size of the atrium relative to the parent building.

A quantitative account of these effects is given by the Buffer-space Thermal Savings tables of the LT Method 2.0 [12.8]. Figure 9.16 shows the modelled results for a typical atrium building in the UK, giving an indication of the orders of magnitude. The graph gives the annual heating load for a number of ventilation options.

The biggest step is in the difference between an independently ventilated atrium (b) and having no atrium at all (a). Here the saving is all due to the reduced conductive losses through the separating wall. The modelled building has a rather high protectivity ratio of about 2.5, which accounts for this significant effect.

Energy saving can be increased by ventilation coupling between the atrium and the parent building. The ventilation pre-heat mode (c) is particularly appropriate for atria of high solarity, when during sunny hours the atrium temperature might go unnecessarily high without the ingress of ambient air. The ventilation dumping mode (d) causes slight savings but carries the advantage of higher atrium temperatures, particularly appropriate on cloudy days in winter.

The recirculation mode (e) is interesting. At first sight this should be ruled out on grounds of air quality, since

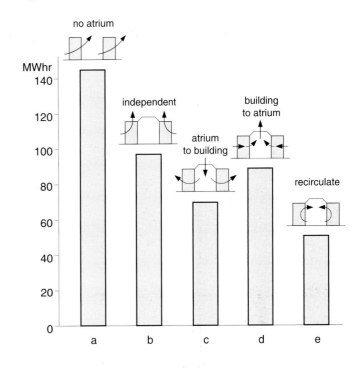

9.16 *Heating energy consumption by a building with an atrium for different ventilation modes.*

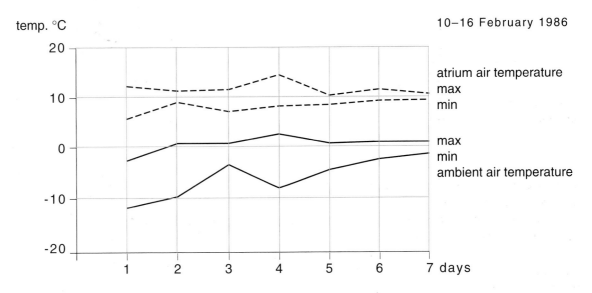

10–16 February 1986

atrium air temperature
max
min

max
min
ambient air temperature

9.15 *Measured temperature in unheated atrium at Cambridge Consultants Ltd over seven days in winter.*

there is no obvious source of fresh air. However, unavoidable infiltration through the atrium envelope takes place over 24 hours (and is allowed for in this simulation), whilst the building is typically occupied for about 10 hours. Furthermore, atria often contain large quantities of green plants which absorb CO_2 and other contaminants. The notion of the atrium being in symbiosis with the building is an attractive one, but must be treated with some caution. In practice, a mix of all three modes (c), (d) and (e) could probably be used to advantage, controlling the temperature swings and air quality. This would certainly demand fairly sophisticated automatic controls. A serious threat to systems of this kind is the provision for fire safety. However, with certain constraints, ventilation linking between building and atrium is not ruled out.

It must be reiterated here that in many non-domestic buildings heating energy forms only a small part of the total energy consumption. The thermal energy benefits of an atrium can easily be compensated by the loss in daylighting and natural ventilation.

9.3 Summer performance

The main concern is to prevent overheating. Three passive measures, in descending order of effectiveness, may be employed to attain this: shading, ventilation, and the incorporation of thermal mass.

Shading

Shading is the first line of defence reducing the ingress of solar gain. Shade can also reduce the effective temperature, as experienced by an occupant, by up to 8°C. It also reduces glare, which is of psychological benefit during times of heat stress.

Ideally the shading should be movable. Fixed shading, or tinted glazing, will reduce daylighting levels all year round, creating a need for artificial lighting for the atrium and the adjacent spaces in winter. To a large extent the discussion on shading device types [6.4] applies here also. If movable shading cannot be adopted, it is better to reduce the glazing area by having opaque well-insulated areas in the atrium envelope. If fixed shading is applied to the south-facing slopes, the shading function is maximised. If applied to north-facing roof slopes, this allows useful winter solar gains but performs less well to prevent summer overheating. A good compromise for relatively cool climates is where steep-angled south-facing glazing is left unshaded, and the shallow-angled north-sloping atrium envelope is opaque insulation.

Alternatively, geometrically selective louvres and overhangs can shade summer sun and admit winter sun, but these will inevitably reduce daylight from the diffuse sky.

The advantage of external shading is often stressed. The performance of external shading certainly is better, particularly in windows, as illustrated in Figure 5.10. However, when shading devices are positioned well away from and above the occupants, re-emission of heat by radiation and convection is far less significant. If the devices are light coloured and well ventilated, then internal shading can be highly effective. This has the advantage of significant cost reductions compared with external devices, and facilitates control and maintenance.

Ventilation

Many atria are sealed and mechanically ventilated, even cooled. Sensitive to the need to limit cooling loads, the designer uses heavily tinted glazing and permanent shading, reducing lighting levels to such an extent that artificial lighting is required even in the daytime. The choice of subtropical plants then adds to the demand for year-round thermal conditions. Thus the spiral of energy consumption is born.

Natural ventilation can provide high rates of air change for zero energy cost. The ventilation of the atrium can also induce cross-ventilation of the surrounding occupied spaces.

Heat can be rejected by ventilation when the outside temperature is below the atrium temperature [5.4]. Natural ventilation is driven by wind pressure and thermal buoyancy. The limiting case is likely to be the latter, i.e. when there is no breeze. Two kinds of buoyancy driven ventilation can be identified. They are *mixing ventilation* and *displacement ventilation*, and are defined by the position of the openings.

9.17 Mixing ventilation *from a high-level opening in an atrium minimises stratification.*

9.18 Displacement ventilation *by low-level and high-level openings encourages stratification which may be useful in summer to keep warm air away from occupied floors.*

cold plume entrains
warmer air

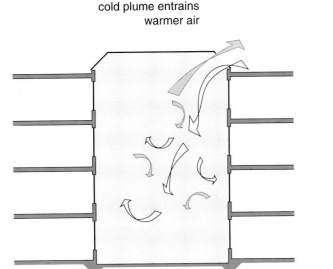

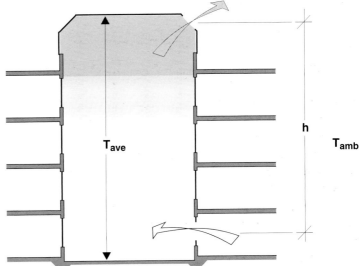

T_{ave}

h

T_{amb}

Figure 9.17 shows the effect of openings at the top only of an atrium. Warm air leaves the atrium, reducing the pressure and allowing cool air to enter via the same opening. This cool, dense air then falls to the floor, mixing with the warm air as it falls. This results in the air temperature at floor level being above ambient by an amount dependent upon the size of the opening – the larger the opening the closer to the outside temperature. This is known as mixing ventilation and leads to a relatively uniform vertical temperature distribution.

Figure 9.18 shows the effect of openings at the top and bottom of an atrium. Warm air leaves the upper opening and cooler air enters the lower opening. Assuming there is a steady heat input from a sunpatch or other source, then an equilibrium is reached where a stationary boundary between the upper warm air and the cool air exists. Reducing the size of the openings lowers this boundary and increases the temperature of the upper zone, but the temperature of the lower zone remains at or close to the ambient temperature. This ventilation mode is known as displacement ventilation or stack effect.

In most situations, displacement ventilation is appropriate for summer conditions. In most atria, occupation occurs at floor level (excepting galleries and staircases) and thus it is important to keep the temperature at floor level as low as possible. The position of the boundary is important. Ideally, the hot layer will be confined to a level above adjacent occupied spaces. This suggests that atria should have extra height to ensure this, as indicated in Figure 9.18. The boundary is not sharp – there is a mixing layer as indicated in the diagram. The temperature distribution is known as *stratification,* and is clearly an advantage in summer conditions. However, it is wrong to suggest that the stack effect is driven by stratification. It is driven by the difference in the mean temperature of the column of air and the outside air, integrated over the height of the stack.

For displacement ventilation, driven by stack effect, openings will be required at the top and bottom of between 5% and 10% of the roof glazing area of a top-lit atrium. For atria with large areas of vertical glazing facing between south and west, the openable areas should relate similarly to these glazing areas. The more shading that can

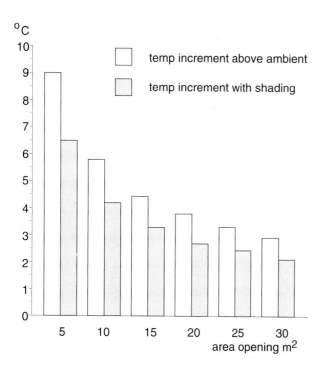

9.19 *The effect of ventilation openings and shading on average atrium temperature.*

Height between inlet and outlet	12m
Area of roof glazing	144m²
U-value of glazing	6.0
Solar gain factor	0.65/0.4
Peak solar radiation	850 W/m²

Note – area is value for each top and bottom opening

be provided, the smaller the openings need be for a given thermal performance, as illustrated in Figure 9.19, which is for a predominantly top-lit atrium. These temperature increments are averaged over the height of the atrium. With displacement ventilation, temperature increments at ground level will be much lower.

It must be emphasised that the stack effect only works when the average temperature of the air in the stack is greater than the ambient temperature. In summer conditions this may be too hot for comfort in the upper parts of the atrium. At night, however, heat retained in massive elements in the atrium will drive the stack effect to provide useful night cooling.

Stack effect in the atrium may also induce cross-ventilation in the adjacent spaces, where the lower inlet airflow paths are via these spaces (Figure 9.20). However, the designer should not be too optimistic about this; the stack effect is quite weak and large openings will be required. A further complication is that the stack height varies floor by floor, demanding careful control of opening areas.

One set of openings can often serve the function of summer ventilation and smoke-extract vents. Both shading and vents can be mechanically operated and controlled by heat sensors.

Thermal mass

The principle of limiting overheating by thermal mass has already been described [5.5] and the same recommendations broadly apply. Typical finishes in atria tend to be massive – brick, stone, concrete, etc., and this is an advantage over rooms which although massive structurally, will often be lined with lightweight finishes. It was pointed out that mass is only effective if it can be cooled at night and in this respect the height of the atrium is an advantage in setting up strong buoyancy driven ventilation (stack effect).

The downside of massive finishes is their lack of acoustic absorption which in combination with large volumes can lead to excessive reverberation time and hence noise problems. Solutions to this problem include the provision of acoustically absorbing banners or panels. Vegetation improves the situation to a limited extent.

9.4 Heating in atria

Due to its large volume, the atrium is an intrinsically extravagant space to heat, and thus the heating of atria should be avoided if possible. It has already been pointed out that atrium temperatures in winter are usually well above ambient temperatures and may be sufficient for functions such as circulation. However, limited heating may be justified to provide local areas of comfort for sedentary occupants.

9.20 *Gateway 2 at Basingstoke where stack effect in the atrium draws air through the adjacent offices (Architects: Arup Associates).*

9.21 *The use of reflecting surfaces to direct sunlight to the occupied zone of the atrium.*

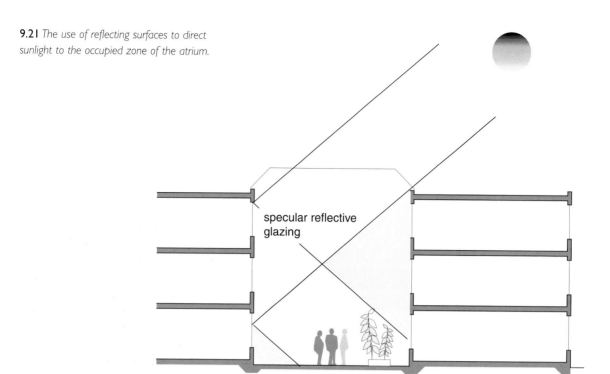

specular reflective glazing

Stratification is undesirable in winter when it is obviously advantageous to realise any heat gains at floor level. Mixing ventilation leads to very little stratification and so if ventilation is necessary for fresh air supply (further to uncontrolled infiltration), it should be provided by high-level vents only. Stratification may occur in winter if there are large heat inputs from a sunpatch high up in the atrium. The position of the sunpatch is related to the geometry of the atrium. It may also be controlled by the use of specular (mirror) reflecting surfaces as shown in Figure 9.21.

Another cause of stratification is a large heat input from a convective (warm air) source. This is a totally inappropriate form of heating for an atrium since it has to fill up the atrium with warm air from the top down before it benefits the occupants (Figure 9.22).

If comfort heating is to be provided in an atrium it should be from local radiant sources. Indeed it should be regarded as heating the occupants rather than space heating of the atrium. A high temperature source can be used from an elevated position and could be regarded as an 'artificial sun'. An alternative is to use underfloor heating, at low temperature. It may be necessary to provide minimal heating for the survival of plants. This demand can be minimised by the following:

1   Make good use of free heat gains – for example, solar gains stored in massive elements, and 'dumping' exhaust air from the parent building.
2   Consider making movable shading devices function also as night insulation.
3   Choose plant species which can tolerate low temperatures. Remember that the plants occupy the building 24 hours per day, 7 days a week – four times longer than human occupants.
4   If heating is necessary use local radiant sources or underfloor heating. Do not use convective (warm air) heaters.

9.22 *If heating has to be provided in an atrium it should not be a convective input, i.e. warm air. It should be limited to where the occupants are, e.g. underfloor heating or a local radiant source.*

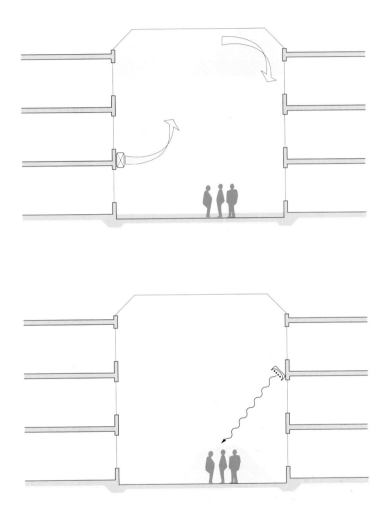

Atria are not automatically energy-saving features. The energy saving and the temperature conditions of an unheated atrium can vary quite widely and are dependent upon the configuration, the conductance of the separating wall and the atrium envelope, and ventilation exchange between the atrium and the parent building.

For an atrium to provide useful daylighting to adjacent spaces it should be designed to maximise the sky view and have high reflectance walls and floor. Overheating in summer can be reduced by shading and ventilation. Ideally shading should be movable to allow maximum daylight penetration during dull winter conditions. Suitable planting should be chosen to avoid demands for heating and lighting which often cause significant energy consumption.

10

Energy systems

As buildings have become more dependent upon services, and services have grown in complexity, the architect has become increasingly divorced from the services design process. Services design has become more and more reactive to the wishes of the architect, which in turn has given the impression to the architect of almost complete freedom.

It is now evident that this has been a recipe for high energy consumption, high capital costs, and often buildings which are not enjoyed by their occupants. With a renewed interest in passive design, where the building shares the important role of providing a satisfactory environment, there must be more dialogue between architect and engineer. Increasingly the need for the design team approach is being recognised.

Services engineering design is a topic outside the scope of this volume. The following section is intended to provide only the most basic background to some of the more strategic decisions that have to be made by the design team.

10.1 Energy sources

The choice of energy source for environmental systems has a considerable influence on cost. It also has a significant impact on environmental pollution, in particular CO_2 as shown in Table 10.1. Atmospheric CO_2 is now identified as the largest single cause of global warming, and as part of the Kyoto Treaty the UK government is committed to reducing emissions by 20% of present levels by the year 2010. To get a complete picture, CO_2 production per useful kWh must be considered, since certain fuels have a considerably lower conversion efficiency than others, as shown in Table 10.1.

Table 10.1 CO_2 and relative cost for fuel options

Fuel	Cost factor	kg CO_2/kWh delivered	CO_2/kWh useful
Electricity	5.2	0.83	0.83
Gas	1.3	0.2	0.24
Oil (class D)	1.0	0.3	0.37
Coal	0.8	0.33	0.44

Source: BRECSU (9)

This shows that the best conventional fuel for heating is natural gas, from the point of view of impact on the global environment. However, clearly this would be a short-term solution only. Advances in coal-handling technologies have extended the applicability of coal to a range of non-domestic buildings. There have also been advances in efficiency and clean burning, although due to the inherent chemistry CO_2 output remains higher than for gas or oil. Coal suits buildings requiring large and continuous heating loads. For example, the initial design study for a new low-energy hospital at Ashington in Northumberland showed that coal would be an economically viable option for the main fuel source.

The use of electricity for heating incurs far higher inefficiencies – largely at the power station – than other conventional fuels, and consequently results in a high output of carbon dioxide. This is why it is misleading to add delivered units of electricity to delivered units of other fuels. For some applications, of course, there is no choice of energy source – electricity is required for lighting and mechanical ventilation systems, for example. It may be possible, however, to consider replacing electricity use for certain applications such as heat pumps with mechanical energy from a prime mover, or to generate electricity in a combined heat and power (CHP) installation [10.3].

Non-conventional options such as solar thermal, geothermal, photovoltaic and wind power provide energy which, after the manufacture of the plant, has no penalty in terms of carbon dioxide production and emission of other environmentally damaging substances such as sulphur dioxide and dust particles. Other renewable sources, such as biomass in the form of timber, fuel crops and agricultural waste, do produce carbon dioxide when burnt – but this is the same in quantity as the carbon dioxide which has been removed from the atmosphere during the growth of the crop.

10.2 Renewable sources of heat

Solar energy

Good design exploits the potential for passive solar gain by consideration for glazing area, thermal mass and orientation. Control systems also play a vital part in solar utilisation. However, as illustrated by the LT Method, solar thermal systems have a relatively small potential in most non-domestic buildings, except those of a domestic scale and without large internal heat gains.

Active solar technologies (which usually require a conventional energy input to collect energy from a renewable source) include the use of solar collectors to pre-heat air or hot water supplies. A backup system using a conventional fuel is always required, increasing the capital cost of the system which for most applications will have a long payback period. However, with increasing availability of such systems and rising costs of conventional fuels, their economic viability improves steadily.

The most appropriate application of active solar water heating with current energy costs is where it replaces electrical heating, because of the non-availability or inconvenience of conventional fuels. Its viability is also increased in buildings operating only in summer, such as holiday centres, camping and sports facilities. Swimming pools, especially outdoor pools, which require large quantities of low temperature heating, are particularly appropriate for solar water heating. It is interesting to note that in southern European countries such as Spain, Italy and Greece, solar water heating is commonplace and especially associated with the tourist and hotel industry.

Heat pumps

Heat pumps can provide usable heat from low temperature sources such as the ambient air or water. Due to the consumption of electricity to power the compressor and circulating pumps, the efficiency of such a system in terms

10.1 *The St. Mary's Hospital, Isle of Wight, uses heat recovered from the incinerator flue gases to pre-heat hot water.*

of primary energy use must be considered carefully. The efficiency is described as the Coefficient of Performance (CoP), which is defined as the ratio of the thermal energy output to the electrical energy input. Typical values for building applications lie in the range 2 to 4.5. A CoP of about 3 for an electrically driven system means that its CO_2 output is comparable with the best gas-fired boiler.

Greater efficiency is achieved by using the heat pump as part of a heat recovery system from a local source of waste heat, perhaps from an industrial process, flue gases, rejected hot water, etc. The low energy St. Mary's Hospital, Isle of Wight (Figure 10.1), uses a system of this kind. Underground aquifers may also be used as low tempera-

ture heat sources for heat pump systems. Figure 10.2 illustrates a heat pump system. Thermal storage is used when the supply of low-grade heat is intermittent and not coincident with heat demand.

10.3 Electricity generation

Combined heat and power (CHP)

To by-pass the inefficiency of centralised electricity generation, with the waste of the rejected heat and the subsequent waste of energy in distribution from the power station, electricity can be generated on site by a system

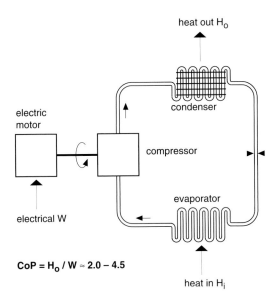

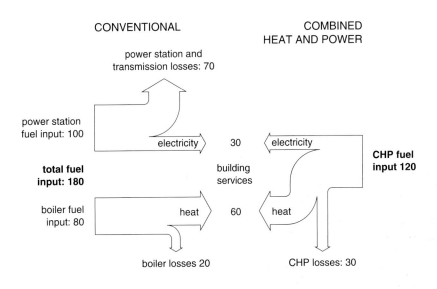

which utilises the waste heat production at source. The principle is illustrated in the Sankey diagram in Figure 10.3. There is increased interest in 'mini-CHP' installations which are matched to the heat load of one building, with the possibility of surplus electricity being sold back to the grid.

Windpower

Wind generation of electricity has a promising future at both small and large scales. Countries such as Denmark and The Netherlands have many operating 'wind farms', each comprising a number of individual machines. Test sites exist in the UK, and studies show that, due to the long coastline, wind resources in this country are the best in Europe.

Most large machines are connected to the grid. The main problem associated with stand-alone wind-power systems is the need for storage, so that power is available when the winds are too light to be useful for generation. Chemical storage, the use of gravity stores (pumping water uphill as a store of potential energy, for example), or thermal storage in tanks or underground aquifers are possible solutions to this problem.

It is doubtful whether generation local to specific buildings is generally viable. Due to the generating potential of the wind being proportional to the wind-speed to the power three, $(W)^3$, installations on remote and exposed sites will always be much more economically viable than sheltered sites. Thus the decision to utilise windpower is largely out of the architect's control.

Hydropower

The UK currently uses less than 2% hydro-generated electricity on the National Grid. There is considerable potential for the use of small-scale hydro plants, particularly in remote upland areas where the cost of connection to the grid makes local generation attractive.

The economics of small-scale generation is continually changing, due to technological advances and the new buy-back policy introduced by the Electricity Generation Act. The policy of the regional electricity boards differs; this can have a profound effect on the viability of such systems on particular sites.

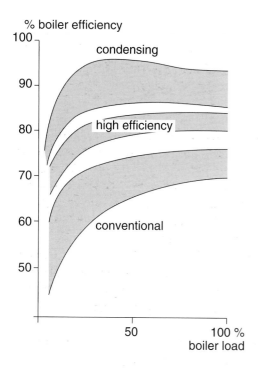

10.4 *Boiler efficiencies as a function of boiler load. Source: BRECSU (10).*

Technical advances, such as the development of condensing boilers, are making high efficiency equipment available for a wide range of applications. Figure 10.4 shows how operating efficiencies reduce for boilers running under part load. Note that condensing boilers have an efficiency around 90%, even at half load. Other important factors include the proper sequencing of boilers to ensure full load operation and reduce standing losses, and the provision of proper maintenance.

Services generally have a shorter life expectancy than building fabric elements; in refurbishment projects, boilers and other plant may need to be replaced in any case, and so the extra cost of high-efficiency systems is marginal. The replacement of plant and controls in many cases will have little disruptive effect on the fabric and operation of the building, and is thus an attractive option for such projects. Improvements to plant in buildings with intrinsically poor performance (building design factors [Chapter 2]), e.g. poor values of insulation, will show greater savings in absolute terms than buildings with intrinsically good performance.

Distribution of heat around a building or site will inevitably lead to some losses. These are minimised if service runs are as short as possible, in particular if zones of the building which are especially heavily serviced (for example, which require full air-conditioning) are located close to one another, and close to the main plant room.

Distribution ducts and pipes – for hot water, air or steam – should be appropriately insulated. Low-temperature distribution will result in lower losses, but may require larger heat emitters.

Losses will be reduced if pipes or ductwork run through heated spaces, but thought should then be given to minimising the volume of space occupied: water distribution systems will take up less volume than air systems.

Sufficient space should be provided for maintenance and access. Recent experience with sick-building syndrome (SBS) has drawn attention to the need for access to clean the inside of ductwork and air-handling equipment.

In some situations, savings may be made by servicing the building or site as several separate systems rather than distributing heat from a centralised boiler house. Similarly, water heating at point of use could be considered where

10.4 Heat production and distribution

Substantial energy savings are possible from maximising the efficiency of plant and control systems. This is discussed in Chapter 2, and Figure 2.1 indicates that plant design is as important as building design and the effect of occupants. Building Energy Management Systems (BEMS) have developed in the past decade, with the purpose of improving overall operational efficiency.

For a typical application to an office building, fuel savings attributed to the use of an energy management system break down as follows:

7%   boiler efficiency;
11%   improved controls, including optimum start and stop;
10%   accurate adaptation to patterns of use, holiday scheduling, temperature control, etc.

demand is low; this could be economic even if electricity is used as the fuel.

10.5 Heat emitters

The basic differentiation is between delivery of heat by convective and radiant means. Some emitters are almost entirely convective (warm air); some almost entirely radiant (high-level radiant tubes); some such as water-filled radiators use a combination of both heat transfer mechanisms.

Convective emitters

Warm air systems are most appropriate where:

1   air handling is required for humidity control, dust control, cooling;
2   quick response is needed (perhaps in response to fluctuating solar gains);
3   internal surfaces are lightweight and will respond quickly.

However, the higher rates of air movement typical of convective systems may cause discomfort due to the perception of draughts, particularly when lower delivery temperatures are used to minimise distribution losses.

Air is heated (and cooled) either locally or centrally. Local heating may be by natural convection or more commonly by fan-assisted units. These are referred to as fan-coil units (see [7.5], Figure 7.18). Heat (or 'coolth') is delivered to the local unit by heated (or chilled) water. Room air is drawn into the unit, heated and ejected into the room. If units are located on or close to the external wall they may introduce a fraction of fresh air.

Larger fan-coil units may be located in ceiling voids or in local plant rooms and are usually referred to as air-handling units (AHUs). With local air-handling systems, the need for ductwork to be routed around the building is avoided and they can respond to local heating or cooling demands.

If central air-handling systems are used, they may have constant or variable air volume (CV or VAV).

1   CV systems typically require smaller, more efficient fans.

2   VAV systems are appropriate where loads are concentrated in particular areas at particular times of day, for example in catering facilities.

Radiant emitters

Radiant systems can operate at high or low temperatures. Low-temperature installations (for example, heated floor slabs) have a surface temperature which is comfortable to the touch and can thus be located close to or touching the building occupants. High-temperature systems, such as panel emitters or radiant tubes, must be carefully positioned to avoid discomfort. Radiant panels may be water heated; tubes are usually heated by the direct combustion of gas. Electrical radiant heaters are also available but should only be used where heating is highly intermittent.

Radiant systems are advantageous where:

1   stratification of air temperature is undesirable such as in tall spaces, particularly atria [9.4];
2   the space is lightly occupied and heating need is localised – reception desks, warehouses, etc.;
3   heavy buildings are to be intermittently heated.

Systems with a strong radiative component enable comfort to be achieved at a slightly lower air temperature, thus saving energy. Note that water-filled panel 'radiators' emit only about 30% of their energy as radiation and this is reduced further for multi-layer panels and thus should be considered as convective emitters.

10.6 Heat recovery

Heat recovery systems operate on one of two basic principles. Firstly, there is the direct exchange of heat by thermal wheels, run-around coils, and plate heat exchangers: these always downgrade energy since it is not possible to raise the output temperature above that of the source. Secondly, various types of heat pumps can be used to raise the temperature of the system above that of the source, but these require an input of high grade (mechanical) energy. This has already been discussed [10.2].

It is essential that heat recovery systems should more than recover their own operating costs, including maintenance, and lead to an overall reduction in CO_2 emission. Remember that many recovery systems will require electrical energy to power fans or heat pumps, and consequently are relatively heavy users of primary energy.

High temperature sources (for example, flue gases) will in general provide the easiest and most economical ways of recovering heat. As with waste heat sources discussed above, it is important to match heat sources to the end use. Ideally, the source and the end use will be physically located close together and have similar patterns of utilisation. High temperature sources, such as incinerator flues, can be used to provide hot water supplies; low temperature sources such as return air or waste water are useful for pre-heating incoming air and mains water.

To improve the match between supply and demand, heat can be stored in well-insulated water tanks. The use of stores, however, will inevitably lead to some storage losses and consequent reduction in system efficiency.

10.7 Controls

Effective controls are essential to obtain the best possible performance from low-energy design features. The low-energy building may in fact require a more sophisticated control regime than a conventional highly serviced building – which makes less use of ambient conditions for 'free' heat or ventilation potential.

Controls must therefore be capable of responding to the complex interaction of a number of variables, including the characteristics of controls, emitters and the building itself. The controls should always have a faster response time than the emitters, and the emitters a faster response than the building.

Automatic controls are becoming increasingly sophisticated, and there are a number of Building Energy Management Systems (BEMS) on the market which can be customised to control all aspects of the building's environment. Nevertheless, there are advantages to manual controls, or manual overrides on automatic control systems. Personal preferences for degrees of warmth, for example, can vary quite widely and energy is wasted if an individual is forced to endure an environment that he finds too hot or (in summer) too cold. Furthermore, several studies have shown that there is an important psychological element to 'comfort' – a high degree of personal control over the immediate environment may lessen sensitivity, for example, to occasional overheating in summer.

Manual controls must be user friendly; that is, easily accessible and simple to operate correctly. Even more important is that they should be adapted to the social and ergonomic needs of the building's occupants: controls are useless if those who would benefit from their operation are not motivated – or empowered – to use them. The following points should be considered:

Heating and cooling

1   appropriate target temperatures, bearing in mind the typical activity level and clothing of building occupants – a building which is 1°C too warm may cost 5-10% more to heat.;
2   zoning – areas with different use patterns should be independently controllable; so should the spaces behind façades of different orientation in buildings with large solar gains;
3   optimum start controls to adjust warm-up periods for intermittently occupied spaces according to internal and external temperatures – intelligent controls are capable of learning from patterns of previous use.

Lighting

1   zoning – correct levels of lighting for different areas;
2   use of dimmers to reduce artificial light levels gradually in response to increasing daylight – controlled by a photocell-operated automatic system;
3   provision of task lighting to enable background lighting levels to be reduced;
4   group switching of lights, so that (for example) perimeter lights can be turned off as daylight levels rise;
5   time control to ensure that all lights are switched off at lunchtime and the end of the working day; pull cords or I. R. controllers should be available as manual overrides;

6   use of occupancy detecting switches using infra-red detectors are particularly useful during times when the building is very lightly occupied – e.g. for cleaning.

10.8 Management issues

Human factors have a high degree of influence on the actual energy use of a building (see Figure 2.1). These factors are not directly within the designer's control; however, the 'feel' of the building has an impact on how well its occupants respond to the designer's intentions, and thus contribute to its overall energy efficiency.

Motivation

The use of manual controls, opening windows, etc. involves the building occupants in decisions which affect energy use. It is important that occupants are motivated to use controls sensibly. This is facilitated by good design of controls so that their mode of operation is clearly apparent and there is immediate feedback on the result of an instruction. Where practicable, control systems should be designed to fail safe, with the default mode governed by an intelligent energy management system.

Maintenance

Provision for regular maintenance is essential to the efficient functioning of the building and its services. This includes window cleaning, replacement of filters, cleaning of flues and ducts, and replacement of failed lamps. Sufficient space must be provided within the plant room and service runs for a straightforward, logical arrangement of the installation and for maintenance access.

Targets

Building users need to be aware of targets for the optimum performance of the building. Where this information has been calculated as part of the design process, it should be included in the users' manual. Procedures for monitoring energy use should be set up and the results publicised.

> *Environmental systems and controls can contribute at least as much as the fabric and form of the building to its energy performance. Improvements in this area can be highly cost effective, especially for refurbishment projects.*

10.5 *The Cutty Sark represented the peak of development of the working ship and a fine example of sustainable technology. Her best grain run from Sydney to London was 84 days and, until recently, held the world record six-day run of 2,180 miles, with only the use of renewable energy. Modern, highly serviced buildings such as the Canary Wharf tower represent the other end of the spectrum, consuming large amounts of energy just to provide light and air for the occupants.*

10.5

Bibliography

1   Building Research Energy Conservation Support Unit (BRECSU) Energy Consumption Guide No. 10.

2   Humphreys, M. and Nicol, F., Theoretical and practical aspects of thermal comfort, BRE Current Paper CP 14/71

3   Building Research Energy Conservation Support Unit (BRECSU) Energy Consumption Guide No. 19.

4   van Dijk, H. A. L. and Arkesteijn, C. A. M., Windows and space heating requirements. TNO Institute Applied Physics, Delft 1987.

5   ETSU (Yannas, S). Passive solar energy efficient house design.

6   Building Research Energy Conservation Support Unit (BRECSU) Energy Consumption Guide, No. 35.

7   Szokolay, S. V., Passive and low energy design. *Proc Conf. PLEA*, Pergamon 1985.

8   Estimating daylight in buildings, parts 1 and 2. *BRE Digests 309 and 310*. Building Research Establishment 1986.

9   Building Research Energy Conservation Support Unit (BRECSU), Good Practice Guide No. 28.

10 Building Research Energy Conservation Support Unit (BRECSU), Guide for installers of condensing boilers in commercial buildings. Good Practice Guide No. 16.

11 Building Research Energy Conservation Support Unit (BRECSU). *Selecting Air-Conditioning Systems*. Good Practice Guide No. 71.

For further information contact the Enquiries Bureau, Building Research Energy Conservation Support Unit (BRECSU), Building Research Establishment, Garston, Watford, WD2 7JR. Tel no. 01923 664258. Fax no. 01923 664097.

The LT Method

Chapter 11

Introduction to the LT Method

Energy performance in non-domestic buildings varies over a wide range, even when comparing buildings of similar use type. We have identified three factors which lead to this variation:

1 building design;
2 services design;
3 occupant behaviour.

The first factor is of particular relevance early in the development of the design by the architect. It is clear that basic building design is not amenable to later modification, whereas services can be improved and good management can reduce the often detrimental effects of occupants.

How does the energy consumption of a building relate to the early design parameters? Lighting energy and fan power represent the major energy input to most larger buildings and have to be provided permanently to the deep areas away from the perimeter. Thus these areas should be kept to a minimum. The LT Method is concerned with the design and maximising of the perimeter zones, or *passive zones*, of the building, and provides a means of estimating the relative energy performance of different options.

The interactions between the heating, cooling and lighting energy of a building are complex and a mathematical model of such a system requires many input parameters. Most of these are unavailable early in the design process, or are often of peripheral interest to the architect. The LT Method, a manual design tool for the calculation of energy consumption in non-domestic buildings, uses energy performance data produced by a mathematical model, where most of these parameters have been given assumed values. Only a few key design variables, mainly relating to building form and façade design, are left for the user to manipulate.

It follows from the need to use assumed values, that the LT Method should not be regarded as a precision model producing an accurate estimate of the performance of an actual building. Rather LT should be used to evaluate the energy performance of a number of options and to make comparisons. Furthermore, the energy breakdowns of heating, cooling and lighting, which are evident from carrying out the LT Method, will give a picture of the relative importance of various energy components.

The Method can be applied to a range of non-domestic building types, in particular schools, offices, institutional buildings and health buildings. It has limited application to certain manufacturing buildings. It is a manual procedure requiring pencil and calculator. Proposed building data and energy values from the graphs are combined onto a single worksheet.

It must be stressed again that the LT Method only responds to relatively few of the many design parameters of a building. It is beyond the scope of simplified methods to deal with the full range of these parameters and their interactions quantitatively. Many of these other factors are dealt with descriptively in Part One.

11.1 Technical background

Amongst the considerations early in the development of a building design, the designer is concerned with two issues: the form of the building (its plan depth, section, orientation, etc.), and the design of the façades (in particular the area and distribution of glazing). It is useful to know the implications for energy use of the designer's early decisions. The plan form, the façade design, and proportion of perimeter (or passive) areas play a crucial part.

Any calculation method employed must be quick and easy to use in order to allow the designer to explore a number of options. Secondly, it must be able to respond to the main design parameters under consideration. Energy consumption will also depend upon other parameters

such as artificial lighting levels and plant efficiencies. However, these can be regarded as engineering parameters and to some extent can be considered independently.

The LT Method (LT stands for Lighting and Thermal) is an energy design tool which has been developed expressly for this purpose. A computer-based model has been used to predict annual primary energy consumption per square metre of floor area as a function of:

1 local climatic conditions;
2 orientation of façade;
3 area and type of glazing;
4 obstructions due to adjacent buildings (or parts of the same building);
5 the inclusion of an atrium (optional);
6 occupancy and vacation patterns;
7 lighting levels;
8 internal gains.

The basis of the design tool is the sets of graphs, the LT curves, giving annual primary energy consumption per square metre for north, east/west and south orientations of the façade, plus one for horizontal glazed apertures (rooflights). Curves are presented for lighting, heating, ventilation and cooling, and total energy, for two climatic zones, northern UK and southern UK.

The model used to derive the curves, described in more detail later [A.2], takes account of the energy flows associated with inputs for heating, cooling, ventilation and lighting, and ambient energy flows due to fabric and ventilation heat losses, solar gains and useful daylight, as illustrated in Figure 11.1.

Many of the input parameters for the model are given assumed values. It is important to be aware of these, and the basic principles upon which the model works, in order to fully appreciate the applicability and limitations of the LT Method. A fuller description and a list of the main parameter values is given later [A.3].

The definition of the climatic zones is not precise and this is indicated by the fuzzy boundary (Figure 11.2). LT is influenced by temperature, solar radiation and sky luminance. It also integrates over the day and the year and is

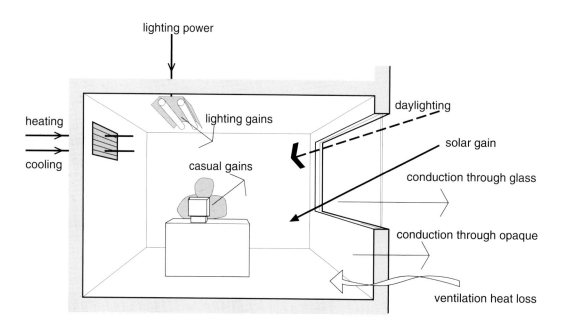

11.1 *Energy flows in the LT model*

therefore sensitive to day length and heating/cooling season length. This results in certain combinations of these parameters being significant. In defining these zones the most relevant characteristics are:

Northern   Cold winters with low solar radiation and short days, and mild summers.

Southern   Cool winters with low solar radiation, warmer summers.

11.2 Limitations of the LT Method

The LT Method is a tool for strategic energy design and it is very important that its limitations and applicability are understood. The main points to bear in mind are as follows:

The LT Method should not be regarded as a precision energy model, but should be used to test the relative performance of a number of design options. The precision of the actual number produced is far less important than the trends shown by comparison with other LT calculations.

As a manual method, only a very limited number of design parameters are required for input. A much larger number of parameters have already been given assumed values, which in some cases already represent good practice in low-energy design. These are listed later [A.1].

The Method predicts the potential performance of the building, assuming that both systems and occupants function optimally. This is in order to concentrate on the effect of building design parameters.

It follows that direct comparison of the LT-calculated energy performance with a real building is not likely to be relevant, unless it is known that the assumptions made by LT accurately describe conditions in the real building.

The output of the method is annual primary energy per square metre. Primary energy relates well to both cost and environmental impact. Building energy data and energy targets are often given in delivered energy units. This must be borne in mind if compared with LT outputs.

11.2 *Northern and southern UK climatic zones for LT curves*

Chapter 12

How to use the LT Method

The LT Method uses the concept of *passive* and *non-passive zones*. Passive zones can be daylit and naturally ventilated and may make use of solar gains for heating in winter; they may also suffer overheating by solar gains in summer. They are defined by orientation. Non-passive zones have to be artificially lit and ventilated and in many cases cooled.

There are four main steps in using the LT Method:

Step 1 Define and measure the areas of passive and non-passive zones, and enter into worksheet.

Step 2 Define a proposed glazing ratio for each of the passive zones.

Step 3 Choose the appropriate LT curve for each zone and read off specific energy consumption. Enter into worksheet.

Step 4 Multiply areas by the appropriate specific energy consumptions and calculate totals to complete worksheet.

For predicting the effect of the overshadowing of adjacent buildings or an atrium, further steps are required and are described later [12.7] and [12.8].

12.1 Step 1: the passive zone

On the plan of the building, identify the *side-lit* passive zones as in Figure 12.1, including the top floor. The passive zone depth (distance from the façade) is normally twice the floor to ceiling height. Enter the areas on the worksheet.

12.1 *Passive and non-passive zones in plan and section*

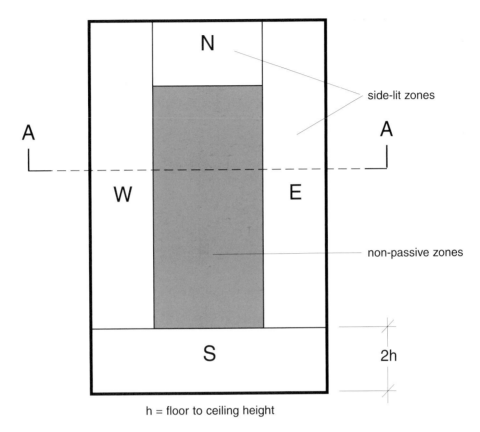

h = floor to ceiling height

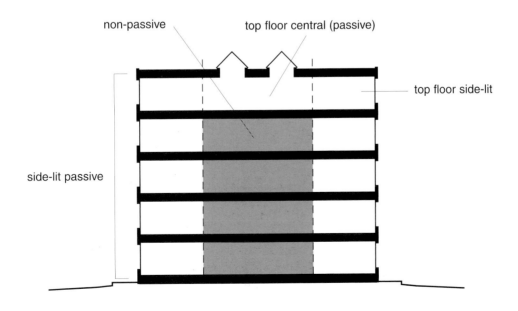

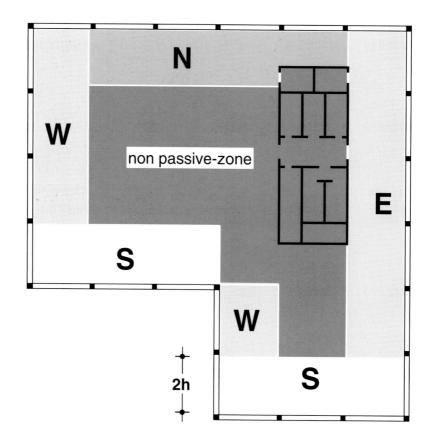

N

W

non passive-zone

E

S

W

S

2h

12.2 *Passive and non-passive zones in L-shaped plan*

When defining the orientation of a passive zone in a corner always choose the best performer – for example, south in preference to east and west, unless this is precluded by a blank wall. The zone behind an inside corner is poorly provided with light and natural ventilation and it is best to designate this as non-passive, as in Figure 12.2.

For the top floor, enter the central area separately on the worksheet under *roof*. This is the area which is not side-lit but may (or may not) be top-lit.

All the remaining area is designated *non-passive*. The proportion of passive zone to the total building floor area is a good indicator of its potential energy performance. There is a box for the passive zone ratio in the worksheet.

If some zones are adjacent to buffer spaces, e.g. atria or sunspaces, enter these separately in the 'buffer adjacent' section of the worksheet. This is explained in more detail later [12.8].

Top floor side-lit zone

Note that the top floor side-lit zone would actually have conductive losses through both the walls and the roof. The side-lit curves account for the losses through the walls; the roof losses can be added as a correction, although in most cases it is small and can be neglected. It has most impact in a small single-storey building where neglecting these losses will underpredict heating energy by up to 12%, but for larger multi-storey buildings this will be typically less than 5%.

If this error is unacceptable, then for the *side-lit top floor areas*, also read off the horizontal curve for heating only at zero glazing ratio (assuming that these are not top-lit as well). The heating energy for the ventilation has to be deducted from this since it has already been accounted for in the side-lit curve. The remainder is then added into the heating total to account for heat losses through the roof

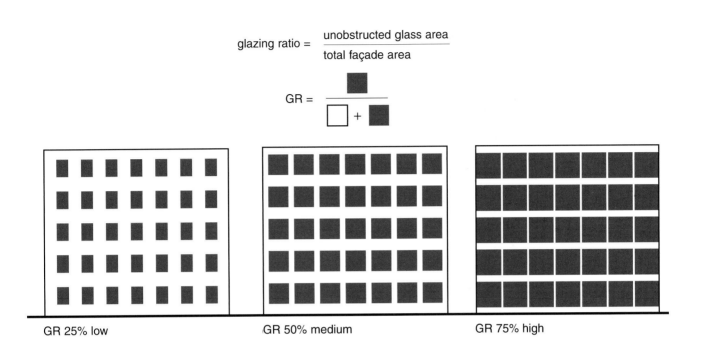

glazing ratio = $\dfrac{\text{unobstructed glass area}}{\text{total façade area}}$

GR 25% low   GR 50% medium   GR 75% high

12.3 *Definition of glazing ratio*

of the side-lit areas. Heat losses through the vertical glazing and opaque wall are already accounted for by the side-lit curves. This procedure for making the correction is described in more detail in the worked example [13.1].

12.2 Step 2: the glazing ratio

For the elevations (and the roof plan if glazed) propose a glazing ratio. This is defined as the ratio of the glazed area to the total area of the façade. This need not be precise and could be estimated using Figure 12.3 as a guide. Note that it is not the ratio of the glazing to opaque wall area. Note also that it is the nominal glazing area, and allows for obstruction to daylighting by framing and glazing bars of 20%.

If the actual value of framing obstruction is known to be significantly different from this, compensation should be made when reading off the lighting energy curve. For example, if the glazing design results in only 5% obstruction, which is possible for very large panes of glass, then for a 30% nominal glazing area read off the lighting energy at 30% + (30 × (20-5))% = 34.5%.

Even when a façade is nominally all glass, when viewed from outside, about 10% is obstructed by the structural floor zones. Thus for a façade which viewed from inside the room is floor to ceiling and wall to wall glazing, this would in fact be entered as 90%.

12.3 Step 3: the LT curves

An example of an LT curve is shown in Figure 12.4. The vertical axis represents the annual primary energy consumption in MWh/m², and the horizontal axis is the glazing area as a percentage of total façade area. Curves are

12.4 *Example LT curve for office in southern UK*

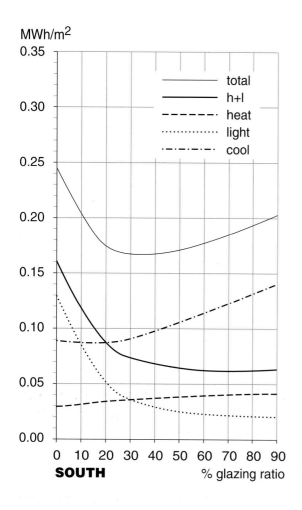

12.5 *The LT curve reading aid made from drawing film*

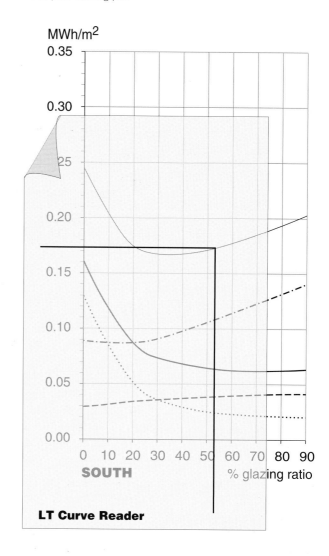

LT Curve Reader

provided for vertical glazing orientated south, east/west, and north, and for horizontal apertures (rooflights). The main set of curves for different building types, lighting levels and internal gain levels are found in Chapter 14.

Two totals are shown, heating + cooling + lighting (total), and heating + lighting (h+l). The cooling curve includes an allowance for fan power as well as refrigeration. The total without cooling can be used to indicate the energy use of a non-air-conditioned, naturally ventilated building. However, a fixed allowance for fresh air mechanical ventilation must be added for all non-passive zones. This

value is given at the bottom of each set of four graphs. For buildings with high internal gains, these non-passive areas would be air-conditioned and the cooling and fan power should be read off from the LT curves at the zero % glazing intercept. The ventilation heating energy is also indicated numerically at the bottom of the page; this is only used when making the correction for side-lit top floor areas.

Choose the set of curves corresponding to the location and building type. A separate index to the curves is provided on page 127, Chapter 14. Study the curves for different lighting levels and internal gains and note how the

12.6 *Rules for rooflights*

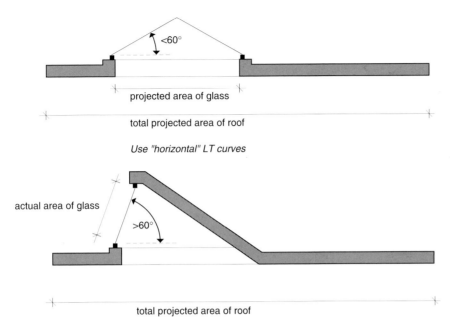

projected area of glass

total projected area of roof

Use "horizontal" LT curves

actual area of glass

>60°

total projected area of roof

Use "side-lit" LT curves of appropriate orientation for lighting only

proportion of heating, cooling and lighting energy changes. It may also be interesting to look at other building types to get a feel for the effect of occupancy. Note how steeply the lighting curve drops as daylight becomes available.

The summation of the curves shows a fairly distinct optimum for glazing ratio. Note that this is much smaller for the horizontal apertures due to the higher illuminance of horizontal surfaces compared with vertical surfaces.

For vertical glazing most curves show only a slow increase in energy consumption after the minimum. However, the overheating risk will increase significantly with large glazing areas. So too will other comfort problems such as glare and 'cold radiation'. Thus glazing ratios well away from the optimum in either direction should be avoided.

Reading off values from the LT curves is made much easier by the use of an LT curve reading aid (Figure 12.5). On a small piece of tracing paper, about 100mm × 150mm, draw two narrow lines about 20mm from the top and the right-hand edge and accurately at right angles to each other. Place the point of intersection of the lines on the curve so that the vertical line intersects the chosen

glazing ratio. Then, by eye, make this line parallel to the vertical grid lines, and read off the energy value where the horizontal line cuts the vertical axis.

Rooflights

For rooflights with horizontal apertures the use of the *horizontal* curve for the *central top-lit* areas is straightforward. However, rooflights often do not have horizontal apertures. Monitors, northlights, or 'sheds' have sloping or vertical glazing. For these cases the following rules apply:

1   If the glazed aperture is 60° to horizontal or less, use the horizontal curve specifying the glazing ratio as the actual area of glass, to the area of the roof projected in plan.
2   If the glazed aperture is greater than 60° to horizontal, read off the lighting energy and the cooling energy from the *side-lit* curve for the appropriate orientation; the heating is still read from the horizontal curve; the glazing ratio is defined as the ratio of the actual glazing area to area of roof projected in plan as in Figure 12.6.

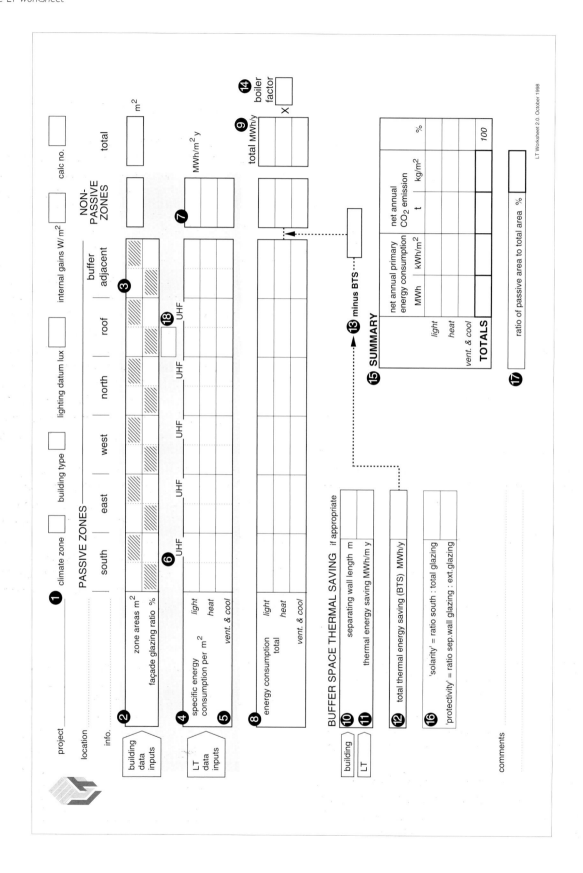

Non-passive zones

The energy for non-passive zones can be calculated by reading from the side-lit curve at zero glazing ratio. The non-passive zones must always have a fan power allowance (value printed at bottom of page), at least for fresh air supply. For non-passive zones in buildings with high internal gains and high lighting levels, a cooling energy obtained from the zero glazing intercept of the cooling curve should be added.

Orientation

LT curves have been produced for four orientations only, in order to keep down the total number of curves. This means that specific curves have to be used when they are within 45° of the orientation of the façade. The overall energy consumption is not highly sensitive to orientation and this procedure is compatible with the overall accuracy of the method.

In the rare event of a building façade being orientated at exactly 45° to one of the four cardinal directions, define the zones for the principal façades (i.e. the longest) as south or north in preference to east or west.

12.4 Step 4: the LT worksheet

The passive and non-passive zone areas, and the specific energy consumptions read from the LT curves, are entered into the LT worksheet (Figure 12.7). These values are multiplied together and totalled for lighting, heating and cooling.

The heating energy has been calculated assuming a boiler efficiency of 65%. High-efficiency boilers or condensing boilers are significantly better than this. In order to take account of different boiler efficiencies, the heating energy is multiplied by a boiler factor B, defined by: B = 0.65 / (boiler efficiency). Boiler efficiency was discussed earlier [10.4].

The summary table can be completed to show the total energy consumption for the building, or as energy per square metre. CO_2 emissions can be calculated by applying the factors given in the next section [12.5].

12.5 Primary energy and CO_2

Primary energy is the energy value of the fuel at source. For fuels such as gas or oil, there is an *energy overhead* required for extracting, refining and distribution. There is a further loss at the point of use due to flue and distribution losses, defined by the *boiler efficiency*. In the case of electricity, used for lighting, and mechanical power for cooling and ventilation, an energy overhead occurs at the power station due to the thermodynamic efficiency of the conversion of heat to mechanical power. This is a large factor – 1 unit of delivered electricity is equivalent to 3.7 units of primary energy. The first reason that *primary* energy is used is that it allows the different 'fuel' inputs for lighting, heating and cooling to be reduced to one common unit. Adding *delivered* energy units together would give a distorted picture, grossly understating the impact of electricity use.

For energy sources which are fossil fuels, the expression of energy in primary energy units is satisfactory in that it relates well to CO_2 and other pollutant production, and to cost.

However, certain fuels produce more CO_2 than others, for the same *primary* energy value. For example, coal produces more CO_2 than gas, for a given amount of primary energy, due to its high carbon content. Where improvement in environmental performance is a criterion rather than energy cost, and the heating fuel is known, the CO_2 production for the heating fuel can be calculated separately instead of using the overall conversion factor. These factors are given in Table 12.1.

Table 12.1 CO_2 production for different types of fuel

Tonnes CO_2/MWh primary or kg CO_2	kWh primary
All energy types	0.24
Electricity	0.22
Gas	0.19
Coal	0.31
Oil	0.28

12.8 *The definition of Urban Horizon Angle (UHA) – the average elevation of the skyline from the centre of the façade being considered*

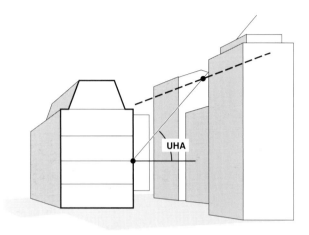

12.8

Problems may arise where a substantial proportion of the electricity is generated by renewable (mechanical) sources such as hydro or wind. It also presents problems where electricity is generated by nuclear sources since the concept of primary (nuclear) energy is not really equivalent to primary energy of conventional sources. However, in the UK 80% of electricity is generated from fossil fuels, and a primary/delivered energy ratio of 3.7 is generally accepted.

Furthermore, it is argued that, since the overriding objective is to reduce CO_2 emissions, reductions in energy demand will be used to displace CO_2-emitting sources rather than clean sources.

12.6 Interpretation of cooling energy

The LT value for *cooling energy consumption* consists of *fan power* and *heat rejection*. The fan power is a fixed value derived from typical observed performance. The energy for heat rejection (that is, the energy used to drive the refrigeration equipment) is variable and responds to cooling load. This is calculated assuming a typical refrigeration plant efficiency. These components are indicated separately on the curves as illustrated in Figure 12.4. Note that there is also a smaller fan-power component numerically indicated for fresh air supply only, as distinct from full air-conditioning systems.

The fact that LT includes cooling energy as an output should not be taken as a recommendation for mechanical cooling. Rather the cooling energy should be used to indicate the *potential* energy consumption if the building were air-conditioned. The *overheating* risk if it is not air-conditioned is indicated by the growth of the heat rejection component. By reducing this indicated value to a minimum, it is likely that with the proper use of measures such as shading, ventilation and thermal mass, the need for mechanical cooling will be avoided.

It follows that although the *lighting + heating energy* may rise slowly or even drop in some cases with increasing glazing area, the minimum of the *total energy* value should be used to indicate an optimum value for glazing ratio, even if the building is not air-conditioned.

A more detailed discussion of overheating risk is given in Chapter 5.

12.7 Step 5: the Urban Horizon Factor

In most cases the view of the horizon will not be free of obstructions in all directions; this is particularly true of urban sites where other buildings often block out large areas of the sky. This will affect energy use in three ways by reducing the availability of daylight, the useful heating in winter due to solar gain, and the cooling load due to solar gain in summer. The degree to which it affects the annual total will depend upon the angle of elevation of the sun (dependent upon latitude), the orientation of the façade under consideration, and of course the angle of elevation of the obstruction relative to the façade (Figure 12.8).

Using the computer-based LT model, a correction factor has been derived to modify the specific energy consumption value as read from the curves. Tables are provided in Chapter 14 for each building type, lighting level, internal gains level, and climatic zone. An example is given in Figure 12.9. Each table gives a correction factor for lighting, heating and cooling, for the four orientations and for two Urban Horizon Angles (UHA). The Urban Horizon Factor (UHF) is also dependent upon the glazing ratio. It is evident that the factors for lighting and heating vary quite strongly for some combinations of parameters, and interpolation between values of horizon angle and glazing ratio can be made.

12.9 *Example of Urban Horizon Factor (UHF) table – corrections for different orientations, obstruction angles, and glazing ratios*

12.10 *Limit of obstruction-forming horizon in plan for UHF*

orientation	UHA deg.	glazing ratio %	correction factors		
			heating	cooling	lighting
south	15 - 45	20	1.4	1.01	1.5
		40	1.9	0.93	1.5
		60	2.0	0.89	1.7
		80	2.3	0.86	1.5
	>45	20	1.3	0.99	2.1
		40	1.9	0.81	2.3
		60	2.2	0.70	2.6
		80	2.8	0.62	2.2
east / west	15 - 45	20	1.1	1.01	1.4
		40	1.1	0.93	1.5
		60	1.2	0.89	1.7
		80	1.2	0.86	1.6
	>45	20	1.0	1.02	2.0
		40	1.0	0.88	2.5
		60	1.2	0.78	2.6
		80	1.3	0.71	2.3
north	15 - 45	20	0.9	1.04	1.4
		40	1.0	0.97	1.5
		60	1.0	0.94	1.5
		80	1.0	0.91	1.6
	>45	20	0.9	1.09	2.0
		40	0.8	0.97	2.4
		60	1.0	0.89	2.4
		80	1.0	0.84	2.4

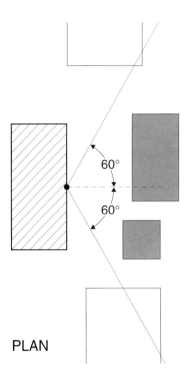

PLAN

To determine the UHA for a design proposal requires a degree of approximation. It is the average angle of elevation from the centre of the façade to the top of the obstruction as shown in Figure 12.8. There are only three angle ranges provided for in the tables. For UHA less than 15° no correction factor is necessary; 15° to 45° corresponds to moderate obstruction; and above 45° heavy obstruction. Obstructions that are outside of a line at 60° to the normal (a line at right angles) to the façade in plan, can be ignored, as in Figure 12.10.

For example, an east-facing façade has a UHA of 30°, and a proposed glazing ratio of 40%. Using the table as shown in Figure 12.9, UHF values of 1.1 for heating, 0.9 for cooling and 1.5 for lighting are obtained. Thus the main effect of overshadowing is to increase the demand for artificial lighting. Comparing this with a similar case but for south orientation, the heating factor has now increased from 1.1 to 1.9. This increase in heat demand is due to the loss of useful solar gains, whilst the heat loss through the glazing remains unaffected by the overshadowing.

In most cases the UHA will vary significantly from ground to top storey, and may vary in different parts of the plan. The quickest method is to use a single average UHA, as in Figure 12.8, but it is more accurate to divide the building into parts and apply the appropriate UHA to each. This may lead a designer to provide larger glazing ratios on the lower floors than on the higher, less-obstructed floors. This procedure, dividing the building into parts, will necessitate filling in an LT worksheet for each part and adding the sub-totals together for the whole building.

These factors can also be applied to buildings which, due to their plan shape, are self-obstructing. It is relatively easy to determine the UHA for a courtyard façade at a point well away from the corners; it is in effect

12.11 *Limit of self-obstruction in courtyard for UHF*

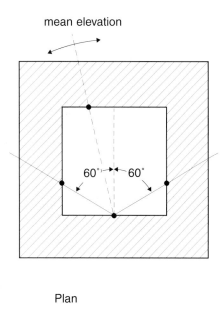

Plan

12.12 *Reduced passive-zone depth for buffer-adjacent zone*

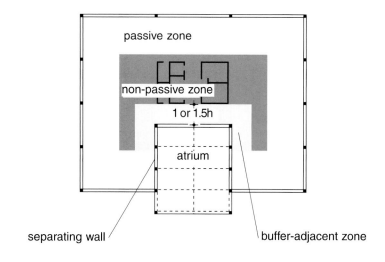

h = floor to ceiling height

the same as shown in Figure 12.8. However, at positions closer to the corners, the side walls of the courtyard will also cause significant obstruction. These can be evaluated from the elevation of the sky line at the limiting angle of 60° to the normal in the horizontal plane (Figure 12.11). An example of self-obstruction is given in the next chapter [13.4].

Only where obstructions are distant does the UHA remain truly constant over the whole building façade. This will usually be the case in mountainous country.

12.8 Step 6: atria and sunspaces

For zones protected by unheated atria or sunspaces (buffer-spaces), the LT Method takes account of the fact that a buffer-space will reduce heating load, but in most cases will also impair the daylighting of the adjacent rooms. Due to the reduction in both temperature difference and air movement, the potential for natural ventilation will also be reduced. On the other hand, the atrium may represent

an opportunity for ventilation, where a noisy polluted atmosphere would rule out ventilation from outside.

Step 6A: the effect on daylighting of adjacent spaces

It is not possible to account with precision for the reduction in availability of daylight brought about by the installation of a glazed buffer-space. There are too many unknowns – geometry, obstruction, reflections, etc. For the purpose of the LT Method, a simplified approach is taken. The daylit zone is reduced from the full twice floor-to-ceiling depth, according to the estimated light transmittance characteristics of the buffer-space. By reducing the depth of the daylit zone, the non-passive zone area is increased and the extra lighting energy accounted for (Figure 12.12).

Table 12.2 is used to determine the buffer-adjacent passive zone depth. Calculate the total area of this zone and enter it on the worksheet.

If an atrium is open to the parent building – that is, it has no separating wall – this procedure does not apply. In this case the atrium must be considered as normal internal space with energy consumption predicted from the horizontal or side-lit LT curve as appropriate.

Step 6B: the effect on heating and cooling of adjacent spaces

The heating and cooling energy for the buffer-adjacent zone is initially calculated from the LT curves in the same way as the other passive zones. However, because the penetration of direct radiation via the buffer-space is likely to be slight, the east/west curve is used irrespective of the orientation of the buffer-adjacent zone.

In summer, an atrium can overheat and transmit gains to adjacent fully occupied spaces, creating a cooling load or overheating. Quantification of this is outside the scope of the LT Method, but guidance on the avoidance of this problem, by shading and ventilation, can be found elsewhere in this volume [9.3].

An unheated atrium or buffer-space affects the heating load of the adjacent building in two ways – by reducing the conductive losses through the separating wall, and reducing the ventilation heat losses. This is more complex than it may seem since the reduction of conductive loss is strongly influenced by the geometry of the atrium, and the effect on ventilation heat loss is dependent on the mode of ventilation coupling between the atrium and the building.

The LT Method calculates the effect by applying a Buffer-space Thermal Saving (BTS) component which is dependent upon the length (in plan) of separating wall between the buffer-space and the building. A table of these savings has been prepared for a range of buffer-space configurations and ventilation modes and for each building type and climatic zone, by running a computer-based model.

To calculate the reduction in heating load (reduced from that predicted on the curve), first determine the separating wall-plan length as in Figure 12.12, and enter in the worksheet. Then consult the BTS table for the appropriate building type, included with each set of LT curves. An example of a BTS table is shown in Figure 12.13.

Table 12.2 Buffer-adjacent zone depth

Characteristic	Score 0	Score 1
Shading	Fixed	Movable
Glazing	Tinted/reflective	Clear
Internal finishes	Dark coloured	Light coloured
Horizon angle*	Greater than 45°	Less than 45°

Total score	Buffer-adjacent passive zone depth
0 or 1	0
2 or 3	1.0 h
4	1.5 h
	(h = floor to ceiling height)

Note: *Horizon angle is defined in much the same way as UHA. In the case of an enclosed atrium the effect of the obstructing side walls may have to be estimated to give an effective horizon angle. Very deep atria or lightwells, where the depth is more than 2–3 times the average width, should not be considered for the provision of light to adjacent spaces, and thus the passive-zone depth becomes zero, irrespective of the other characteristics. However, on the upper floors the horizon angle will be reduced and there will be a daylit zone.

The different ventilation modes are (a) independent (b) buffer-space to building, (c) building to buffer-space and (d) recirculated. These values are further subdivided into single glazing (×1) and double glazing (×2) referring to the external glazing of the buffer-space. The types of buffer-space configuration and orientation are illustrated in the left-hand column of the BTS table and are numbered 1 to 7. Choose the closest atrium configuration type or interpolate.

Considering the ventilation type, note that types (b) and (c) can only be guaranteed to occur all the time, with mechanical ventilation. Natural ventilation may be able to create these flow paths but the effect of varying wind direction and strength, and temperature difference, will affect the flow.

12.13 *Buffer-space Thermal Savings (BTS) table for southern UK*

config. type \\ vent mode	a		b		c		d	
	x1	x2	x1	x2	x1	x2	x1	x2
1 ▲N	0.52	0.60	0.58	0.63	0.54	0.57	1.02	1.12
2 ▲N	0.55	0.71	0.70	0.84	0.59	0.71	1.02	1.24
3 ▲N	0.41	0.53	0.51	0.62	0.48	0.58	0.83	1.02
4 ▲N	0.36	0.49	0.53	0.69	0.42	0.53	0.84	1.10
5 ▲N	0.35	0.46	0.46	0.64	0.38	0.50	0.56	0.80
6 ▲N	0.57	0.83	0.75	1.03	0.61	0.85	0.93	1.30
7 ▲N	0.47	0.63	0.58	0.74	0.54	0.70	0.83	1.03

Type (d) is most likely to occur passively, but only in a shallow zone around the atrium, and it is important to realise that a small conservatory or atrium could not provide fresh air for a large building for more than a small fraction of the day, unless the atrium itself was being refreshed at very high rates of infiltration.

Note that in deriving the savings value, it was assumed that the fraction of ventilation involved was proportional to the separating wall area (or length, assuming constant floor to ceiling height) in relation to the external wall of the building. Implicit in this assumption is that the atrium only reduces the heat demand of the buffer adjacent zone; i.e. the maximum saving would occur when this heat demand becomes zero. However, for atria with high solar input, and designed to provide ventilation pre-heating to parts of the building other than the adjacent zone, it is reasonable to apply the full BTS value, i.e. the heat demand of the buffer-adjacent zone itself may become negative.

The tables give the Buffer-space Thermal Savings in annual primary energy per metre separating wall length. These values are calculated for an eleven-hour office day. For other building types multiply the value from the table by the appropriate occupancy factor as given in Table 12.3, and enter the value on the worksheet in the "Buffer-space Thermal Saving" box. The occupancy factor is defined as the ratio of occupied hours for the actual building to those of the office type, including the effect of holidays and night

Table 12.3 Buffer-space occupancy factors

Building type	Occupancy factors
Schools	0.55
Colleges	0.75
Offices	1.0
Institutional	1.5

set-back. Note that occupancy refers to occupancy of the whole building, not just the atrium.

Tables 12.2 and 12.3 are reproduced alongside the BTS charts in the main data section [14], for convenience.

The thermal performance of an atrium is strongly dependent upon two parameters, the protectivity and the solarity. The protectivity is the ratio of the glazing area of the separating wall to the glazing area of the atrium external envelope. The solarity is the ratio of the south-facing glazing of the atrium to the total external glazing area of the atrium. An important performance indicator is the temperature prevailing in an unheated atrium. A procedure for evaluating this from early design parameters including the protectivity is given in section [9.2].

13

LT Method worked examples

These worked examples demonstrate the LT Method in use and illustrate the kind of investigations and comparisons that can be carried out.

The first two examples show the LT worksheets. The remaining examples are more concerned with the principles and the assumptions made, and less with the mechanics of the method. These latter examples also show the more flexible use of the LT curves, which for the experienced user can greatly increase the power of the method.

13.1 Five-storey office building

The first proposal being investigated is an office building with an L-shaped plan. The building is five storeys high (floor to ceiling height 3m) and is on a site which is heavily overshadowed from the east, slightly overshadowed from the north and open to the south and west. It will not have particularly high internal gains (from office machines etc.) and will have lighting for normal office use. The site location is southern UK.

Passive zones

Figure 13.1 shows the building on an urban site, with dimensions and the areas of the zones indicated. In designating the 6m passive zones at outside corners the best performer for light and heat is assumed, i.e. south rather than west or east. Note that the inside corner is designated a non-passive zone.

The top floor is all passive zone; we will assume that the centre of the plan is roof-lit with a side-lit perimeter zone, i.e. we enter only the central rooflit area under 'roof' initially. The areas are now summed up in the rough working

13.1 *Worked example of five-storey office building*

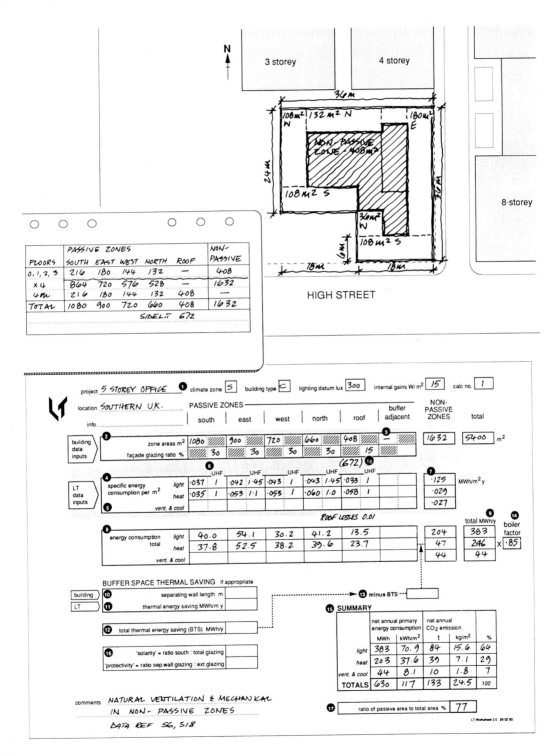

table, and then entered in the LT worksheet. The top-floor side-lit zone (total area) is counted a second time to calculate heat losses through the roof and entered at (18).

The LT curves

First the building type has to be selected. It is obviously type C, and from the brief we assume the 'low' internal gains of 15W/m² and the 300 lux lighting datum. This defines the set of curves on Chart S6.

The next step is to enter the glazing ratios for the façades. Let us start off with 30% all round – maybe we will change it later.

It is possible that the fenestration has already been designed as part of the initial concept. If working from a pre-conceived glazing pattern, then remember that the glazing ratio refers to the area of structural opening. A 20% obstruction due to framing and glazing bars is already allowed for in drawing the curves. Also, the glazing ratio is the ratio of the area of opening to the total wall area (as seen from the outside of the building), not just the area of opaque wall.

For the rooflights, the 'horizontal' total curve shows a minimum at about 15% – let us choose that. Note that we are already using the curves to influence our choice here, whereas for the vertical glazing we are working from an initial proposal which might have originated from aesthetic considerations.

If the top floor is lit with monitor or other rooflight configurations with the aperture tilted to more than 60° to horizontal, use the vertical glazing curve of appropriate orientation and calculate the glazing ratio as the ratio of the actual area of glazing to the area of roof projected in plan (Figure 12.6). Here we will assume that the rooflights are low-pitched 'shed' type with horizontal roof apertures.

Next, on the appropriate graphs, the specific energy consumption for light and heat is read off on the vertical axis for the appropriate values of glazing ratio. It is possible to estimate the third decimal place, i.e. divide the smallest division in 10 parts. The LT curve reading aid is a great help here, or a pair of compasses or dividers can be used to measure off the curves and transfer to the vertical axis. The values are entered on the worksheet in the second box of inputs, at *specific energy consumption* for the appropriate orientations. For the non-passive zone the value for zero % glazing ratio is entered – any side-lit curve – they are all the same for a given climatic zone.

For ventilation and cooling, if the building is not air-conditioned, the passive zones will be naturally ventilated; there will be no mechanical cooling so zeros are entered here. However, the non-passive zone will have to be mechanically ventilated to supply fresh air only. This value is given at the bottom of the page of LT curves. If it is a space in which there are high gains, it may be necessary to air-condition this zone, in which case the cooling energy (including fan power) should be read off from the cooling curve at zero % glazing ratio. (Advice can be obtained from the EEO publication *Selecting Air-Conditioning Systems* (3), available from BRECSU.)

The Urban Horizon Angle

From the site plan (by making a sketch section) we have deduced that the UHA from the centre of the third storey is less than 15° for south and west, between 15° and 45° for north, and greater than 45° for east. Reading off the Urban Horizon Factor table for southern offices, 300 lux, 15W/m², Chart S18, we can find the appropriate values of UHF for each orientation, and enter them in the worksheet. This table is difficult to read – it helps to mask off all but the relevant part. The UHF for the roof-lit area is always 1.0.

The next step is simply multiplying the areas by the appropriate specific energy consumption values and UHFs, adding across the page in the third box, at (8), to give totals for lighting, heating and cooling. (The procedure accounting for the heat loss through the side-lit roof zones is described in the next example [13.2].)

In the summary box the totals and the specific energy consumption in kWh/m² are entered. It is also interesting to enter the ratio of the area of passive zone to the total floor area to indicate the 'passivity' of the design.

This gives the first base case. The value of total primary energy per square metre is shown in the summary box. This is a very low value, because the test case has adopted a low energy strategy – minimising non-passive area, maximising use of daylight and natural ventilation. The LT default values assume good insulation standards and efficient lighting [A.3]. A boiler efficiency of 70% has been applied corresponding to a high efficiency modular gas boiler with zonal control.

The real value of the LT Method is to make comparisons. Many more options and conditions could be evaluated. The effect of rotating the plan through 180° in order to reduce the area overshadowed to the north and east can be calculated by redistributing the passive areas in relation to orientation, but in this case keeping the UHFs the same. The glazing ratio could be increased to the north and east, to offset the overshadowing effect, but in this case new values of UHF would have to be read from the table. Another more drastic change would be to reduce the plan to a square, decreasing the surface area but increasing the non-passive zone.

Filling in many worksheets is quite a chore. To reduce the effort a little, it is useful to work on a sheet of tracing paper placed over the base case LT worksheet, since unaltered data can be read through. Much better, of course, is to set up the worksheet on a computer using a spreadsheet application programme.

Heat loss correction for top floor side-lit areas

As previously explained [12.3], these areas have conductive heat loss through both the roof and the walls. Losses through the walls are included in the LT side-lit curves, but the conductive loss through the roof has to be added as a correction.

On the worksheet under the *roof* column, the total area of side-lit roof zone (all orientations) is entered below the *building data inputs* box, in this case: 672m^2.

The specific energy consumption is obtained from the horizontal curve for zero glazing ratio (or other glazing ratio if the side-lit zone also has rooflights). The value read from the curve includes the ventilation heat loss and this must be deducted. This value is shown at the bottom of the page, and for LT Chart S6 it is 0.03MWh/m^2. This results in the specific heating energy for the roof due to conduction being: 0.04 − 0.03 = 0.01. This value is entered in the space below the *specific energy consumption* box.

The product of the two values above, 6.7MWh/y, is added as a correction to the existing heating energy total of 237, an increase of only 3% to the heating energy and only 1% to the total energy. As is shown in this example, the effect is small and for most multi-storey buildings it can be neglected. It has more significance for shallow-plan single-storey buildings where the side-lit area under the roof forms the major part of the building.

13.2 Four-storey office building with atrium

This building has a south-facing atrium and is four storeys high with floor-to-ceiling height of 3m. It is on a 'greenfield' site with no significant obstructions and so there is no application of UHFs. The climatic zone is northern UK.

Passive zones

The passive and non-passive zones are taken off the plan and set out in the working table as shown in Figure 13.2. (We have not bothered with the top-floor side-lit heat loss correction.) With reference to Table 12.2 we have assumed movable shading, clear glazing and light internal finishes. From the geometry of the atrium, the effective sky angle is less than 45°. This results in a buffer-adjacent zone of 4.5m deep.

Note also that the south-facing zone takes precedence over the buffer adjacent zone. The top floor (to be used as a daylit studio) has rooflights and very small vision windows in the walls, and is thus designated as all roof-lit. The areas are entered on the worksheet.

Proposed values for the glazing ratios are as follows: north, east and west-facing 25%, south-facing 40%, roof 15%, and buffer-adjacent 60%.

Specific energy consumption values are read off from the LT curves on chart N6. Note that the buffer-adjacent space is read off from the east/west curve irrespective of orientation. The energy consumption for the zones is calculated, but before totalling the heating energy the Buffer-space Thermal Saving (BTS) is calculated.

13.2 *Worked example of four-storey office building with atrium*

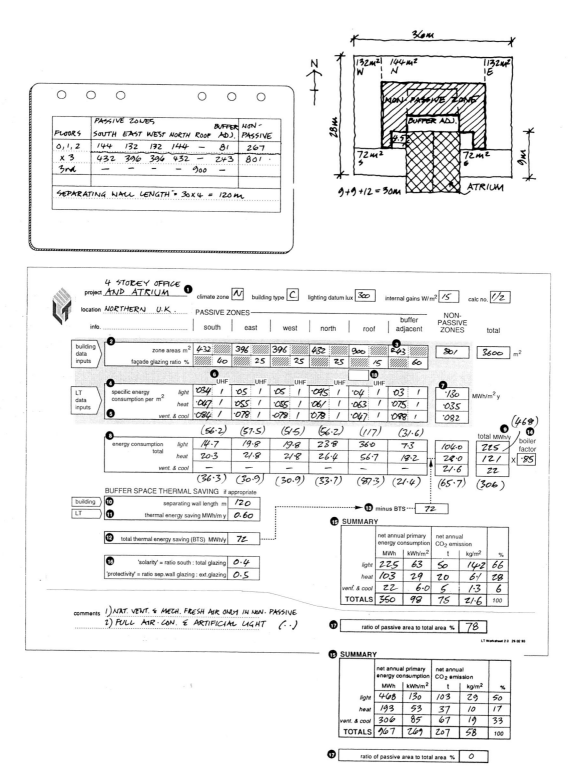

Buffer-space Thermal Saving

First the separating wall length is measured, as indicated on Figure 13.2. Since the plan is the same on all four floors, we simply multiply by four to get the total length. Note that this length, together with the storey height, implies an area which is a measure of the thermal coupling between the unheated atrium and the parent building.

Now, referring to the Buffer-space Thermal Saving chart N25 for northern UK, clearly the atrium is of type 4 (in the left-hand column). Assuming that the external glazing of the atrium is single, and that ventilation pre-heating will be used if possible, as in mode B, the Specific Buffer-space Thermal Saving (BTS) is 0.60MWh/my. This is entered on the LT worksheet.

The BTS is multiplied by the separating wall length to get the total Buffer-space Thermal Saving. Enter this in the buffer-space box and transfer it to the insert box in the main worksheet, as indicated by the dotted line.

Two other values are requested – the Protectivity Ratio and the Solarity Ratio, although they are not actually required for the LT calculation. We can use the Protectivity Ratio to calculate the average atrium temperature in absence of solar radiation using the nomogram in section [9.2].

The final totals are calculated with the BTS deducted from the total heating energy, not just that for the buffer-adjacent zone. This is because in the ventilation pre-heating mode the thermal benefit of the atrium can be considered to benefit a much larger area of the building since it is not just reducing conduction losses.

However, for a very large atrium the method may predict a BTS as great as the heating energy for the rest of the building. This is obviously unrealistic. A safe compromise would be to allow the BTS to be deducted from up to half of the heating energy of the rest of the building.

The primary energy consumption per m² of 98 kWh has been calculated without including the area of the atrium since it is assumed that this is not serviced. However, an allowance for the potentially useful atrium space could be made in which case the specific energy consumption figure will be reduced further. This is a matter of choice, but whatever is decided should be noted on the worksheet.

Comparison with non-passive building

It is always difficult to know how to define the non-passive building with which to make the comparison. But supposing we consider a building of the same plan and section but with no atrium. There is 60% glazing (probably tinted) all round, but there are no photo-electric controls and we know that the electric lighting will be used all day. The whole building will be air-conditioned. This may sound like a horror story, but it is not at all unusual!

If we interpret this as a zero passive zone building, i.e. take the specific energy consumptions off the zero glazing ratio intercept, we shall get the correct value for lighting, but it will be an underestimate for heating and cooling since it assumes an opaque envelope with U-value 0.35. So for clear glazing, we should use the actual glazing ratios for heating and cooling. Tinted or reflective glass will reduce cooling loads, and this could be estimated by reading off the cooling load for a reduced glazing ratio, corresponding to the shading factor of the glass.

Using the LT curves for the same lighting datum of 300 lux and the low internal gains of 15W/m², the annual primary energy is 269kWh/m²y; that is, over 2.5 times as much as the passive atrium building above. It must be pointed out, however, that most of the difference is due to the non-utilisation of daylight, rather than the presence of the atrium.

Using the higher lighting datum of 500 lux and the high internal gains of 30 W/m², the energy consumption for this case goes up to 392kWh/m²y, nearly four times that for the passive building. Furthermore, when combined with inefficiencies in operation such as simultaneous heating and cooling, and poor maintenance leading to reduced system efficiency, even worse performance can occur in reality. These figures begin to explain the large variations in energy consumption observed in non-domestic buildings, and underline the importance of the early design strategies.

13.3 School with conservatory

In this example an early design objective is to create a 'solar' design with an unheated single-glazed conservatory

13.3 *Worked example of school with conservatory.*

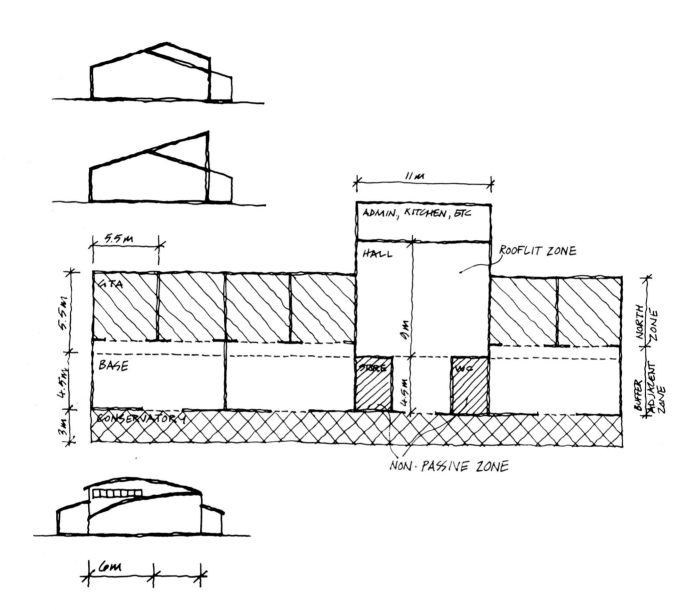

running along the south side acting as both a main circulation route and a sunspace to provide pre-heated ventilation air. The building is located in southern UK on an open site. A particular question is investigated – how does the performance compare with a more conventional linear plan, where the circulation runs in a heated corridor on the north?

The first step is to designate passive zones as shown in Figure 13.3. The conservatory has clear glazing with movable shading giving a buffer-adjacent zone depth of 4.5m. This, with a passive zone depth of 6m from the north, indicates that some effort needs to be made to light the centre – this could be achieved with a generous ceiling height to the south with clerestory lighting, or even a small area of rooflighting. We will assume that it is achievable with sidelighting only, and with a roof-lit hall, the whole floor area becomes passive except for the toilet and stores. The specific energy consumptions are read off from the curves for type A buildings, in the normal way. The side-lit spaces are also under the roof and the heating energy is corrected for heat loss through the roof as described previously [12.3]. However, the effect is less than 8% in this case, since for a well-insulated roof, heating energy is dominated by ventilation losses and heat loss through glazing. The east/west curves are used for the buffer-adjacent zone, to allow for the reduction of direct solar gain by obstructions in the atrium.

In calculating the Buffer-space Thermal Savings, the conservatory is clearly type 6 and the ventilation mode is B. This gives total savings of 14.8MWh/y for the 44m separating wall, after an occupancy correction factor of 0.55 has been applied. A boiler factor of 0.85 (efficiency 75%) is applied to the heating total to account for a lightweight boiler. This gives an annual specific heating requirement of 65.5kWh/m^2.

The value of the BTS is 26% of the gross heating requirement and a simplistic interpretation is that this is the contribution of the conservatory. However if we simply 'remove' the conservatory, this would not give a realistic alternative, since firstly there would be no circulation area, and secondly it would not take account of useful solar gains which would be made by the now-unobstructed south-facing glazing. So the comparison is made redesig-

nating the buffer-adjacent zone as the south zone, and adding a non-passive area which would result from adding a 2m heated corridor to the north side.

In fact the result of this is to increase the specific heating energy to 81.8kWh/m^2, an increase of 25% on a square metre basis, close to the BTS value. However, this is an increase of 40% in absolute heating energy due to the 12% increase in heated area of the circulation zone.

This example is loosely based upon Netley Infants School in Hampshire. This building was monitored for three years, and it is interesting to note that after initial difficulties with control systems, the annual heating demand was 74kWh/m^2 primary, 12% more than the LT Method prediction. This can be regarded as good agreement for this type of model; the discrepancy could be partly explained by slightly higher U-values and areas of single glazing in the real building, and non-optimal control of the building by the occupants.

In the LT prediction, lighting energy is very low, as it should be in a school where the occupied period is short and falls in the middle of the day. In reality this will only be achieved with a high degree of cooperation by the occupants, or more reliably by photo-electric lighting controls. At Netley, electricity use was much higher, due to poor control.

13.4 Nucleus hospital

Figure 13.4 shows two Nucleus planning templates in the normal grid configuration, serviced by the hospital street. In this LT example the alternatives of using rooflights, or increasing floor-to-ceiling height to improve sidelighting, is investigated for a two-storey module. The original floor-to-ceiling height is 2.7m.

Because conditions differ on the ground and first floor, a total of four LT worksheets are completed as follows:

1   Ground floor 2.7m floor to ceiling (f/c) with UHFs for S, W and N façades due to self-overshadowing.
2   First floor 2.7m f/c with no overshadowing.
3   Ground floor 3.5m f/c with UHFs for S, W and N façades.

4   First floor 2.7m f/c no overshadowing and with rooflights.

The passive-zone depths are defined as twice the f/c height and this has the effect of reducing the non-passive area for the greater f/c height. The base case assumes that there is mechanical fresh air only in all perimeter spaces, with air-conditioning in the non-passive zones. For the top-floor roof-lit option it is not assumed that the whole area would become passive; some service spaces would always require high ventilation rates or air-conditioning. The results are shown in Table 13.1.

Table 13.1 LT analysis of Nucleus hospital for effect of ceiling height and incorporation of rooflights, kWh/m²y

Annual energy (kWh/m²y)	Light	Heat	Vent.	Total
Ground floor 2.7m f/c	230	131	192	553
First floor 2.7m f/c	219	129	192	540
Ground floor 3.5m f/c	214	139	180 (86)	533 (439)
First floor rooflights	185	145	150 (35)	480 (365)

The base case shows that the influence of overshadowing is slight, with only a 5% increase in lighting energy for the ground floor and a negligible reduction in useful solar energy. This is due to the generous spacing of the Nucleus templates, giving a UHA of about 18° from the centre of the ground-floor windows. This would increase rapidly if the building was more than two storeys.

Increasing the floor to ceiling height of the ground floor reduces lighting energy from 230 to 214MWh, a reduction of 7%. This is rather disappointing and would be insufficient on its own to justify the extra f/c height. The use of rooflights has a much greater effect, reducing the base case top-floor lighting energy by 16%. It is interesting to note, however, that due to the 24-hour occupation, improvements to daylighting have less impact, in proportion, than in building types with predominantly daytime occupancy.

Heating shows only slight variation, the most being a slight increase due to the top-floor rooflights. This is much less than the decrease in lighting energy.

To evaluate the effect on ventilation and cooling-energy, certain assumptions have to be made. Mechanical fresh-air supply is common practice in the Nucleus system, but it could be argued that the need is marginal. Increasing the f/c height to 3.6m, and/or using rooflights with ventilation opportunities on the top floor, could allow natural ventilation in all ward areas, as was common practice in the traditional Nightingale wards. (The greater vertical distance between the ingress of cool air and the occupants allows for more mixing and is less likely to cause discomfort.) If this is the case, much more significant savings can be made, as indicated by the numbers in parentheses in Table 13.1.

If all ground-floor perimeter areas, and all perimeter and roof-lit areas on the top floor were naturally ventilated, ventilation energy is reduced from 180 to 86MWh and 150 to 35MWh respectively, an overall reduction in ventilation energy of 37%.

Combining the two, and comparing the base case with the 3.6m ground floor and the roof-lit top-floor, the resulting reduction in annual total primary energy would be 26%.

13.4 *Nucleus hospital 'planning template' used in example.*

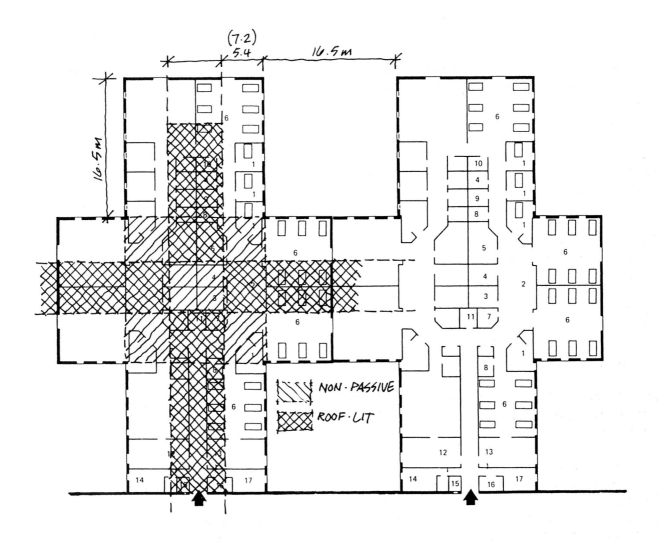

14

LT data and worksheet

Index

Northern UK

	Lighting datum (lux)	Internal gains (W/m²)	Data ref. nos.		Page nos.	
			LT curves	UHF		
Type A (schools)	150	20	N1	N13	122	136
	300	20	N2	N14	123	136
Type B (colleges)	150	20	N3	N15	124	137
	300	20	N4	N16	125	137
Type C (offices)	150	15	N5	N17	126	138
	300	15	N6	N18	127	138
	500	15	N7	N19	128	139
	150	30	N8	N20	129	139
	300	30	N9	N21	130	140
	500	30	N10	N22	131	140
Type D (institutional)	150	10	N11	N23	132	141
	300	10	N12	N24	134	141
Buffer-space thermal saving:			ref. no. N25		142	

Southern UK

	Lighting datum (lux)	Internal gains (W/m²)	Data ref. nos.		Page nos.	
			LT curves	UHF		
Type A (schools)	150	20	S1	S13	143	157
	300	20	S2	S14	144	157
Type B (colleges)	150	20	S3	S15	145	158
	300	20	S4	S16	146	158
Type C (offices)	150	15	S5	S17	147	159
	300	15	S6	S18	148	159
	500	15	S7	S19	149	160
	150	30	S8	S20	150	160
	300	30	S9	S21	151	161
	500	30	S10	S22	152	161
Type D (institutional)	150	10	S11	S23	153	162
	300	10	S12	S24	155	162
Buffer-space thermal saving:			ref. no. S25		163	

14.1 LT data

Type A (schools)
150 lux, 20 W/m²,
Northern UK

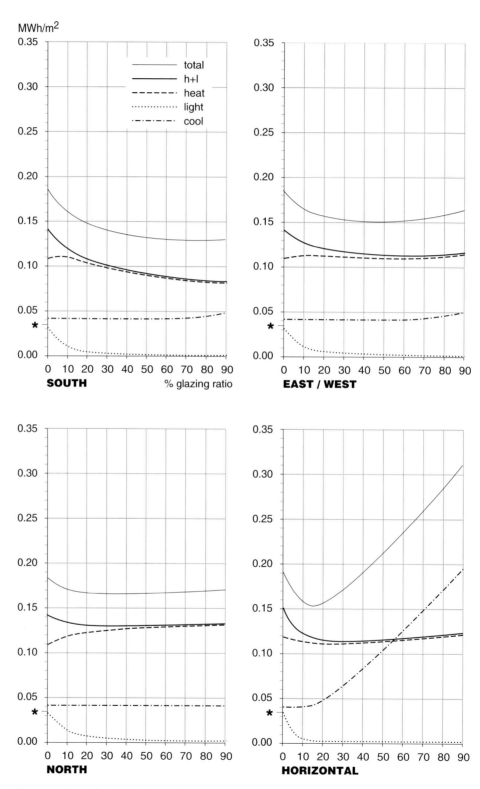

*Mechanical vent fresh air only 0.035MWh/m²

Ventilation heating energy 0.100MWh/m²

MWh/m²

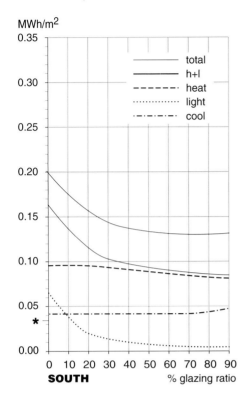

SOUTH   % glazing ratio

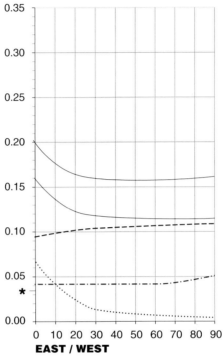

EAST / WEST

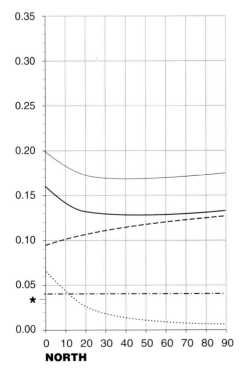

NORTH

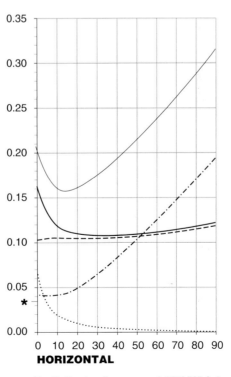

HORIZONTAL

*Mechanical vent fresh air only 0.035MWh/m²

Ventilation heating energy 0.087MWh/m²

N2

Type A (schools)
300 lux, 20 W/m²,
Northern UK

Type B (colleges)
150 lux, 20 W/m²,
Northern UK

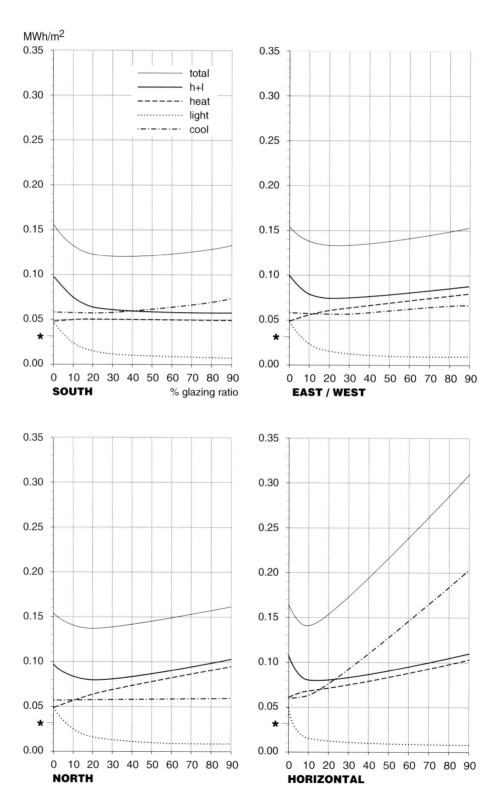

*Mechanical vent fresh air only 0.031MWh/m²

Ventilation heating energy 0.045MWh/m²

Type B (colleges)
300 lux, 20 W/m²,
Northern UK

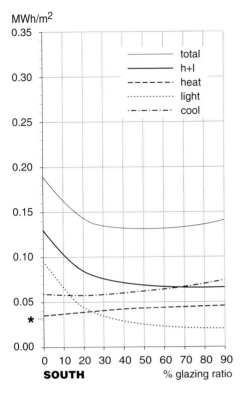

MWh/m²

total
h+l
heat
light
cool

SOUTH   % glazing ratio

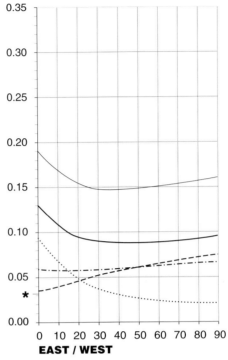

EAST / WEST

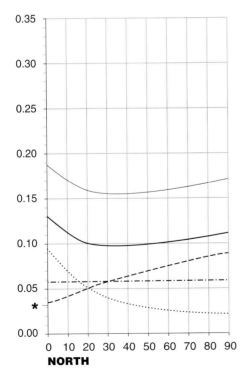

NORTH

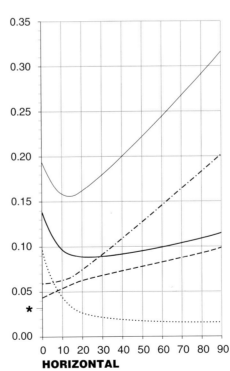

HORIZONTAL

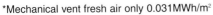

*Mechanical vent fresh air only 0.031MWh/m²

Ventilation heating energy 0.032MWh/m²

Type C (offices)
150 lux, 15 W/m²,
Northern UK

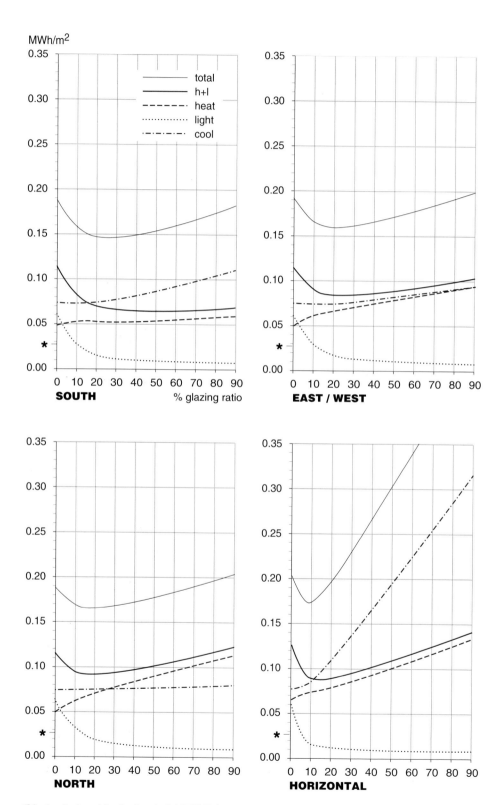

*Mechanical vent fresh air only 0.027MWh/m²

Ventilation heating energy 0.043MWh/m²

Type C (offices)
300 lux, 15 W/m²,
Northern UK

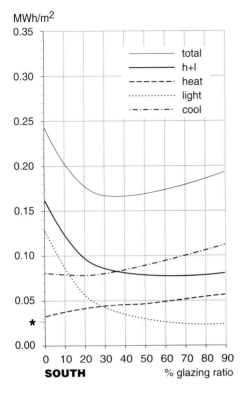

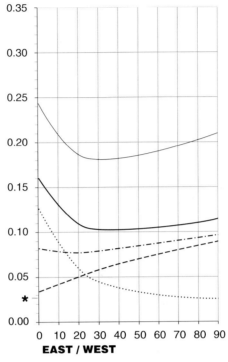

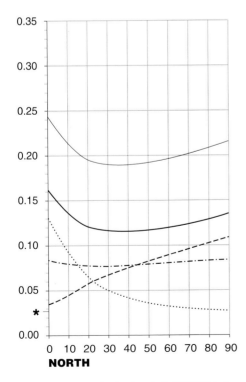

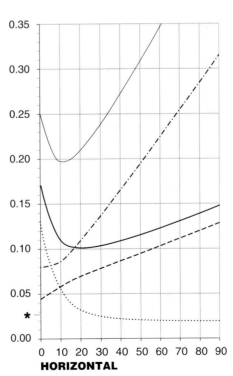

*Mechanical vent fresh air only 0.027MWh/m²

Ventilation heating energy 0.030MWh/m²

N7

Type C (offices)
500 lux, 15 W/m², Northern UK

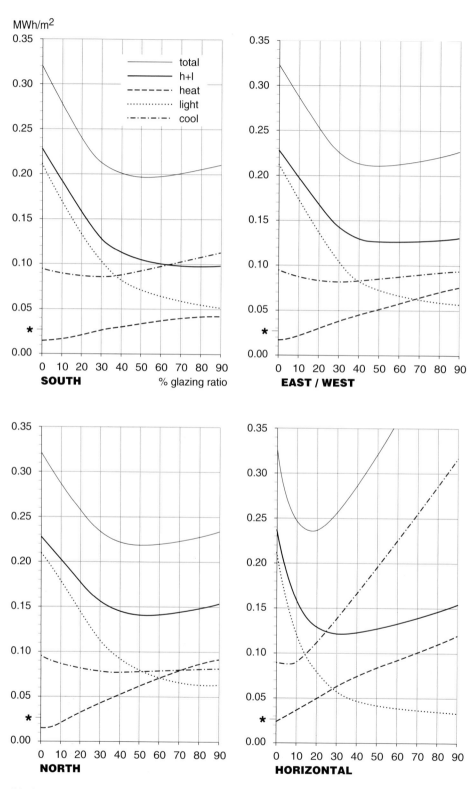

MWh/m²

SOUTH
% glazing ratio

- total
- h+l
- heat
- light
- cool

EAST / WEST

NORTH

HORIZONTAL

*Mechanical vent fresh air only 0.027MWh/m²

Ventilation heating energy 0.014MWh/m²

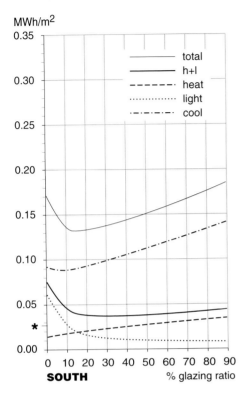

MWh/m²

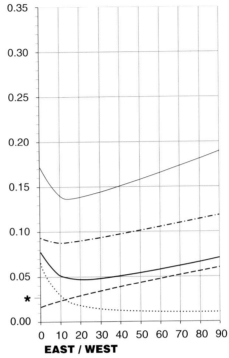

Type C (offices)
150 lux, 30 W/m²,
Northern UK

Legend:
— total
— h+l
-- heat
··· light
-·- cool

SOUTH — % glazing ratio

EAST / WEST

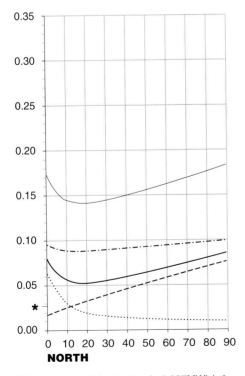

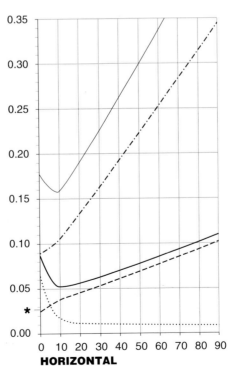

NORTH

HORIZONTAL

*Mechanical vent fresh air only 0.027MWh/m²

Ventilation heating energy 0.014MWh/m²

Type C (offices)
300 lux, 30 W/m², Northern UK

MWh/m²

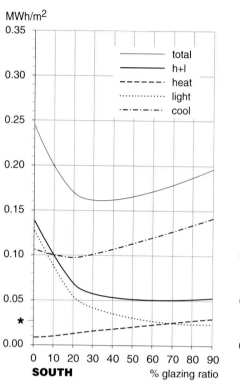

total
h+l
heat
light
cool

SOUTH   % glazing ratio

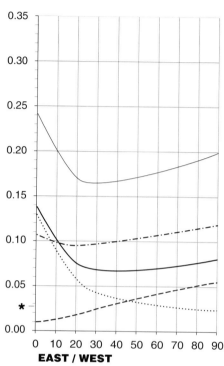

EAST / WEST

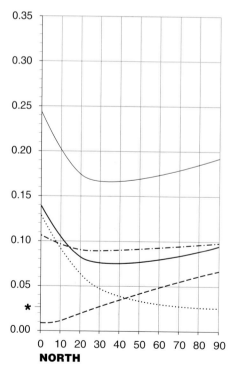

NORTH

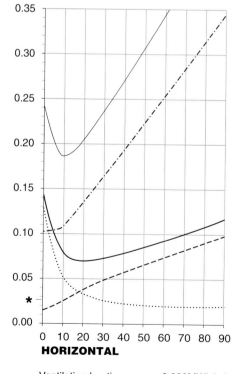

HORIZONTAL

*Mechanical vent fresh air only 0.027MWh/m²

Ventilation heating energy 0.009MWh/m²

Type C (offices)
500 lux, 30 W/m²,
Northern UK

MWh/m²

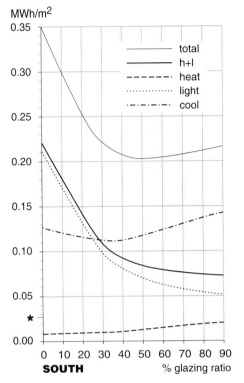

SOUTH   % glazing ratio

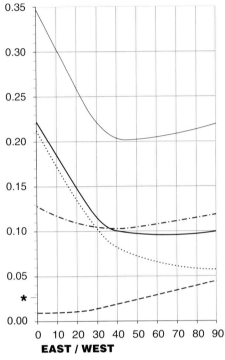

EAST / WEST

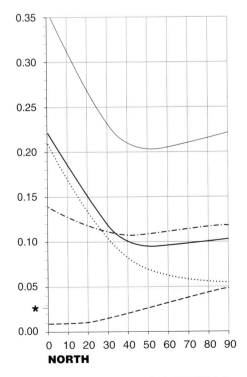

NORTH

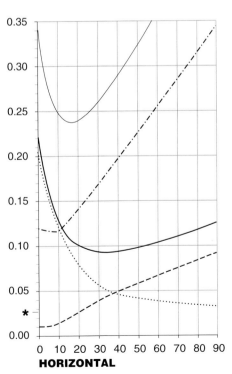

HORIZONTAL

*Mechanical vent fresh air only 0.027MWh/m²

Ventilation heating energy 0.008MWh/m²

Type D
(institutional)
150 lux, 10 W/m²,
Northern UK

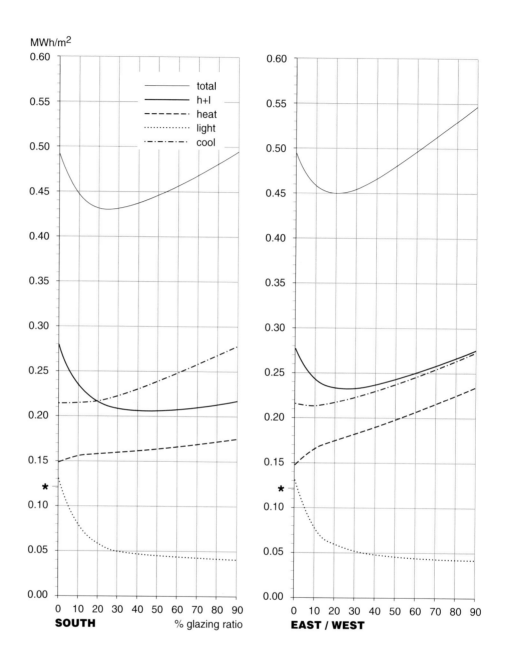

MWh/m²

SOUTH   % glazing ratio

EAST / WEST

*Mechanical vent fresh air only 0.121MWh/m²   Ventilation heating energy 0.132MWh/m²

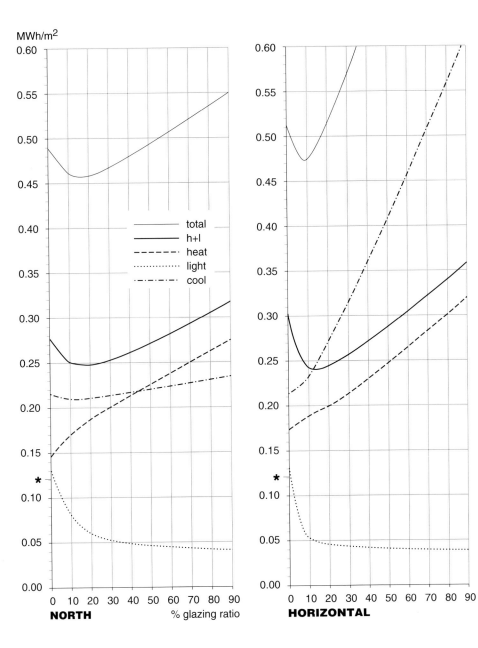

MWh/m²

NORTH % glazing ratio

HORIZONTAL

Legend:
- total
- h+l
- heat
- light
- cool

*Mechanical vent fresh air only 0.121MWh/m²

Ventilation heating energy 0.132MWh/m²

Type D
(institutional)
300 lux, 10 W/m²,
Northern UK

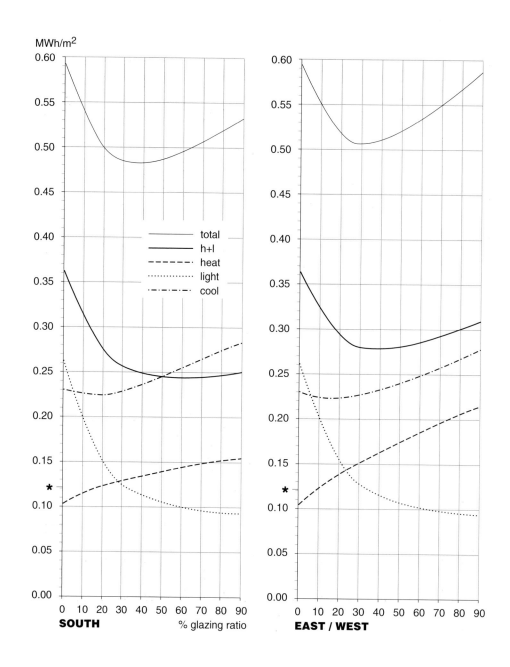

MWh/m²

total
h+l
heat
light
cool

SOUTH   % glazing ratio

EAST / WEST

*Mechanical vent fresh air only 0.121MWh/m²   Ventilation heating energy 0.094MWh/m²

MWh/m²

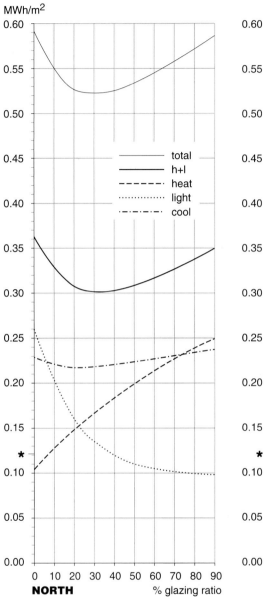

NORTH　　% glazing ratio

total
h+l
heat
light
cool

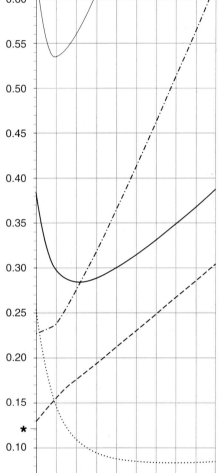

HORIZONTAL

*Mechanical vent fresh air only 0.121MWh/m²　　　Ventilation heating energy 0.094MWh/m²

Urban Horizon Factors

Type A (schools)
150 lux, 20 W/m²,
Northern UK

orientation	UHA deg.	glazing ratio %	correction factors		
			heating	cooling	lighting
south	15 - 45	20	1.1	1.00	1.9
		40	1.2	1.00	2.4
		60	1.3	1.00	2.0
		80	1.4	1.00	1.8
	> 45	20	1.1	1.00	3.5
		40	1.4	1.00	4.4
		60	1.5	1.00	3.4
		80	1.7	1.00	3.9
east / west	15 - 45	20	1.0	1.00	1.9
		40	1.1	1.00	2.6
		60	1.1	1.00	2.0
		80	1.1	1.00	2.3
	> 45	20	1.0	1.00	3.5
		40	1.1	1.00	4.9
		60	1.2	1.00	3.4
		80	1.3	1.00	3.9
north	15 - 45	20	1.0	1.00	1.6
		40	1.0	1.00	2.5
		60	1.0	1.00	2.1
		80	1.1	1.00	1.7
	> 45	20	1.0	1.00	3.0
		40	1.1	1.00	4.5
		60	1.1	1.00	3.0
		80	1.1	1.00	3.2

Type A (schools)
300 lux, 20 W/m²,
Northern UK

orientation	UHA deg.	glazing ratio %	correction factors		
			heating	cooling	lighting
south	15 - 45	20	1.1	1.00	1.7
		40	1.1	1.00	2.0
		60	1.3	1.00	1.9
		80	1.3	1.00	2.4
	> 45	20	1.1	1.00	2.5
		40	1.3	1.00	3.6
		60	1.5	1.00	3.6
		80	1.6	1.00	4.6
east / west	15 - 45	20	1.0	1.00	1.6
		40	1.0	1.00	1.9
		60	1.1	1.00	2.0
		80	1.1	1.00	2.0
	> 45	20	1.0	1.00	2.3
		40	1.1	1.00	3.6
		60	1.1	1.00	3.9
		80	1.2	1.00	4.2
north	15 - 45	20	1.0	1.00	1.5
		40	1.0	1.00	1.6
		60	1.0	1.00	2.1
		80	1.0	1.00	2.1
	> 45	20	0.9	1.00	2.2
		40	1.0	1.00	3.1
		60	1.1	1.00	3.4
		80	1.1	1.00	3.6

Type B (colleges)
150 lux, 20 W/m², Northern UK

orientation	UHA deg.	glazing ratio %	correction factors		
			heating	cooling	lighting
south	15 - 45	20	1.2	1.00	1.4
		40	1.3	0.98	1.5
		60	1.5	0.95	1.3
		80	1.6	0.93	1.2
	> 45	20	1.2	1.00	2.1
		40	1.5	0.97	2.1
		60	1.8	0.92	1.8
		80	2.0	0.86	1.7
east / west	15 - 45	20	1.0	1.00	1.4
		40	1.1	0.99	1.5
		60	1.2	0.95	1.3
		80	1.2	0.92	1.3
	> 45	20	1.0	1.00	2.2
		40	1.2	0.99	2.2
		60	1.3	0.95	1.8
		80	1.3	0.91	1.7
north	15 - 45	20	1.0	1.00	1.3
		40	1.0	1.00	1.5
		60	1.0	1.00	1.3
		80	1.1	0.99	1.2
	> 45	20	1.0	1.00	2.0
		40	1.0	1.00	2.2
		60	1.1	1.00	1.7
		80	1.1	0.99	1.7

Type B (colleges)
300 lux, 20 W/m², Northern UK

orientation	UHA deg.	glazing ratio %	correction factors		
			heating	cooling	lighting
south	15 - 45	20	1.2	1.01	1.3
		40	1.3	0.98	1.5
		60	1.5	0.96	1.5
		80	1.6	0.93	1.5
	> 45	20	1.1	1.00	1.8
		40	1.4	0.97	2.2
		60	1.7	0.92	2.2
		80	1.9	0.85	2.2
east / west	15 - 45	20	1.0	1.00	1.3
		40	1.1	0.99	1.4
		60	1.1	0.96	1.5
		80	1.2	0.92	1.5
	> 45	20	1.0	1.01	1.8
		40	1.0	0.99	2.2
		60	1.1	0.95	2.2
		80	1.2	0.91	2.2
north	15 - 45	20	1.0	1.00	1.3
		40	1.0	1.00	1.3
		60	1.0	1.00	1.5
		80	1.0	0.99	1.5
	> 45	20	0.9	1.01	1.7
		40	0.9	1.00	2.1
		60	1.0	1.00	2.2
		80	1.1	0.99	2.1

Type C (offices)
150 lux, 15 W/m², Northern UK

orientation	UHA deg.	glazing ratio %	correction factors		
			heating	cooling	lighting
south	15 - 45	20	1.2	0.99	1.4
		40	1.4	0.96	1.5
		60	1.5	0.92	1.3
		80	1.6	0.88	1.3
	> 45	20	1.3	0.99	2.3
		40	1.7	0.91	2.1
		60	1.9	0.83	1.8
		80	2.1	0.74	1.8
east / west	15 - 45	20	1.1	1.00	1.5
		40	1.1	0.96	1.5
		60	1.2	0.91	1.3
		80	1.2	0.89	1.3
	> 45	20	1.1	1.00	2.3
		40	1.2	0.95	2.3
		60	1.3	0.90	1.9
		80	1.4	0.85	1.7
north	15 - 45	20	1.0	1.00	1.4
		40	1.0	1.00	1.5
		60	1.1	0.98	1.3
		80	1.1	0.95	1.2
	> 45	20	1.0	1.00	2.2
		40	1.1	1.00	2.2
		60	1.2	0.98	1.8
		80	1.2	0.95	1.7

Type C (offices)
300 lux, 15 W/m², Northern UK

orientation	UHA deg.	glazing ratio %	correction factors		
			heating	cooling	lighting
south	15 - 45	20	1.2	1.03	1.4
		40	1.4	0.97	1.5
		60	1.5	0.93	1.4
		80	1.6	0.88	1.5
	> 45	20	1.2	1.02	2.0
		40	1.5	0.90	2.3
		60	1.8	0.82	2.2
		80	2.0	0.74	2.2
east / west	15 - 45	20	1.0	1.02	1.4
		40	1.1	0.96	1.5
		60	1.1	0.92	1.4
		80	1.2	0.89	1.4
	> 45	20	1.0	1.03	1.9
		40	1.1	0.95	2.3
		60	1.2	0.90	2.3
		80	1.3	0.84	2.2
north	15 - 45	20	1.0	1.02	1.3
		40	1.0	0.99	1.4
		60	1.0	0.98	1.5
		80	1.0	0.95	1.4
	> 45	20	0.9	1.05	1.8
		40	0.9	1.00	2.2
		60	1.0	0.98	2.3
		80	1.1	0.95	2.1

Type C (offices)
500 lux, 15 W/m², Northern UK

orientation	UHA deg.	glazing ratio %	correction factors heating	cooling	lighting
south	15 - 45	20	1.3	0.98	1.1
		40	1.4	1.06	1.5
		60	1.5	0.97	1.5
		80	1.6	0.90	1.5
	> 45	20	1.3	1.04	1.4
		40	1.4	0.97	2.1
		60	1.6	0.86	2.4
		80	1.9	0.73	2.3
east / west	15 - 45	20	1.0	0.96	1.1
		40	1.0	1.04	1.6
		60	1.1	0.95	1.4
		80	1.1	0.91	1.5
	> 45	20	1.0	1.06	1.4
		40	0.9	1.04	2.1
		60	1.0	0.93	2.3
		80	1.2	0.85	2.3
north	15 - 45	20	1.0	0.99	1.1
		40	1.0	1.05	1.4
		60	1.0	1.01	1.5
		80	1.0	0.95	1.5
	> 45	20	0.9	1.10	1.4
		40	0.8	1.09	1.9
		60	0.9	1.02	2.3
		80	1.0	0.95	2.2

Type C (offices)
150 lux, 30 W/m², Northern UK

orientation	UHA deg.	glazing ratio %	correction factors heating	cooling	lighting
south	15 - 45	20	1.3	0.98	1.4
		40	1.5	0.94	1.5
		60	1.7	0.90	1.3
		80	1.9	0.87	1.3
	> 45	20	1.3	0.92	2.3
		40	1.7	0.79	2.1
		60	2.1	0.71	1.8
		80	2.3	0.64	1.8
east / west	15 - 45	20	1.1	0.97	1.5
		40	1.1	0.92	1.5
		60	1.2	0.88	1.3
		80	1.2	0.85	1.3
	> 45	20	1.0	0.96	2.3
		40	1.2	0.85	2.3
		60	1.3	0.78	1.9
		80	1.4	0.72	1.7
north	15 - 45	20	1.0	1.00	1.4
		40	1.0	0.96	1.5
		60	1.0	0.94	1.3
		80	1.1	0.92	1.2
	> 45	20	0.9	1.00	2.2
		40	1.0	0.92	2.2
		60	1.1	0.88	1.8
		80	1.2	0.85	1.7

Type C (offices)
300 lux, 30 W/m²,
Northern UK

orientation	UHA deg.	glazing ratio %	correction factors		
			heating	cooling	lighting
south	15 - 45	20	1.2	1.02	1.4
		40	1.6	0.95	1.5
		60	1.9	0.91	1.4
		80	1.9	0.88	1.5
	> 45	20	1.2	1.00	2.0
		40	1.6	0.85	2.3
		60	2.1	0.72	2.2
		80	2.2	0.64	2.2
east / west	15 - 45	20	1.0	1.02	1.4
		40	1.1	0.94	1.5
		60	1.1	0.89	1.4
		80	1.2	0.85	1.4
	> 45	20	0.9	1.05	1.9
		40	1.0	0.91	2.3
		60	1.1	0.80	2.3
		80	1.2	0.73	2.2
north	15 - 45	20	1.0	1.03	1.3
		40	1.0	0.99	1.4
		60	1.0	0.95	1.5
		80	1.0	0.93	1.4
	> 45	20	0.9	1.09	1.8
		40	0.9	1.00	2.2
		60	1.0	0.91	2.3
		80	1.1	0.86	2.1

Type C (offices)
500 lux, 30 W/m²,
Northern UK

orientation	UHA deg.	glazing ratio %	correction factors		
			heating	cooling	lighting
south	15 - 45	20	1.0	0.96	1.1
		40	1.5	1.04	1.5
		60	1.9	0.95	1.5
		80	2.1	0.89	1.5
	> 45	20	1.0	1.03	1.4
		40	1.3	0.94	2.1
		60	1.6	0.82	2.4
		80	2.1	0.68	2.3
east / west	15 - 45	20	1.0	0.96	1.1
		40	1.1	1.03	1.6
		60	1.2	0.94	1.4
		80	1.2	0.88	1.5
	> 45	20	1.0	1.07	1.4
		40	0.9	1.03	2.1
		60	0.9	0.92	2.3
		80	1.1	0.80	2.3
north	15 - 45	20	1.0	1.00	1.1
		40	1.0	1.07	1.4
		60	1.0	1.01	1.5
		80	1.0	0.95	1.5
	> 45	20	1.0	1.12	1.4
		40	0.8	1.13	1.9
		60	0.8	1.03	2.3
		80	0.9	0.93	2.2

orientation	UHA deg.	glazing ratio %	correction factors		
			heating	cooling	lighting
south	15 - 45	20	1.1	0.99	1.3
		40	1.2	0.97	1.2
		60	1.3	0.94	1.1
		80	1.4	0.92	1.1
	> 45	20	1.2	0.98	1.7
		40	1.4	0.92	1.5
		60	1.6	0.86	1.4
		80	1.7	0.80	1.3
east / west	15 - 45	20	1.0	0.98	1.3
		40	1.1	0.96	1.2
		60	1.1	0.93	1.2
		80	1.2	0.90	1.1
	> 45	20	1.1	0.98	1.7
		40	1.2	0.92	1.6
		60	1.3	0.87	1.4
		80	1.3	0.82	1.3
north	15 - 45	20	1.0	1.00	1.2
		40	1.0	0.97	1.2
		60	1.1	0.95	1.1
		80	1.1	0.94	1.1
	> 45	20	1.0	1.00	1.7
		40	1.1	0.97	1.6
		60	1.1	0.94	1.4
		80	1.2	0.92	1.3

Type D
(institutional)
150 lux, 10 W/m², Northern UK

orientation	UHA deg.	glazing ratio %	correction factors		
			heating	cooling	lighting
south	15 - 45	20	1.1	1.01	1.2
		40	1.2	0.98	1.3
		60	1.3	0.95	1.2
		80	1.4	0.92	1.2
	> 45	20	1.1	1.01	1.6
		40	1.3	0.94	1.7
		60	1.5	0.86	1.6
		80	1.7	0.79	1.5
east / west	15 - 45	20	1.0	1.00	1.2
		40	1.1	0.97	1.3
		60	1.1	0.93	1.2
		80	1.1	0.90	1.2
	> 45	20	1.0	1.01	1.5
		40	1.1	0.94	1.7
		60	1.2	0.87	1.6
		80	1.3	0.81	1.6
north	15 - 45	20	1.0	1.01	1.2
		40	1.0	0.99	1.3
		60	1.0	0.96	1.3
		80	1.0	0.95	1.2
	> 45	20	0.9	1.04	1.5
		40	1.0	0.99	1.7
		60	1.0	0.94	1.7
		80	1.1	0.91	1.5

Type D
(institutional)
300 lux, 10 W/m², Northern UK

Buffer-space
Thermal Savings
(BTS) MWh/my
glazing options
(×1, ×2) refers to
atrium envelope
glazing

config. type	vent mode a x1	x2	b x1	x2	c x1	x2	d x1	x2
1 ▲N	0.62	0.71	0.71	0.77	0.65	0.72	1.27	1.39
2 ▲N	0.62	0.84	0.82	1.01	0.69	0.84	1.24	1.50
3 ▲N	0.47	0.64	0.60	0.75	0.57	0.71	1.02	1.27
4 ▲N	0.39	0.60	0.60	0.80	0.49	0.62	1.01	1.34
5 ▲N	0.35	0.49	0.47	0.67	0.41	0.54	0.60	0.89
6 ▲N	0.62	0.95	0.84	1.22	0.71	0.99	1.09	1.57
7 ▲N	0.56	0.75	0.67	0.90	0.65	0.81	1.01	1.34

Table 12.2
**Buffer-adjacent
zone depth**

characteristic	score 0	score 1
shading	fixed	movable
glazing	tinted/reflective	clear
internal finishes	dark coloured	light coloured
horizon angle	greater than 45°	less than 45°

total score	buffer-adjacent passive zone depth
0 or 1	0.0
2 or 3	1.0 h
4	1.5 h

h = floor to ceiling height

Table 12.3
**Buffer-space
occupancy
factors**

building type	occupancy factors
schools	0.55
colleges	0.75
offices	1.0
institutional	1.5

MWh/m²

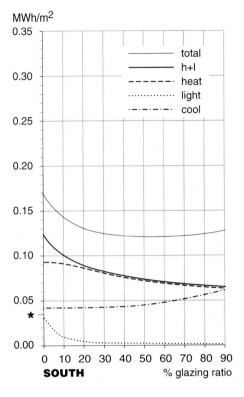

- total
- h+l
- heat
- light
- cool

SOUTH % glazing ratio

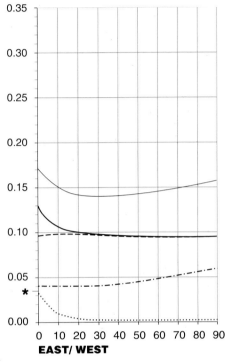

EAST/ WEST

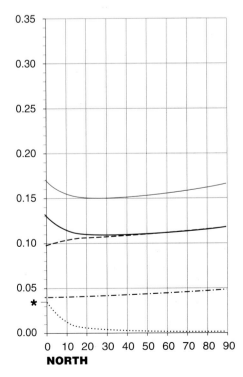

NORTH

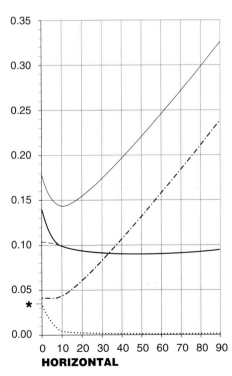

HORIZONTAL

*Mechanical vent fresh air only 0.035MWh/m²

Ventilation heating energy 0.090MWh/m²

S1

Type A (schools)
150 lux, 20 W/m²,
Southern UK

S2

Type A (schools)
300 lux, 20 W/m², Southern UK

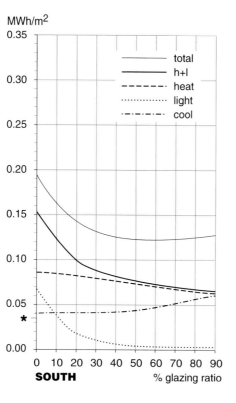

SOUTH   % glazing ratio

MWh/m²

total
h+l
heat
light
cool

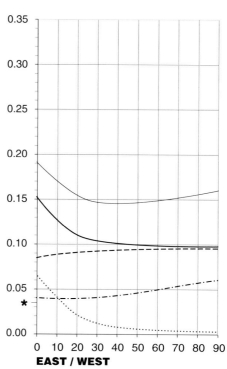

EAST / WEST

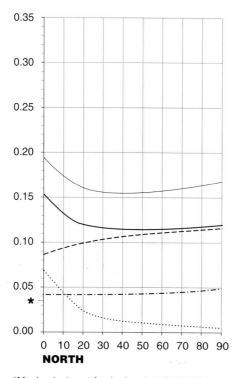

NORTH

*Mechanical vent fresh air only 0.035MWh/m²

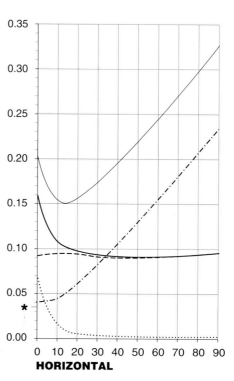

HORIZONTAL

Ventilation heating energy 0.077MWh/m²

MWh/m²

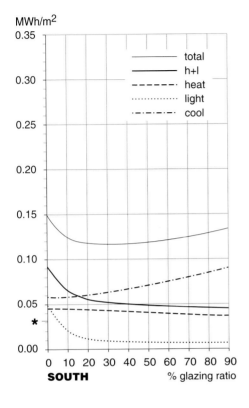

SOUTH   % glazing ratio

Legend:
- total
- h+l
- heat
- light
- cool

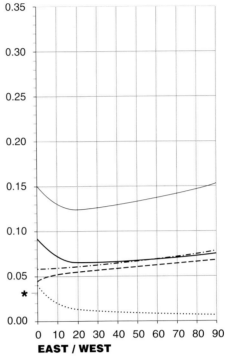

EAST / WEST

Type B (colleges)
150 lux, 20 W/m²,
Southern UK

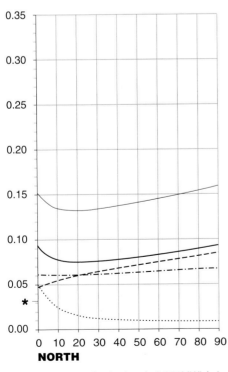

NORTH

*Mechanical vent fresh air only 0.031MWh/m²

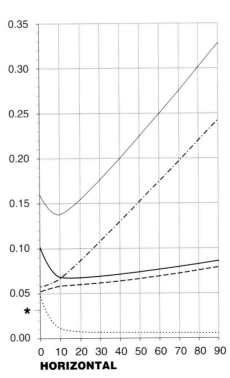

HORIZONTAL

Ventilation heating energy 0.040MWh/m²

Type B (colleges)
300 lux, 20 W/m², Southern UK

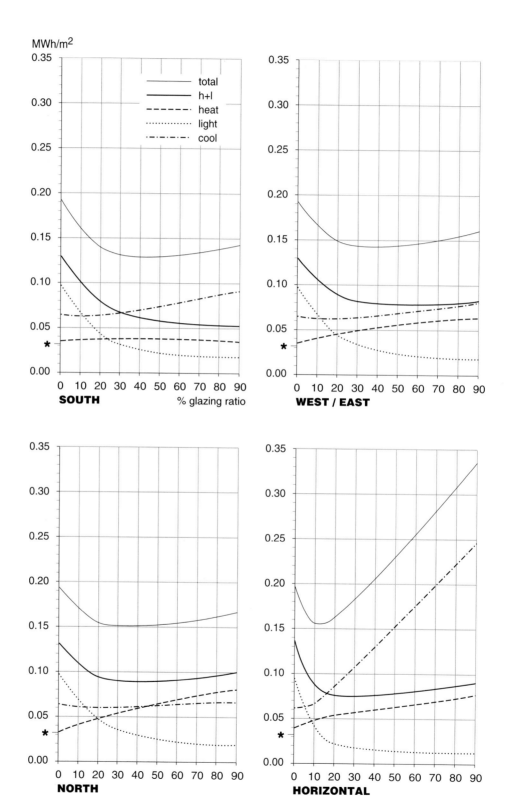

*Mechanical vent fresh air only 0.031MWh/m²

Ventilation heating energy 0.030MWh/m²

MWh/m^2

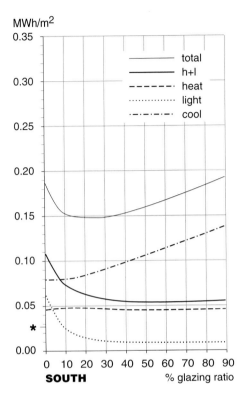

SOUTH   % glazing ratio

Legend:
- total
- h+l
- heat
- light
- cool

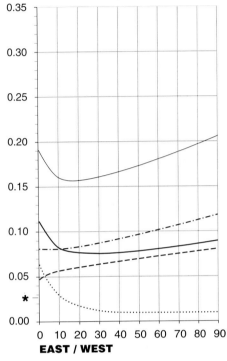

EAST / WEST

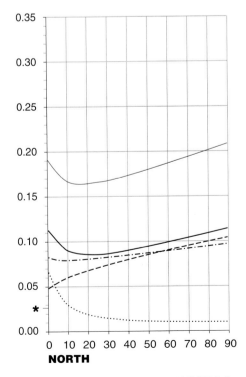

NORTH

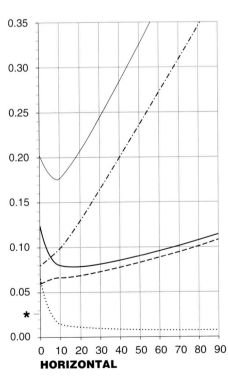

HORIZONTAL

Type C (offices)
150 lux, 15 W/m^2,
Southern UK

*Mechanical vent fresh air only 0.027MWh/m^2

Ventilation heating energy 0.040MWh/m^2

Type C (offices)
300 lux, 15 W/m²,
Southern UK

MWh/m²

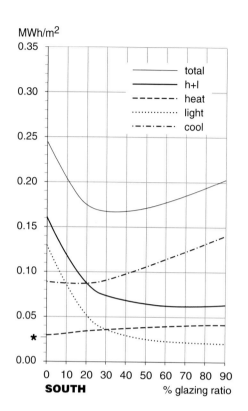

SOUTH   % glazing ratio

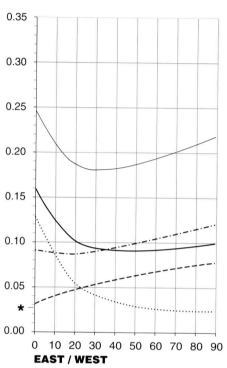

EAST / WEST

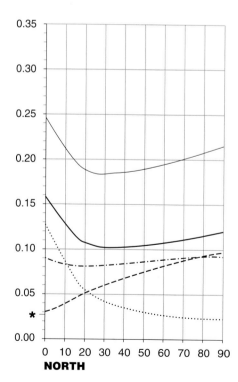

NORTH

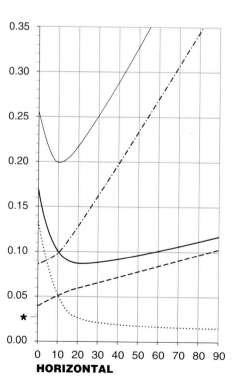

HORIZONTAL

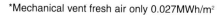

*Mechanical vent fresh air only 0.027MWh/m²

Ventilation heating energy 0.026MWh/m²

MWh/m²

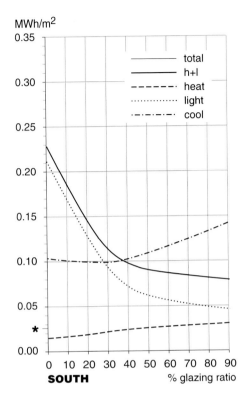

SOUTH % glazing ratio

Legend:
- total
- h+l
- heat
- light
- cool

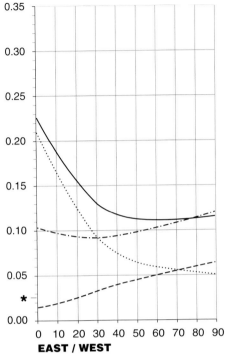

EAST / WEST

Type C (offices)
500 lux, 15 W/m²,
Southern UK

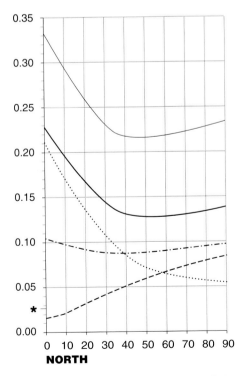

NORTH

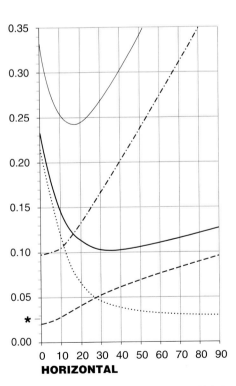

HORIZONTAL

*Mechanical vent fresh air only 0.027MWh/m²

Ventilation heating energy 0.013MWh/m²

S8

Type C (offices)
150 lux, 30 W/m²,
Southern UK

MWh/m²

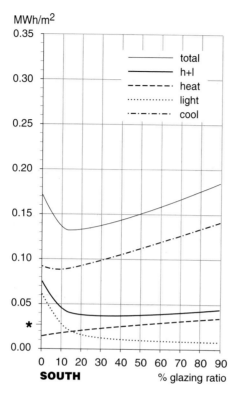

SOUTH   % glazing ratio

Legend:
- total
- h+l
- heat
- light
- cool

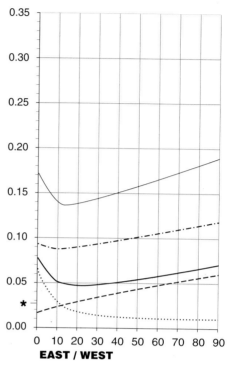

EAST / WEST

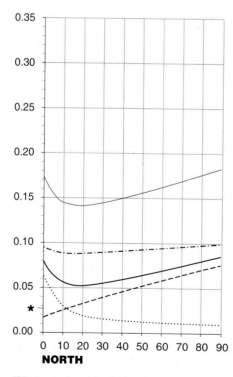

NORTH

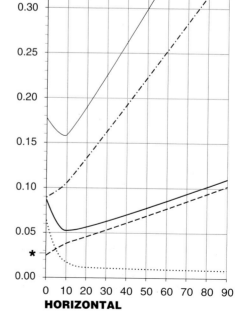

HORIZONTAL

*Mechanical vent fresh air only 0.027MWh/m²

Ventilation heating energy 0.013MWh/m²

Type C (offices)
300 lux, 30 W/m²,
Southern UK

MWh/m²

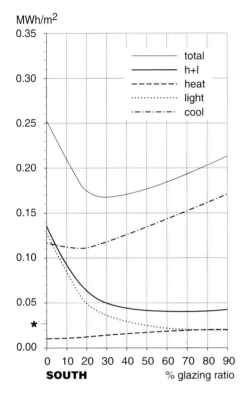

SOUTH   % glazing ratio

legend:
total
h+l
heat
light
cool

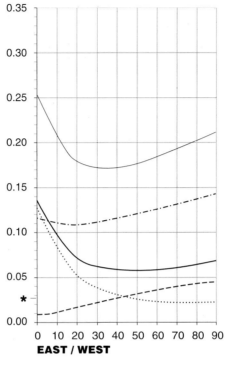

EAST / WEST

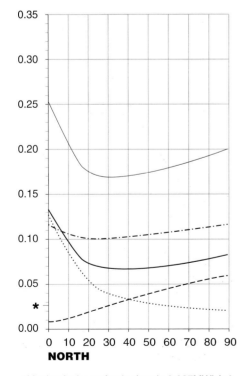

NORTH

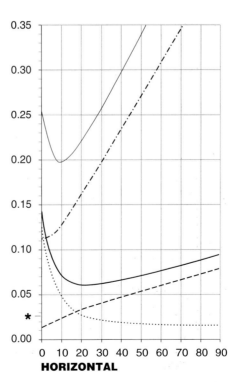

HORIZONTAL

Type C (offices)
500 lux, 30 W/m²,
Southern UK

MWh/m²

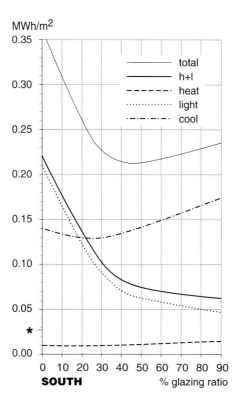

Legend:
- total
- h+l
- heat
- light
- cool

SOUTH — % glazing ratio

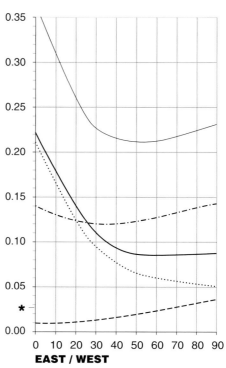

EAST / WEST

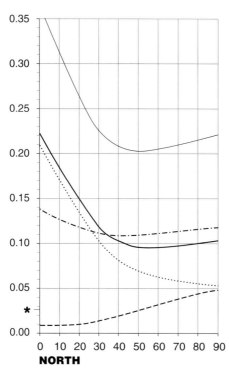

NORTH

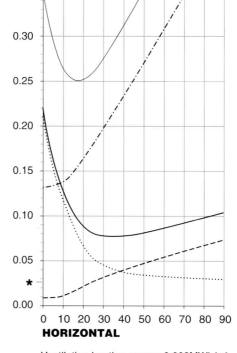

HORIZONTAL

*Mechanical vent fresh air only 0.027MWh/m²

Ventilation heating energy 0.008MWh/m²

MWh/m^2

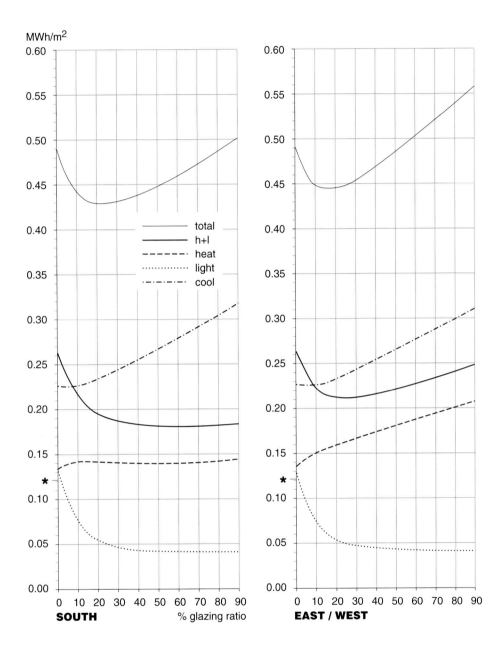

SOUTH % glazing ratio

EAST / WEST

legend:
- total
- h+l
- heat
- light
- cool

S11

Type D
(institutional)
150 lux, 10 W/m^2,
Southern UK

*Mechanical vent fresh air only 0.121MWh/m^2 Ventilation heating energy 0.122MWh/m^2

Type D
(institutional)
150 lux, 10 W/m²,
Southern UK

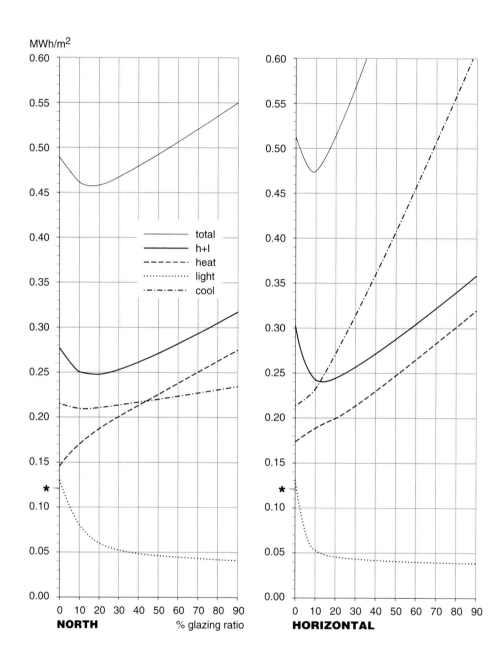

*Mechanical vent fresh air only 0.121MWh/m²   Ventilation heating energy 0.122MWh/m²

Type D
(institutional)
300 lux, 10 W/m²,
Southern UK

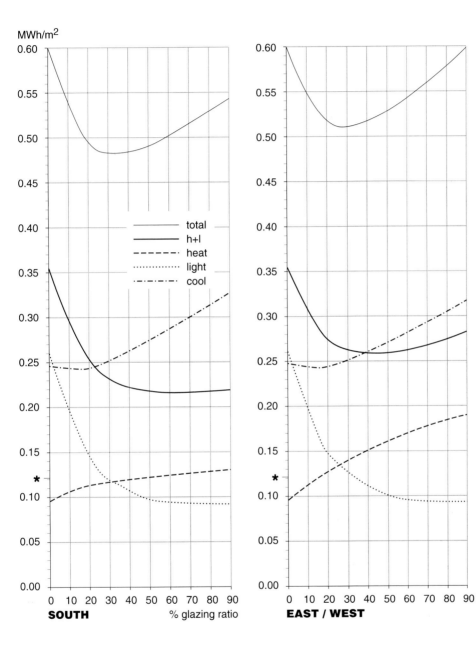

MWh/m²

Legend:
- total
- h+l
- heat
- light
- cool

SOUTH   % glazing ratio

EAST / WEST

*Mechanical vent fresh air only 0.121MWh/m²   Ventilation heating energy 0.085MWh/m²

Type D
(institutional)
300 lux, 10 W/m²,
Southern UK

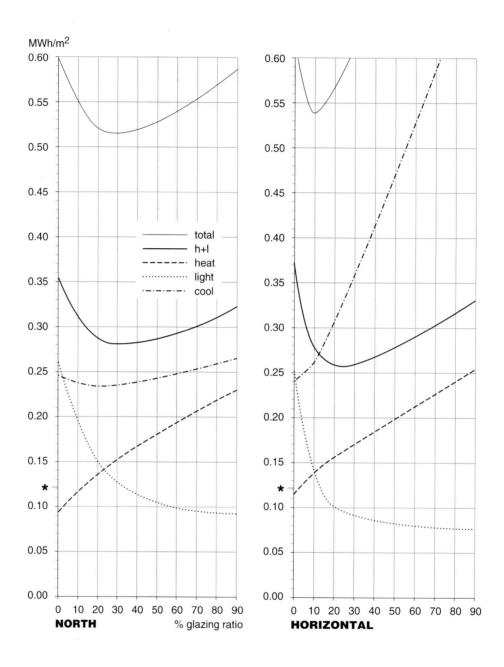

MWh/m²

NORTH   % glazing ratio

HORIZONTAL

Legend:
- total
- h+l
- heat
- light
- cool

*Mechanical vent fresh air only 0.121MWh/m²   Ventilation heating energy 0.085MWh/m²

orientation	UHA deg.	glazing ratio %	correction factors		
			heating	cooling	lighting
south	15 - 45	20	1.1	1.00	2.0
		40	1.2	1.00	2.9
		60	1.4	0.97	2.6
		80	1.5	0.96	2.0
	> 45	20	1.2	1.00	3.7
		40	1.4	1.00	4.9
		60	1.6	0.97	6.7
		80	1.8	0.93	4.5
east / west	15 - 45	20	1.0	1.00	2.0
		40	1.1	1.00	2.9
		60	1.1	1.00	3.1
		80	1.2	0.97	2.0
	> 45	20	1.0	1.00	4.3
		40	1.1	1.00	5.7
		60	1.2	1.00	8.1
		80	1.3	0.97	4.5
north	15 - 45	20	1.0	1.00	2.1
		40	1.0	1.00	2.7
		60	1.0	1.00	2.9
		80	1.1	1.00	2.6
	> 45	20	1.0	1.00	3.9
		40	1.1	1.00	5.3
		60	1.1	1.00	6.1
		80	1.1	1.00	6.7

Type A (schools)
150 lux, 20 W/m², Southern UK

orientation	UHA deg.	glazing ratio %	correction factors		
			heating	cooling	lighting
south	15 - 45	20	1.1	1.00	1.9
		40	1.2	1.00	2.0
		60	1.3	0.97	3.1
		80	1.5	0.96	2.9
	> 45	20	1.1	1.00	2.9
		40	1.3	1.00	3.8
		60	1.5	0.97	6.4
		80	1.8	0.93	5.4
east / west	15 - 45	20	1.0	1.00	1.7
		40	1.1	1.00	2.2
		60	1.1	1.00	3.2
		80	1.1	0.97	3.4
	> 45	20	1.0	1.00	2.6
		40	1.1	1.00	4.3
		60	1.2	1.00	5.7
		80	1.2	0.97	6.1
north	15 - 45	20	1.0	1.00	1.7
		40	1.0	1.00	2.1
		60	1.0	1.00	2.6
		80	1.0	1.00	2.9
	> 45	20	0.9	1.00	2.6
		40	1.0	1.00	3.9
		60	1.0	1.00	5.1
		80	1.1	1.00	5.7

Type A (schools)
300 lux, 20 W/m², Southern UK

Type B (colleges)
150 lux, 20 W/m²,
Southern UK

orientation	UHA deg.	glazing ratio %	correction factors		
			heating	cooling	lighting
south	15 - 45	20	1.2	0.99	1.4
		40	1.4	0.95	1.5
		60	1.7	0.92	1.2
		80	1.9	0.88	1.2
	> 45	20	1.3	0.97	2.2
		40	1.6	0.88	2.0
		60	2.0	0.80	1.8
		80	2.3	0.72	1.5
east / west	15 - 45	20	1.1	0.99	1.4
		40	1.1	0.96	1.5
		60	1.2	0.92	1.3
		80	1.3	0.90	1.2
	> 45	20	1.0	0.98	2.4
		40	1.2	0.92	2.2
		60	1.3	0.86	2.0
		80	1.4	0.81	1.5
north	15 - 45	20	1.0	1.00	1.5
		40	1.0	0.98	1.6
		60	1.1	0.96	1.4
		80	1.1	0.94	1.2
	> 45	20	1.0	1.00	2.3
		40	1.0	0.97	2.3
		60	1.1	0.94	2.0
		80	1.2	0.91	1.8

Type B (colleges)
300 lux, 20 W/m²,
Southern UK

orientation	UHA deg.	glazing ratio %	correction factors		
			heating	cooling	lighting
south	15 - 45	20	1.2	1.02	1.4
		40	1.4	0.96	1.4
		60	1.6	0.93	1.7
		80	1.9	0.89	1.5
	> 45	20	1.2	1.00	2.0
		40	1.5	0.88	2.2
		60	1.8	0.80	2.6
		80	2.3	0.72	2.2
east / west	15 - 45	20	1.1	1.01	1.3
		40	1.1	0.96	1.5
		60	1.1	0.93	1.7
		80	1.2	0.90	1.6
	> 45	20	1.0	1.01	1.9
		40	1.0	0.93	2.4
		60	1.2	0.86	2.5
		80	1.3	0.81	2.3
north	15 - 45	20	1.0	1.02	1.4
		40	1.0	0.98	1.5
		60	1.0	0.96	1.6
		80	1.0	0.95	1.6
	> 45	20	0.9	1.04	1.9
		40	0.9	0.98	2.3
		60	1.0	0.95	2.4
		80	1.1	0.91	2.4

orientation	UHA deg.	glazing ratio %	correction factors		
			heating	cooling	lighting
south	15 - 45	20	1.2	0.97	1.5
		40	1.5	0.94	1.5
		60	1.7	0.90	1.2
		80	1.9	0.87	1.2
	> 45	20	1.3	0.92	2.3
		40	1.8	0.81	2.0
		60	2.1	0.71	1.9
		80	2.4	0.64	1.6
east / west	15 - 45	20	1.1	0.97	1.4
		40	1.2	0.93	1.5
		60	1.2	0.89	1.3
		80	1.3	0.85	1.2
	> 45	20	1.1	0.95	2.5
		40	1.3	0.86	2.2
		60	1.4	0.79	2.1
		80	1.5	0.72	1.6
north	15 - 45	20	1.0	0.99	1.5
		40	1.0	0.96	1.6
		60	1.1	0.94	1.4
		80	1.1	0.93	1.2
	> 45	20	1.0	0.99	2.4
		40	1.1	0.93	2.3
		60	1.2	0.89	2.2
		80	1.2	0.85	1.9

Type C (offices)
150 lux, 15 W/m², Southern UK

orientation	UHA deg.	glazing ratio %	correction factors		
			heating	cooling	lighting
south	15 - 45	20	1.2	1.03	1.5
		40	1.5	0.95	1.5
		60	1.7	0.91	1.7
		80	1.9	0.88	1.5
	> 45	20	1.2	1.00	2.1
		40	1.7	0.84	2.3
		60	2.0	0.72	2.6
		80	2.4	0.64	2.2
east / west	15 - 45	20	1.1	1.02	1.4
		40	1.1	0.93	1.5
		60	1.2	0.89	1.7
		80	1.2	0.85	1.6
	> 45	20	1.0	1.02	2.0
		40	1.1	0.89	2.5
		60	1.2	0.80	2.6
		80	1.4	0.72	2.3
north	15 - 45	20	1.0	1.04	1.4
		40	1.0	0.98	1.5
		60	1.0	0.95	1.5
		80	1.0	0.93	1.6
	> 45	20	0.9	1.08	2.0
		40	0.9	0.97	2.4
		60	1.0	0.91	2.4
		80	1.1	0.86	2.4

Type C (offices)
300 lux, 15 W/m², Southern UK

Type C (offices)
500 lux, 15 W/m², Southern UK

orientation	UHA deg.	glazing ratio %	correction factors		
			heating	cooling	lighting
south	15 - 45	20	1.4	0.97	1.1
		40	1.6	1.05	1.6
		60	1.9	0.93	1.5
		80	2.1	0.89	1.4
	> 45	20	1.3	1.03	1.5
		40	1.5	0.93	2.2
		60	1.9	0.79	2.5
		80	2.4	0.67	2.3
east / west	15 - 45	20	1.1	0.96	1.0
		40	1.1	1.03	1.5
		60	1.1	0.92	1.5
		80	1.2	0.86	1.4
	> 45	20	1.0	1.05	1.4
		40	0.9	0.98	2.1
		60	1.1	0.89	2.5
		80	1.2	0.76	2.3
north	15 - 45	20	1.0	0.98	1.1
		40	0.9	1.07	1.5
		60	0.9	1.01	1.6
		80	1.0	0.93	1.4
	> 45	20	0.9	1.10	1.4
		40	0.8	1.10	2.1
		60	0.8	1.02	2.5
		80	0.9	0.91	2.4

Type C (offices)
150 lux, 30 W/m², Southern UK

orientation	UHA deg.	glazing ratio %	correction factors		
			heating	cooling	lighting
south	15 - 45	20	1.4	0.96	1.5
		40	1.8	0.92	1.5
		60	2.1	0.88	1.2
		80	2.3	0.85	1.2
	> 45	20	1.4	0.89	2.3
		40	2.0	0.77	2.0
		60	2.5	0.68	1.9
		80	2.9	0.61	1.6
east / west	15 - 45	20	1.1	0.96	1.4
		40	1.2	0.92	1.5
		60	1.3	0.88	1.3
		80	1.3	0.85	1.2
	> 45	20	1.0	0.93	2.5
		40	1.3	0.83	2.2
		60	1.4	0.76	2.1
		80	1.5	0.70	1.6
north	15 - 45	20	1.0	0.99	1.5
		40	1.0	0.95	1.6
		60	1.1	0.93	1.4
		80	1.1	0.91	1.2
	> 45	20	0.9	0.98	2.4
		40	1.0	0.91	2.3
		60	1.1	0.86	2.2
		80	1.2	0.82	1.9

Type C (offices)
300 lux, 30 W/m²,
Southern UK

orientation	UHA deg.	glazing ratio %	correction factors		
			heating	cooling	lighting
south	15 - 45	20	1.4	1.01	1.5
		40	1.9	0.93	1.5
		60	2.0	0.89	1.7
		80	2.3	0.86	1.5
	> 45	20	1.3	0.99	2.1
		40	1.9	0.81	2.3
		60	2.2	0.70	2.6
		80	2.8	0.62	2.2
east / west	15 - 45	20	1.1	1.01	1.4
		40	1.1	0.93	1.5
		60	1.2	0.89	1.7
		80	1.2	0.86	1.6
	> 45	20	1.0	1.02	2.0
		40	1.0	0.88	2.5
		60	1.2	0.78	2.6
		80	1.3	0.71	2.3
north	15 - 45	20	0.9	1.04	1.4
		40	1.0	0.97	1.5
		60	1.0	0.94	1.5
		80	1.0	0.91	1.6
	> 45	20	0.9	1.09	2.0
		40	0.8	0.97	2.4
		60	1.0	0.89	2.4
		80	1.0	0.84	2.4

Type C (offices)
500 lux, 30 W/m²,
Southern UK

orientation	UHA deg.	glazing ratio %	correction factors		
			heating	cooling	lighting
south	15 - 45	20	1.0	0.96	1.1
		40	1.6	1.02	1.6
		60	2.4	0.90	1.5
		80	2.5	0.87	1.4
	> 45	20	1.0	1.02	1.5
		40	1.2	0.92	2.2
		60	2.0	0.78	2.5
		80	2.5	0.65	2.3
east / west	15 - 45	20	1.0	0.95	1.0
		40	1.2	1.02	1.5
		60	1.2	0.91	1.5
		80	1.3	0.87	1.4
	> 45	20	1.0	1.06	1.4
		40	0.9	0.99	2.1
		60	1.0	0.88	2.5
		80	1.2	0.76	2.3
north	15 - 45	20	1.0	0.98	1.1
		40	0.9	1.07	1.5
		60	0.9	1.00	1.6
		80	1.0	0.93	1.4
	> 45	20	1.0	1.11	1.4
		40	0.8	1.11	2.1
		60	0.8	1.03	2.5
		80	0.8	0.90	2.4

Type D
(institutional)
150 lux, 10 W/m²,
Southern UK

orientation	UHA deg.	glazing ratio %	correction factors		
			heating	cooling	lighting
south	15 - 45	20	1.1	0.99	1.3
		40	1.3	0.96	1.2
		60	1.4	0.94	1.1
		80	1.5	0.92	1.1
	> 45	20	1.2	0.95	1.7
		40	1.5	0.88	1.4
		60	1.7	0.82	1.4
		80	1.9	0.76	1.2
east / west	15 - 45	20	1.1	0.98	1.2
		40	1.1	0.94	1.2
		60	1.2	0.90	1.1
		80	1.2	0.87	1.1
	> 45	20	1.1	0.96	1.7
		40	1.2	0.88	1.5
		60	1.3	0.82	1.4
		80	1.4	0.77	1.2
north	15 - 45	20	1.0	0.99	1.3
		40	1.0	0.97	1.2
		60	1.1	0.95	1.2
		80	1.1	0.94	1.1
	> 45	20	1.0	0.99	1.7
		40	1.1	0.95	1.6
		60	1.1	0.92	1.5
		80	1.2	0.89	1.4

Type D
(institutional)
300 lux, 10 W/m²,
Southern UK

orientation	UHA deg.	glazing ratio %	correction factors		
			heating	cooling	lighting
south	15 - 45	20	1.1	1.02	1.3
		40	1.3	0.97	1.3
		60	1.4	0.95	1.3
		80	1.5	0.92	1.2
	> 45	20	1.1	1.00	1.6
		40	1.4	0.91	1.7
		60	1.6	0.83	1.7
		80	1.8	0.76	1.5
east / west	15 - 45	20	1.0	1.00	1.2
		40	1.1	0.95	1.3
		60	1.1	0.91	1.3
		80	1.2	0.88	1.2
	> 45	20	1.0	1.00	1.6
		40	1.1	0.92	1.8
		60	1.2	0.83	1.7
		80	1.3	0.77	1.5
north	15 - 45	20	1.0	1.01	1.2
		40	1.0	0.99	1.3
		60	1.0	0.96	1.3
		80	1.0	0.94	1.3
	> 45	20	0.9	1.04	1.6
		40	1.0	0.98	1.7
		60	1.0	0.93	1.7
		80	1.1	0.89	1.6

vent mode / config. type	a x1	a x2	b x1	b x2	c x1	c x2	d x1	d x2
1 ▲N	0.52	0.60	0.58	0.63	0.54	0.57	1.02	1.12
2 ▲N	0.55	0.71	0.70	0.84	0.59	0.71	1.02	1.24
3 ▲N	0.41	0.53	0.51	0.62	0.48	0.58	0.83	1.02
4 ▲N	0.36	0.49	0.53	0.69	0.42	0.53	0.84	1.10
5 ▲N	0.35	0.46	0.46	0.64	0.38	0.50	0.56	0.80
6 ▲N	0.57	0.83	0.75	1.03	0.61	0.85	0.93	1.30
7 ▲N	0.47	0.63	0.58	0.74	0.54	0.70	0.83	1.03

Buffer-space Thermal Savings (BTS) MWh/my glazing options (x1, x2) refers to atrium envelope glazing

characteristic	score 0	score 1
shading	fixed	movable
glazing	tinted/reflective	clear
internal finishes	dark coloured	light coloured
horizon angle	greater than 45°	less than 45°

total score	buffer-adjacent passive zone depth
0 or 1	0.0
2 or 3	1.0 h
4	1.5 h
h = floor to ceiling height	

Table 12.2
Buffer-adjacent zone depth

building type	occupancy factors
schools	0.55
colleges	0.75
offices	1.0
institutional	1.5

Table 12.3
Buffer-space occupancy factors

The LT worksheet

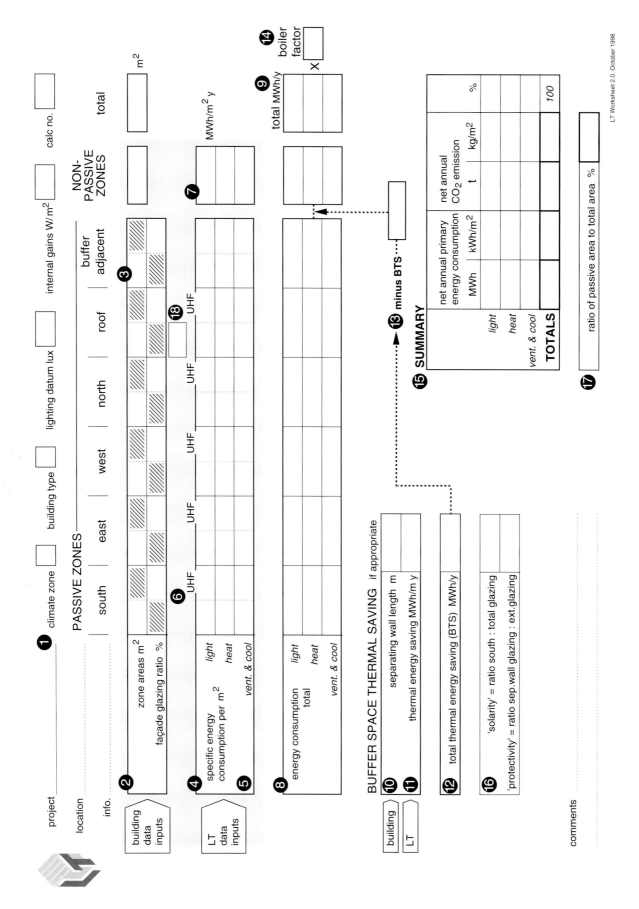

14.2 The LT worksheet and notes

These numbered notes correspond to the circled numbers appearing on the LT Worksheet. Note that the boxes on the shaded background are inputs, whilst the white boxes are for calculated results. To keep the number of digits small, megawatt hours (MWh) are used for energy units: 1MWh = 1000 kilowatt hours (kWh).

1   Enter the climatic zone (N or S), building type A (schools), B (colleges), C (offices) or D (institutional); lighting datum, internal gains and other relevant information.

2   Calculate passive and non-passive zone areas as shown in Figure 12.2 and enter. Enter façade nominal glazing ratio (percentage glass and framing of total wall area) (Figure 12.3).

3   Enter buffer-adjacent area if appropriate (Figure 12.12). Reduce zone depth according to buffer space characteristics as in Table 12.2. Glazing ratio refers to separating wall.

4   Read specific energy consumption for light and heat from LT curves for appropriate climatic zone, building type, lighting level and internal gains, and orientation. For buffer-adjacent zone use east/west curve irrespective of orientation. Enter in worksheet.

5   Read off cooling curve for air-conditioned spaces. For mechanical fresh air supply only, enter fixed allowance shown at bottom of LT curves page.

6   Estimate Urban Horizon Angle for each façade (Figure 12.8). From appropriate chart determine the Urban Horizon Factor (UHF) for appropriate orientation, Urban Horizon Angle (UHA) and glazing ratio, lighting datum and internal gains. For fresh air only mechanical ventilation the factor is always 1.0. The factor for rooflights is also 1.0.

7   Read specific energy consumption for non-passive zone from LT curve at zero glazing ratio for a side-lit curve. For ventilation and cooling of non-passive zones use the value at zero glazing ratio unless low internal gains permit fresh air only – then apply fixed allowance.

8   Multiply areas 2 and 3 by specific energy consumptions 4 and 5 and by UHF 6. To correct for top-floor side-lit spaces see note 18.

9   Sum energy consumption for all zones, by light, heat and cool. If there is a buffer space, do not sum heat until BTS has been calculated (note 12) and subtracted (note 13).

10   For Buffer-space Thermal Savings enter total separating wall length on plan, multiplied by number of storeys; e.g. for three-storey building with 30m of separating wall on plan, enter 90m.

11   From BTS tables choose appropriate buffer-space type 1 to 7 and ventilation mode (a) to (d) and enter specific thermal saving (per metre separating wall), interpolating if necessary.

12   Multiply specific thermal saving by separating wall length and enter total Buffer-space Thermal Saving (BTS), applying occupancy factor for particular building type (Table 12.3) if necessary.

13   Subtract BTS from buffer-space heating and enter total at (9). If this becomes negative then set to zero but see section [12.8].

14   Multiply heating total by appropriate boiler factor: B = 0.65/(boiler efficiency), as defined in [12.4] and enter at (15).

15   Complete summary matrix giving energy totals and energy/m^2 by dividing by the total area. Refer to Table 12.1 [p. 103] for CO_2 conversion factors.

16   Solarity and protectivity are of interest but are not needed for the LT calculation. These are defined in section [9.2].

17   Passive area ratio is of interest but is not essential for the LT calculation.

18   For making the correction for heat losses from top-floor side-lit zones, multiply top-floor side-lit area, by heat loss for 'horizontal', less ventilation heat loss given at bottom of page. Add correction to heating total at (9).

Computer spreadsheets

Those who are familiar with using computer-based spreadsheets will quickly appreciate that the LT worksheet could be installed on one of these. This will greatly simplify the use of the LT Method and in particular will facilitate multiple calculations where a number of alternatives are being investigated, or the use of individual worksheets for each storey in order to account for variation of urban horizon angle or lighting levels more accurately.

Bibliography

Published by the Energy Efficiency Office (EEO), Building Research Energy Conservation Support Unit (BRECSU), Building Research Establishment, Garston, Watford WD2 7JR:

1   *Guide for Installers of Condensing Boilers in Commercial Buildings*, Good Practice Guide No. 16.
2   *Energy Audit and Survey Guide*, Good Practice Guide No. 28.
3   *Selecting Air-Conditioning Systems*, Good Practice Guide No. 71.
4   *Energy Conservation: A Study of Energy Conservation in Building and Possible Means of Saving Energy in Housing*, Building Research Establishment Current Paper, CP 56/75.

3

Case studies

Introduction

Five case study projects are discussed in Part Three, representing a range of building uses and environmental strategies. All have been subjected to LT analysis, either as part of the actual design process or retrospectively to explore alternatives, and thus highlight the potential value of the LT Method.

The discussion of each of the five buildings is structured in a broadly similar way, under the following headings:

— Introduction
— Background
— Built form
— Heating and ventilation strategy
— Daylighting
— Energy efficiency
— LT analysis
— Conclusion

Where appropriate, cost implications are discussed and bibliographies are provided for further information.

The buildings each demonstrate the importance of strategic decisions at the early design stage, relating particularly to questions of building form and façade. The discussion here is not concerned with exploring an aesthetic agenda. In fact, the projects demonstrate the diversity of architectural responses possible within the context of energy-efficient design. However, they also demonstrate that key architectural spaces can be exploited for qualitative and quantifiable environmental advantages – such as the atrium (Ionica HQ and ELA at NUST), glazed street (BRF) or conservatory (Netley). In some cases the environmental strategies become architecturally explicit (such as the wind towers at Ionica), but more often than not the environmental success of the buildings relies on subtle choices of massing, orientation and glazing ratios. It is making appropriate choices at these levels that is likely to result in a robust energy-efficient design.

It is typically easier to fine-tune a building that basically is on the right track (through for example occupant education, introduction of blinds or efficient lighting), than it is to correct for a design that strategically relies on sophisticated, complex and fragile automated systems. An intelligent building is one which can exploit daylight and natural ventilation through modest building depths and vertical shafts; one that can control solar gain through appropriate orientation, shading and thermal mass; one that allows user interaction for control of comfort conditions. Ironically, the term 'intelligent building' often partially refers to a reliance on systems such as ventilated façades with motorised louvres driven by Building Energy Management Systems. Here, as with the introduction of air-conditioning earlier this century, the architecture is 'free' to ignore (for example) orientation, and is reliant on the control systems – until they do not live up to expectation, are not correctly maintained or fail. The life of environmental systems is a fraction of a building's life. We can change the systems, even educate the occupants, but cannot easily adjust the building fabric. A robust design is more likely to ensure energy efficiency for the building's lifetime and reduce obsolescence.

Ionica Headquarters, Cambridge
RH Partnership

Introduction

> The design of the building uses its structure, form and fabric to moderate the environment and to provide comfortable internal conditions for a client and building type that are usually expected to require fully air conditioned space.
>
> *(David Emond, Architect, RH Partnership; quoted in Hawkes et al., 1994)*

The Ionica building, in St. John's Innovation Park, Cambridge, designed by RH Partnership and completed in 1994, is a landmark building with its passive ventilation towers and its strong north–south asymmetrical design responding to the sun (Figure 1). The special considerations of this low-energy office building were its maximum of 24-hour occupancy, heavy use of computer systems and an open-plan workspace. The project also had a very short construction time – the whole scheme, from conception to occupation, took only 18 months to complete. The solution was to exploit the benefits of shallow plans and an atrium in a mixed-mode building which responds to the climate and exploits natural forces, while allowing certain parts of the building at certain times of the year to be mechanically conditioned. The predicted delivered energy use is about $100kWh/m^2/year$, almost half that of a best-practice, air-conditioned building.

Background

St. John's Innovation Park was conceived in 1984 and developed by St. John's College, Cambridge as a way of

1: *View of Ionica from the south*

encouraging technological transfer from academic research to commercial exploitation. The site is located to the north of Cambridge, just within the northern bypass, the A14, which carries a constant stream of traffic just over 100m from the building's northerly façade. The client, Ionica, was a telephone company that needed a new prestigious headquarters. It had been located in the St. John's Innovation Centre, on the same science park, and also designed by RH Partnership.

The brief to the architects, set by the College and Ionica, was for a 4000m² building with offices, boardroom, restaurant, crèche and ancillary facilities. Furthermore, Ionica specifically required an energy-efficient, high-quality working environment with individual control.

The architects co-ordinated a team consisting not only of structural (Hannah Reed Associates) and services engineers (Rybka Smith Ginsler and Battle) with a QS (Davis Langdon & Everest), but also M&E design consultants (Battle McCarthy), acoustics, lighting and thermal analysis specialists (Cambridge Architectural Research Ltd) and wind researchers (Bristol University). The environmental aspects of the project were thus particularly strongly supported, although due to the fast design programme, analysis was limited and there was reliance on expertise and tried and tested principles to develop a robust design. The LT Method in particular provided fast and important feedback in the early stages of the design, which, due to the fast-track approach, proved influential in terms of the building's final resolution.

2: *Openings to the north*

3: *Detailed view of the south façade*

Built form

The three-storey building is planned in layers from north to south. On the north side, and facing the noise of traffic, a gently curving brick façade with moderately sized openings (Figure 2) protects a 10m-deep office zone within. This zone can be sublet and subdivided, and contains all the ancillary and service areas (including restaurant and WCs).

To the south, behind a stepped, glazed façade with a filigree of shading devices (Figure 3), and overlooking a pond and landscaped gardens, are the open-plan offices ranging in depth from 8m to 12m. The west and east façades are closed by brick-clad escape stairs and service cores.

Between the north and south zones is a triple height 54m-long space covered by a rooflight (Figure 4), allowing filtered daylight to enter into the depth of the plan, and creating a passive route for air to rise to the towers above. The maximum depth, across the centre-line of the building, is 26m.

The design of the north and south façades is central to the building's success, responding to the environment of the context. The north side has simple hole-in-the-wall windows which make up about 30% of the façade. This is an optimum value for such office use, as demonstrated

4: *Section and typical floor plan*

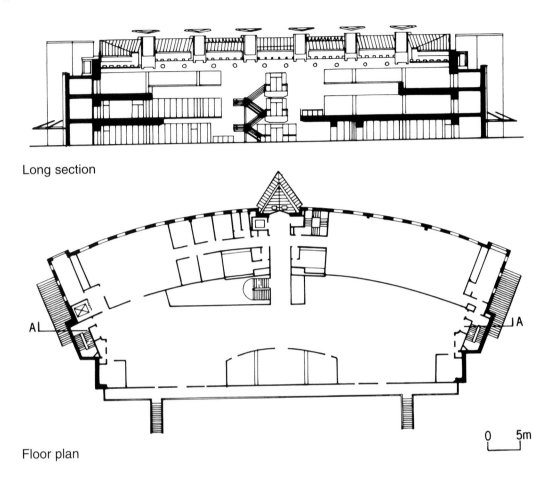

Long section

Floor plan

0   5m

using the LT Method, limiting heat losses while achieving required daylight conditions – not to mention the reduction of noise transmission.

The south façade is more substantially glazed, to 65%. This enables more daylight to enter the deeper office space, but relies on the effective use of a combination of fixed (external) shading louvres and overhangs, and movable internal blinds to minimise overheating risks.

Heating and ventilation strategy

The relationship between mechanical and passive strategies, and between occupant and automated control, is complex and responds to seasonal conditions. In essence, the building is mixed-mode – mechanically and naturally ventilated – substantially exploiting passive stack ventilation during the spring and autumn but relying on mechanical ventilation under more extreme conditions. This can be referred to as *temporal* mixed-mode. However, the building is also *spatially* mixed-mode. The cellular offices to the north are mechanically ventilated, using displacement ventilation, to avoid the need to open windows to the noisy road. A modest degree of cooling is allowed for to cater for extreme summer conditions, where warm external air and high internal heat gains could combine to raise the internal temperature above comfort levels.

5: *View of a wind tower*

internal wood frames, which are controlled by the BEMS and help to cool down the interior at night-time in the unoccupied areas (both north and south offices – traffic noise is not a problem when offices are unoccupied). Windows are composite frames (timber inside, powder-coated aluminium outside) with double, clear glazing and a low-emissivity coating to reduce heat losses in winter.

The interior spaces are exposed to the thermal mass of the concrete ceiling to minimise peak temperatures. When mechanical ventilation is required this is supplied via the floor which can be cooled in advance by night-time structural cooling, again controlled by the BEMS. In the extreme hot situations where cooling is required, this is provided by indirect evaporative cooling and a heat-pump system.

In the winter, windows are closed and fresh air is provided by mechanical supply heated when necessary, and returned by stack effect via the atrium to the rooftop air-handling units. Perimeter heating ensures comfort temperatures by the morning.

Daylighting

The building design exploits daylighting as a means of limiting the need for artificial light to reduce electrical loads, fostering occupant well-being while providing a glare-free daylit interior for VDU use. The building form directly responds to such criteria; shallow plans ensure daylight availability to most workspaces; less-daylight-dependent spaces are placed in the centre of the north block; vertical services are placed on the east and west façades where low-angle sun would make windows problematic in terms of glare and solar gain. The south façade is predominantly and continuously glazed (65%) to benefit from redistributed solar radiation into the deeper office space. The north façade, significantly less transparent (30%), has discrete tall windows with splayed reveals adequate to allow daylight to penetrate the shallower plan, while preserving a level of visual and acoustic privacy from the main road. Finally, the top-lit atrium brings daylight into the core of the building, proving extremely effective at providing daylight throughout the plan, even on overcast days.

The building is predominantly naturally ventilated via manually and mechanically openable windows on the south to afford cross ventilation via the atrium and out from the six distinctive wind towers (Figure 5). The towers have been designed so as to ensure that they will operate correctly, always allowing the air to escape under any wind conditions. Dampers are controlled via sensors (for temperature, wind, humidity and rain) by the BEMS (Building Energy Management System). Windows have motorised upper casements, with the motors set into the

6: *Cross-section showing monitored daylight factors*

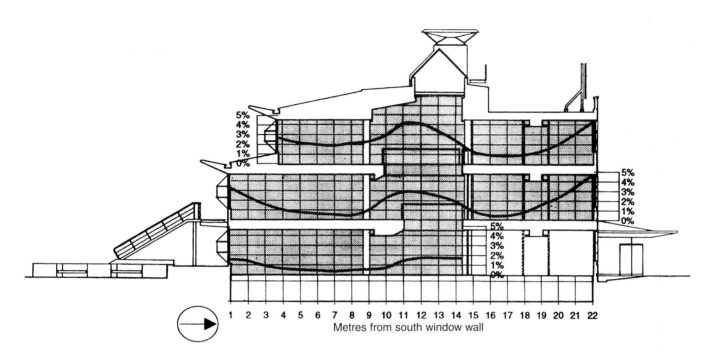

Metres from south window wall

Daylight levels

Independent daylight monitoring (Jackaway and Greene, 1996) has shown that, with all furniture and screens in place, the interior has an even distribution of daylight ranging from a maximum daylight factor (DF) of 5% one metre in, to a minimum of 0.5% (Figure 6). The lowest DFs are found on the ground floor where on the south the balcony obstructs daylight penetration. However, in an intensive VDU-use environment, the distribution of daylight is more important than achieving high levels. This is because glare is a major concern, and light levels for VDU use are lower (perhaps 300 lux) than conventional office use (typically assumed to be 500 lux).

Atrium design

The top-lit atrium without screening would have increased the maximum DFs in the centre of the plan from 10% to 15%, which would have caused potential glare and adaptation problems. A brightness range of 1:20 or 1:30 is too great within the visual field. This risk, as well as excessive summer high-angle solar gains, has been eliminated by introducing fixed white louvres high up in the atrium to intercept direct sunlight as well as to temper diffuse daylight (Figure 7). On sunny days, the louvres create a dynamic effect and reflect light down into the atrium.

The glazed roof allows light to fall on the one opaque wall in the atrium and to be diffused laterally across into the work areas – although this is partially obstructed by structural down-stand beams. The result is a less dramatic change in lighting levels across the section, and the technique (of providing light and a key surface for it to illuminate) has been commended by independent assessors (Jackaway and Greene, 1996) (Figure 8).

7: *Detailed interior view of atrium shading*

8: *Interior view of atrium showing how daylight falls on the opaque atrium wall*

Solar shading

The south façade is heavily shaded with white painted louvred overhangs to intercept unwanted sun penetration during the summer. Manual internal blinds provide user control to both limit solar gains during other parts of the year and to ensure glare is limited. The glazing forms a continuous band from workplane height to the ceiling plane, where the wall-to-ceiling junction is flush. Maximising the window height in this way improves daylight penetration.

Glare

Glare has been addressed on the north façade; windows have splayed reveals to soften the contrast between wall and sky, and manual interior blinds have been provided to intercept unwanted early morning or late evening sun in the summer. Glare is limited to being only a potential problem along the south edge during low-sun winter days, when occupant control is provided by internal louvred blinds. The education of the user was seen as an important part of the building's success, and a series of seminars were held during the first year of occupation.

Artificial lighting

Purpose-made luminaires have been designed for both efficient lighting and acoustic performance. Each fixture provides a combination of uplighting and downlighting to illuminate the ceiling and provide task lighting. Lamps are

9: *Close-up of luminaire with acoustic 'wings'*

controlled by photo-electric sensors and can be dimmed separately in five zones parallel to the façades in response to daylight availability. At night the maximum illuminance has been measured at 420 lux on the working plane. Because the ceiling is exposed to engage with the thermal mass of the concrete floors, acoustic absorption is integrated into the light fixtures as 'wings' without impeding the benefits of thermal mass on comfort (Figure 9).

Energy efficiency

Initial LT calculations, carried out in the early design stages, established the relationship between orientation and appropriate glazing ratios. Simply comparing the LT energy use curves for south and north orientations indicates that optimum glazing ratios are different for each as the result of the change in the energy balance. Thus north façades have an optimum glazing ratio of about 30% and south façades about 55%. The north glazing recommendations were taken directly and have remained in the final design. The south façade has more than the initial recommenda-

tion as a result of two main issues. First, the LT Method assumes movable shading with ideal controls – in the final design manual blinds were used (for individual control) and fixed external shading specified to guarantee limited solar gain and allow the architect to exploit the three-dimensional aspects. The fixed shading reduces daylight availability, causing obstruction to diffuse light, and thus more glazing was recommended. Second, the depth of the south-facing office area was deeper (on the lower two floors) than recommended in LT, therefore an increased glazing ratio was suggested to ensure adequate daylight penetration. The LT Method had thus established a starting point for debate, and had informed the strategy for optimising the energy performance of the façades.

Daylight modelling and analysis demonstrated that 80% of the office areas would receive sufficient natural light for 80% of the working year during daylight hours. The potential savings were only achievable with effective artificial lighting controls in the form of photo sensors and dimming of the high-frequency fluorescent lamps. However, as the building has an occupancy of typically 18 hours, with some areas occupied for 24 hours, daylight energy savings are not as substantial as with a more conventional occupancy pattern. Overall lighting energy savings are estimated to be up to 35% better than traditional design.

Cost savings

The cost comments by the quantity surveyors, Davis Langdon & Everest, highlight some interesting trade-offs. The integrated and low-energy services design produced economic mechanical services but tended to increase the cost of other elements of the building. The work for air routes through the hollow concrete floors cost an extra 1.3% of total building costs; the six wind towers added a further 1.6%; the sealed raised floor for the displacement ventilation supply added 0.4%; but avoiding suspended ceilings saved 1.3%. Overall, compared with a fully air-conditioned building, the cost savings are in the order of 6%. The overall cost of the building was almost £5.5 million, and came to almost £1500/m^2 (1994 prices).

LT analysis

The engineers predicted a delivered energy use of 103kWh/m^2/y and the annual CO_2 emissions to be 67kg/m^2/y. This is equivalent to approximately 250kWh/m^2/y in primary energy. A retrospective and approximate LT analysis (of a simplified version of the final building and its services) supports this predicted energy figure. Furthermore, when compared with a fully air-conditioned version of the same building, the analysis shows energy savings of about 45%.

Conclusion

The value of strategic LT analysis of the energy performance has been shown to be effective in this design, even though the final services and detailing have developed beyond what LT can easily assess. The significant aspect is that LT has supported a robust and effective concept for the building form and façade design that has informed the final solution and resulted in an energy-efficient design. The building is not only significant for its energy performance,

but is also well liked in terms of its qualitative characteristics by client, occupants and independent assessors.

Although long-term monitoring continues, initial user feedback was positive:

The interior is open, comfortable, airy and light. The mechanical and electrical systems are settling down well and we are confident that we can control the building. The building is different and highly technical but it is a fun place to work.
(Bob Lindsey, Head of Operations, Ionica; quoted in Hawkes et al., 1994)

The majority of occupants surveyed a year and a half after occupation feel that the daylighting is a significant quality in their appreciation of the building and contributes substantially to their productivity and well-being. Daylighting in the main workstation areas was consistently deemed 'very satisfactory' and the public atrium was cited as 'exemplary'. It was also felt that the building successfully establishes a relationship between the exterior and interior whereby occupants feel in contact with the outside world.

The building has received critical acclaim in terms of its environmental qualities and design strategy:

It [the building] contributes much to the development of environmental strategies for office buildings, and is a consolidation of the emerging stereotype.
(Professor Dean Hawkes; quoted in Hawkes et al., 1994)

Bibliography

Evans, B. (1993). Low-energy design for a high-tech office, *Architects' Journal*, 17 November, pp. 29-32.

Hawkes, D. et al. (1994). Building Study: Ionica Headquarters, *Architects' Journal*, 1 December, pp. 30-38.

Jackaway, A. and Greene, D. (1996). Shedding light on Ionica, *Architects' Journal*, 28 March, pp. 51-53.

Jones, N. (1995). Composition fit for Cambridge, *Building Design*, 31 March, pp. 12-13.

2

St. Mary's Hospital, Isle of Wight
Ahrends, Burton and Koralek

Introduction

St. Mary's Hospital (Figure 10), near Newport on the Isle of Wight, is a good example of the integration of architectural and services design. As a prototype low-energy hospital for the Department of Health and Social Security, the project benefited from a very detailed analytical process which accompanied the development of the design. Besides a high standard of fabric insulation and infiltration control, the principal low-energy features of the building are its reliance on daylighting and natural ventilation for cooling in ward areas. Environmental control systems are efficiently designed and incorporate heat recovery. The design solution is predicted to save 54% of the energy needed by a conventional hospital.

Background

The project takes as its starting point the principles of hospital planning set out in the Nucleus system developed by the Department of Health and Social Security (DHSS) in the mid-1970s. This locates most health care areas in large cruciform units known as templates, with bed spaces in 6-bed bays and single rooms. The system has been taken as a standard for new hospital construction in the UK and adapted for conditions in other parts of the world.

The DHSS subsequently funded a study into low-energy hospital design, which led in 1981 to the decision to build two such hospitals, one in the south and one in the north of England. The study was carried out by the multi-disciplinary practice BDP, with architectural input from

10: *View of St. Mary's from the west, showing ward blocks*

Ahrends, Burton and Koralek (ABK). St. Mary's is the first demonstration project, for which ABK are also architects.

It was established at an early stage in the study that, in order to reduce the primary energy demand, it was necessary to minimise electrical energy consumption for lighting and cooling. Lighting has been a primary interest in a number of proposals for improved hospital design, from the Nuffield studies in the 1950s and the project for a new hospital in Venice carried out by Le Corbusier's office in the early 1960s. Lighting design within the Nucleus planning system formed the subject of a detailed investigation by Corcoran (1980), which was drawn on in BDP's low-energy hospital study report (DHSS, 1982).

It was found that the Nucleus planning system offered a good basis for energy-efficient design; the templates are cruciform in plan, providing sufficient perimeter length to enable around 80% of treatment space to benefit from natural light and ventilation. This gave a good fit with clinical requirements, since about 18% of space (including operating theatres and the intensive care unit) requires space conditioning.

The low-energy hospital study took a standard 300-bed hospital designed to the Nucleus specification, called Neutral Nucleus, as a basis for comparison. By a combination of energy-saving measures, modelled by the thermal simulation model ESP, it was shown that a low-energy hospital of the same size could save at least 50% of the energy needed by the standard design.

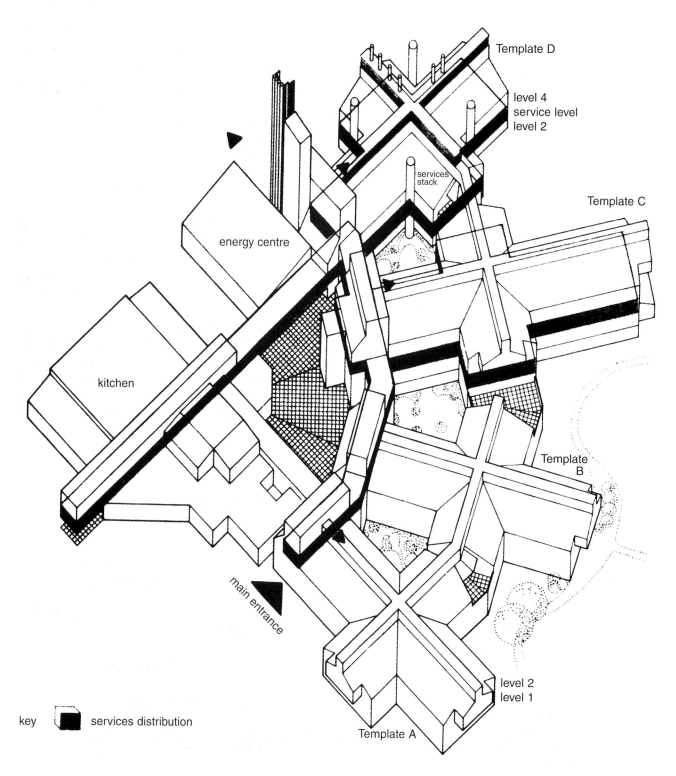

11: *Site axonometric of new building showing servicing route and ward blocks*

Template D

level 4
service level
level 2

services
stack

Template C

energy centre

Template B

kitchen

level 2
level 1

Template A

main entrance

key [ ] services distribution

Built form

St. Mary's low-energy hospital, completed in 1990, is an extension to an existing building; the new building provides 200 new beds, together with some provision for the whole hospital such as a medical records store and new catering facilities. The site chosen for the extension would enable a further phase to be built to the north-east, if required at a later date.

The new building comprises four ward templates, which are linked together by an internal 'street' at one end. The orthogonal arrangement of a standard Nucleus hospital has been varied by splaying the templates apart; this gives more interesting and varied views along the street and shortens service runs from the energy centre at its north end (Figure 11). Catering facilities, a major user of energy in any hospital, are located close to the energy centre, and the northernmost template houses other energy-intensive uses such as pathology labs.

Following the Nucleus principle, the templates are generally two storeys in height. Wards are located on the upper level, with a service space running beneath the roof ridge (Figure 12). The 5m fall across the site has been clev-erly exploited to connect this upper service level from templates A and B to an intermediate service floor in templates C and D. This service floor permits easy access to drainage from pathology labs and air-conditioning ducts serving operating theatres. Template C has an extra lower floor across half its width – this is the children's ward, where a ground-level location was chosen to give access to an outdoor play area.

Heating and ventilation strategy

Ward spaces are arranged to benefit as far as possible from natural lighting and ventilation. It was decided, however, that the use of mechanical ventilation rather than opening windows during winter would reduce the risk of over-ventilation and improve the potential for heat recovery from exhausted air (Figure 13).

Air is therefore supplied to the wards at a temperature between 10 and 16°C, providing 1-2 air changes per hour. A perimeter low-pressure hot water (lphw) heating system, fitted with thermostatic valves, tops up the ward space to the required temperature. The building was designed for high standards of performance: a U-value of

12: *Ward section*

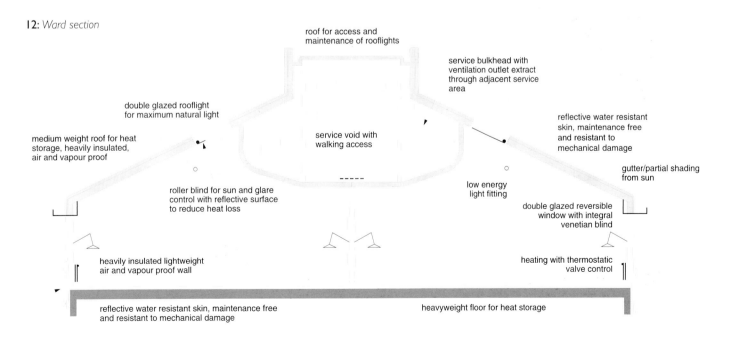

roof for access and maintenance of rooflights

service bulkhead with ventilation outlet extract through adjacent service area

double glazed rooflight for maximum natural light

reflective water resistant skin, maintenance free and resistant to mechanical damage

medium weight roof for heat storage, heavily insulated, air and vapour proof

service void with walking access

gutter/partial shading from sun

roller blind for sun and glare control with reflective surface to reduce heat loss

low energy light fitting

double glazed reversible window with integral venetian blind

heavily insulated lightweight air and vapour proof wall

heating with thermostatic valve control

reflective water resistant skin, maintenance free and resistant to mechanical damage

heavyweight floor for heat storage

13: *Winter day and night modes of the wards*

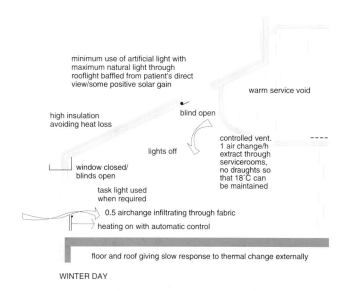

minimum use of artificial light with maximum natural light through rooflight baffled from patient's direct view/some positive solar gain

high insulation avoiding heat loss

blind open

lights off

warm service void

controlled vent. 1 air change/h extract through servicerooms, no draughts so that 18°C can be maintained

window closed/ blinds open

task light used when required

0.5 airchange infiltrating through fabric

heating on with automatic control

floor and roof giving slow response to thermal change externally

WINTER DAY

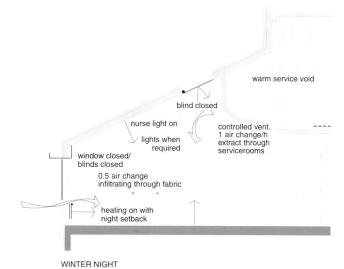

warm service void

blind closed

nurse light on

lights when required

controlled vent. 1 air change/h extract through servicerooms

window closed/ blinds closed

0.5 air change infiltrating through fabric

heating on with night setback

WINTER NIGHT

0.3 and 0.35 for walls and roof respectively, and a maximum infiltration rate of 0.5 air changes per hour.

Initial reactions from hospital users were that this ventilation rate is a little too low to prevent stuffiness in some situations, and that a slightly higher temperature level would be preferable. However, after final commissioning of the environmental systems these problems were ironed out. The energy manager points to one disadvantage of the lphw system: radiator surface temperatures are low, thus making it difficult to receive 'feedback' from adjusting the valves and perhaps leading to some dissatisfaction from patients.

The spaces in the central region of the template are used for ancillary purposes such as stores and bathrooms. Air is extracted from these internal rooms, keeping the ward under a slight negative pressure and preserving air quality in the bed bays (Figure 14).

To minimise the summer load on environmental systems, ventilation is provided as required by openable windows operated by patients or staff. In order to reduce peak summertime temperatures, the effective thermal mass of the construction has been increased with the use of heavyweight partitions, floor slabs covered only with lino (no underlay) and avoidance of suspended ceilings. Rooflights and windows have manually controlled blinds to reduce unwanted solar radiation still further. The influence

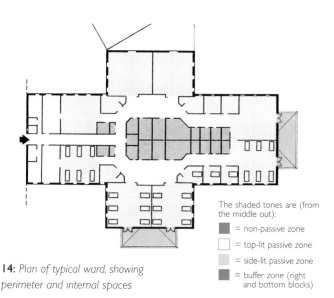

The shaded tones are (from the middle out):

= non-passive zone

= top-lit passive zone

= side-lit passive zone

= buffer zone (right and bottom blocks)

14: *Plan of typical ward, showing perimeter and internal spaces*

of these factors on peak summertime temperatures has been studied by BDP using a thermal simulation model (Figure 15).

Areas of the building which have a daytime use only – for example offices and labs – are generally located on the lower floors of the templates, where thermally lighter-weight finishes have been used. Modelling studies have shown that this is advantageous in minimising energy demand in intermittently heated zones.

Daylighting

An important aspect of the design process was to assess the optimum proportion of glazing which would maximise availability of daylight without compromising the thermal performance of the building fabric.

The standard Nucleus design has 25% glazing in the external envelope, which the energy analysis showed could be increased to 35% in the low-energy hospital design. Upper floor spaces at St. Mary's have 15% wall glazing, with rooflights as the dominant daylighting source. The orientation of windows is critical to their energy balance; unless facing within 30° of south, little useful solar radiation is received. Rooflights, however, are relatively free from this constraint, thus making planning for solar access easier.

The quality of daylighting provided is as important as its quantity. In order to assist both aspects of the design, 1:50 scale models of the ward cross-section were tested under an artificial sky. The basic configuration, with light from above softly modelled by the curved surface of the services bulkhead, was established at an early stage in the design process. Testing assisted decisions on what type of shading device should be incorporated in the rooflights, and helped to confirm that lighting distribution within the space would be adequate without undue glare. Patients do in fact have a direct view of the sky from their bed positions (Figure 16) – but there are few complaints about unwanted sun penetration, say the staff, because the blinds are easy to operate and used when necessary.

This concern for an agreeably daylit environment is carried through to the utility spaces in the centre of the template, which are not directly lit from rooflights. Nevertheless, clerestory glazing is used wherever possible to bring daylight deep into the plan. This clerestory glazing is the cause, however, of one of the few commonly heard complaints about the design: at night, artificial light spilling out from the bathrooms can disturb patients on the ward. This has been rectified by adding blinds to the clerestory windows.

The exterior of the building is given much of its architectural character by the conservatories which are suspended from the gable ends of the ward templates,

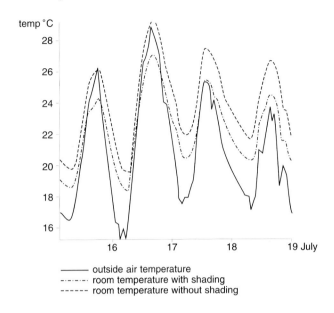

15: *Graph of peak summer temperatures with shading and thermal mass*

overlooking an artificial lake and views out to the south and east. These make use of solar energy through direct gain and have a secondary function in providing fire escape linkages between the two halves of each ward, which can then be operated as two separate 28-bed units. However, they are as yet little used, because there is no adequate way of preventing overheating, which rapidly occurs on sunny days.

The energy-saving benefit of daylighting is only realised if artificial lighting is in fact switched off when daylight is sufficient. Approximately 13% of lighting energy is saved by comparison with the Neutral Nucleus design, making reasonable assumptions of manual light-switching behaviour (the design does not incorporate automatic lighting controls). This saving is further increased to 55% by high-efficiency artificial lighting with polyphosphor fittings, whose colour-rendering capability has been accepted by the DHSS for clinical applications.

Energy efficiency

The low-energy hospital study showed very clearly that hospitals are intensive users of energy for purposes other than space conditioning. This can be termed process energy use, and includes very high temperature operations such as incineration of hospital waste. In a standard hospital, such processes account for 44% of primary energy use, with the most important individual components being the provision of hot water (17%) and catering (22%). There is great potential for heat recovery from these processes to offset space heating loads.

St. Mary's is designed to halve the amount of energy used for these purposes, by both the specification of more efficient systems and a comprehensive strategy of heat recovery and storage.

Considerable scope has been found for improving the efficiency of catering equipment. A careful study of patterns of demand for cafeteria and tray service meals enables large pieces of equipment to be shut down when it is not efficient to run them. Further savings are made by improved specification of equipment – for example, the use of convection ovens.

In the case of hot water, it is difficult to achieve a substantial reduction in load, because a consensus of medical opinion insists on water supply above 60°C to prevent the multiplication of bacteria in the distribution system. Pre-heating mains water with recovered heat is the approach employed in this case.

Recovery uses a number of different systems adapted to particular uses. Heat is recouped from flue gases from the boilers and incinerators by heat exchangers. Run-around transfer systems recover heat from exhausted ventilation air, assisted by heat pumps which can be reversed to operate as chillers in summer. Thermal storage for high-grade and low-grade heat is provided by highly insulated water tanks.

Energy savings for St. Mary's can be compared with a similar-sized hospital to the Neutral Nucleus design (see Table 1). The accuracy of these predictions have been confirmed by results from comprehensive monitoring which was carried out by the Energy Monitoring and Research Centre at Bath University. Crucial to the energy equation on which the low-energy hospital study is based is the distinction between delivered and primary energy. Consideration of delivered energy alone does not make a true reckoning of primary energy consumption (from fossil fuel or nuclear sources). Electricity, for example, uses about 3.7 times as much primary energy as gas for each unit

of delivered energy, due to losses in generation and distribution. This is reflected in pricing for the different fuels. Table 1 also shows the saving in consumption for both fossil fuel and electrical energy from load-reduction methods such as improvement in fabric insulation and air tightness. This amounts to 28% of energy used by the Neutral Nucleus design, while heat recovery boosts the saving to 54%.

Table 1: Predicted percentages of primary energy use in a Standard Nucleus Hospital compared with savings from load reduction and heat recovery at St. Mary's

	Percentage of primary energy use		
	Datum (Standard Nucleus Hospital)	Reduced by load reduction methods	With heat recovery
Fossil fuel			
Space heating	4.3%	2.7%	–
Air heating	21.0%	17.6%	11.3%
Hot water	11.6%	10.3%	–
Catering	14.3%	8.7%	8.7%
Sterilisation & incineration	5.8%	5.8%	5.8%
Total fossil fuel	**57.0%**	**45.1%**	**25.8%**
Electricity			
Lighting	21.5%	8.7%	8.7%
Fan & pump	17.2%	9.3%	10.4%
Refrigeration	1.8%	0.4%	0.3%
Process & humidification	2.5%	6.4%	6.4%
Total electricity	**43.0%**	**24.8%**	**25.8%**
Total	**100.0%**	**69.9%**	**51.6%**
Predicted primary energy per annum (10^6kWh)	19.8	13.8	51.6

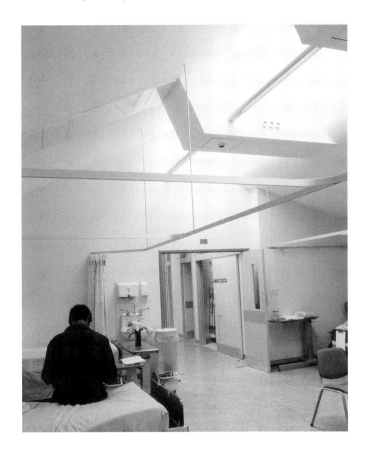

Environmental issues

The materials selected to achieve St. Mary's high performance skin carry a significant energy penalty. Un-recycled aluminium and stainless steel are two of the most energy-intensive construction materials in common use, each using around 250MJ/kg of high-grade energy to produce the sheet metal (aluminium slightly less than stainless steel, but requiring further finishing with anodising or powder-coating). Consequently, the external walls and roof of this hospital contain around three times as much embodied energy as an equivalent load-bearing brick structure with timber windows. For the roof, comparative figures are even more striking; clay tiles would have been seven times 'cheaper' in energy terms, and concrete tiles 14 times cheaper (UNCHS, 1991).

LT analysis

An LT calculation was made to assess the value of the rooflights in the wards of the top floors. In the first calculation the whole wards area is designated as 'passive zone', benefiting from daylight. In the second calculation, assuming no rooflights, the beds away from the perimeter wall are in the 'non-passive zone', requiring permanent artificial light. This leads to a predicted increase in primary energy use of 15%.

Conclusion

Projections of energy savings at St. Mary's Hospital have been based on an extensive series of computer simulations and confirmed by monitoring studies.

The simulation studies necessarily rely on a number of broad assumptions of human behaviour – including the use of windows to regulate ventilation, and control of daylighting. The behaviour of real building occupants could have a substantial impact on actual energy use. Nevertheless, the fact that building users are given control over some aspects of the internal environment will tend to increase their satisfaction with the building; 'comfort' will be improved, and quite possibly the healing process will be assisted.

The success of this project is clearly the result of close collaboration between members of a team from early in the design process, so that theoretical studies and practical implementation of their results have been closely linked. The role of the Nucleus system has been crucial in allowing rapid development of the design and appraisal of options within the constraints of the planning system.

Bibliography

Baker, N. (1990). A machine for healing, *Architecture Today*, June, pp. 47-55.

Corcoran, M. (1980). *Windows in Nucleus Hospitals Multi-bed Wards*, M.Sc. Final Project Report, BDP.

Davies, C. (1991). Hospitality, *Architects' Journal*, 3 July, pp. 24-41.

Dept. of Health and Social Security (1982). DHSS Low Energy Hospital Study, *Vol. 2: Studies and Technical Information*, DHSS.

Hawkes, D. (1982). Energetic nucleus, *Architects' Journal*, 27 October, pp. 45-62.

United Nations Centre for Human Settlements (1991). *Energy for Building*. UNCHS, Nairobi.

Netley Abbey Infants' School, Hampshire
Hampshire County Council Architects' Department

Introduction

The Netley Abbey Infants' School in Hampshire incorporates a number of passive solar features, notably a conservatory corridor connecting the classrooms on the southeast side (Figure 17). This case study briefly reviews the design, the results of a monitoring study of the building, and occupants' reaction to it. The LT Method is used to provide a thumbnail sketch of the building's energy use. It is concluded that the school compares well in terms of energy use with conventional buildings of a similar type, at no extra building cost. However, monitoring showed up early commissioning problems with plant and controls; some user dissatisfaction resulted from this and the passive solar features.

Background

Netley School was the product of a collaboration between the architects (Hampshire County Council Architects' Department) and energy consultants at ECD Partnership. The project put into practice a number of ideas in the field of passive solar design which had been developed in a generic study at the Martin Centre, University of Cambridge, funded by the Science and Engineering Research Council. A previous low-energy school design for Locksheath School had unfortunately not proceeded beyond design stage, but many of the strategies developed for Locksheath were adapted to suit the Netley programme.

17: *View of Netley School from the south showing the conservatory*

The building was completed in September 1984. The project included comprehensive monitoring for the first year of occupation, but due to initial teething problems this monitoring programme was continued for a further year. This gave an almost complete record of energy use and typical temperatures for two years of operation, which was used in the formulation of a targeting method to keep track of energy use in the future. A survey of staff views on a number of issues, including comfort conditions, was also carried out in the third year of use.

Built form

The school is located near Southampton, on the south coast of England. Its site is next to an existing junior school; there is low-rise housing some distance away to the south and playing fields in other directions. Solar access is therefore good (Figure 18).

Around 110 children between the ages of 5 and 7 are accommodated by the school. There are seven general teaching areas (classrooms), arranged in three groups

18: *Site plan*

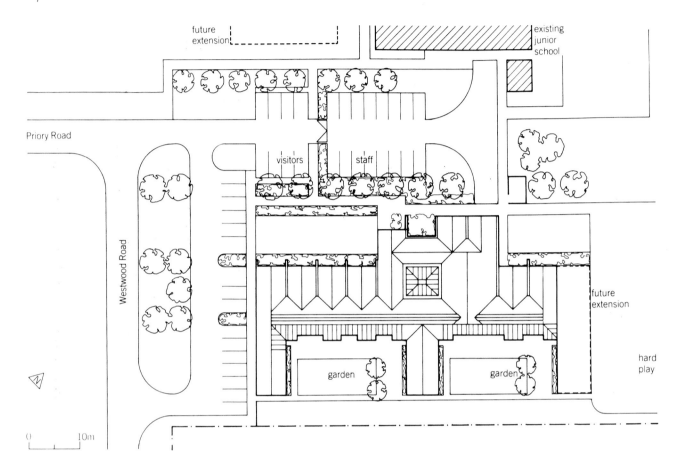

with shared quiet 'home bases', craft areas and toilets. Accommodation also includes music room, resources centre, assembly hall, kitchen, and areas for administrative and maintenance staff.

The building form is predominantly linear, with a highly glazed conservatory corridor running along the southeast side (Figure 19). There is also an atrium which gives light and ventilation to areas such as the resources centre and hall. The principal entrance for staff and parents is through a small roof-lit space to the north, while children can enter through doors opening from the playground into the south conservatory corridor. The conservatory links the classrooms and communal areas, and also pro-vides cloakroom space and some supplementary activity areas (Figure 20).

The building is single storey; each classroom is expressed externally as a pitched roof unit, and these are also apparent as an important feature of the interior. Larger spaces such as the hall project above the general roof line – this gives the opportunity of glazing at high level in the gables, helping to bring daylight deep into the plan.

Heating and ventilation strategy

The principal passive solar strategy is to draw pre-heated air from the conservatory and atrium spaces in order to

20: *Plan of the school*

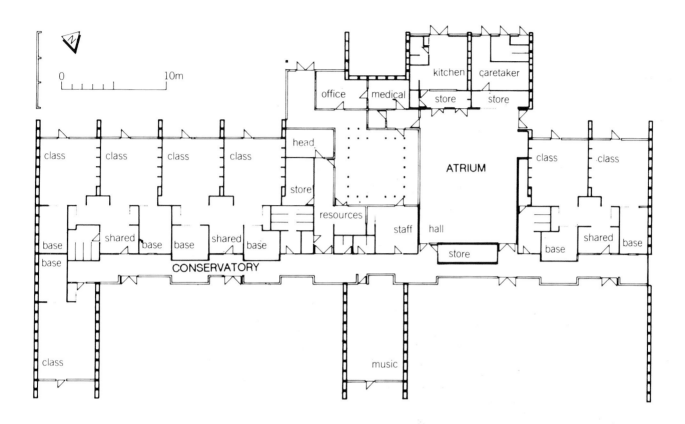

19: *The conservatory space*

offset heat loss – particularly ventilation heat loss. This ventilation pre-heat strategy is particularly appropriate to a school, since the Department for Education requirement is for a ventilation rate of 30m³ per hour per child; heat loss due to ventilation is thus likely to be higher than for most other building types. Fabric loss had already been reduced in Hampshire schools by the adoption of low U-values (0.45W/m²°C compared with the 0.6W/m²°C then required by the Building Regulations) for opaque walls and roofs.

The conservatory is unheated, and its temperature is allowed to float. It therefore also acts as a buffer zone in winter, since its average temperature is higher than that of the outside air (Figure 21) and fabric losses through adjoining walls are consequently reduced.

The seasonal operation of the building is shown in Figure 22. During the heating season, classroom windows are kept closed and all supply air is delivered via air-heater battery units mounted on a gallery adjacent to the conservatory. Heat is supplied to these from a high-efficiency gas-fired boiler. The control system draws fresh air from the conservatory when this will offset the heating load – particularly during sunny conditions in spring and autumn. The fraction of fresh air varies between 10 and 80%, the remainder being recirculated air. Supply air is delivered through a duct suspended at a height of 2.8m along the centreline of each classroom; return air is drawn back along the void between this duct and its outer casing. Each classroom has a thermostatic control which can alter supply air temperature on a scale from –5 to +5, and is equipped with a 'green button' which draws a high level of fresh air from the conservatory on demand. This has a time control which returns the system to recirculation mode after 30 minutes.

During summer, conservatory temperatures can rise above levels that would be considered comfortable in the classrooms (Figure 23). This heat is not needed by other areas, so the design aims to moderate solar gains by the use of shading and raising ventilation levels to remove excess heat as quickly as possible. Automatic 'greenhouse' vents in the top of the conservatory open to allow the hot

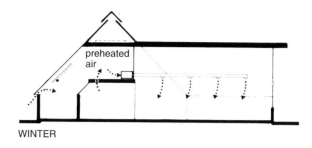
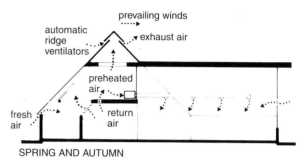
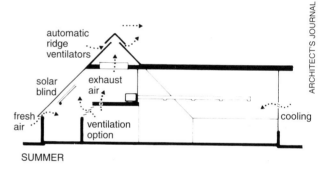
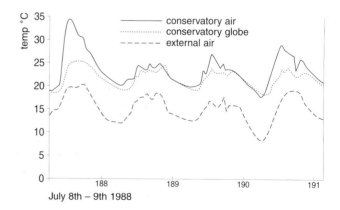

WINTER

SPRING AND AUTUMN

SUMMER

ARCHITECT'S JOURNAL

22: *Cross-sections showing seasonal operation*

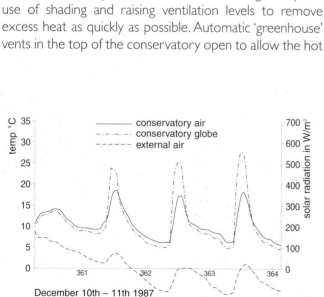

December 10th – 11th 1987

21: *Conservatory thermal performance in winter*

July 8th – 9th 1988

23: *Conservatory thermal performance in summer*

air to escape through a ridge ventilator. The 'green button' system does not operate, but louvres in the external walls can be opened to admit fresh air.

Daylighting

Classrooms receive most of their natural lighting from north-facing windows (Figure 24); east- and west-facing walls are blank. Further light to the classrooms is received from high-level glazing between the shared areas and the conservatory (Figure 25). Low-level windows provide a view out, but most light is received from high-level panels glazed with twin-walled polycarbonate sheet. These extend up into the gables, helping to throw light fairly deep into the plan. Activity rooms adjacent to the conservatory receive borrowed light from it through louvred windows above child's-eye level.

The hall is partially lit from high-level glazing in its gable walls. The atrium assists in lighting this space, the resources centre, staff room and associated offices. Roof glazing to both atrium and conservatory uses twin-walled polycarbonate sheet, which has some diffusing properties and thus helps to avoid glare problems. Internal blinds can be used to block direct sunshine when required.

Artificial lighting in the classrooms is carried on the suspended ventilation ducts, so bringing light sources closer to the working plane. Low-energy light sources are used, but there are no automatic control systems.

Energy efficiency

Energy use, cost savings and environmental issues

Energy consultants to the project have calculated the expected energy use of a similar building with a conventional corridor in place of the conservatory, and compared it with actual energy use of the building in operation. Results (for the second year of operation) show that the conservatory is calculated to save around 28% of the fuel used for space heating (Figure 26). Savings in lighting energy have not been evaluated. However, a comparison with other schools in the district shows that Netley uses only half the total energy (per unit floor area) of some others

24: *North elevation of typical bay*

25: *Interior of typical classroom*

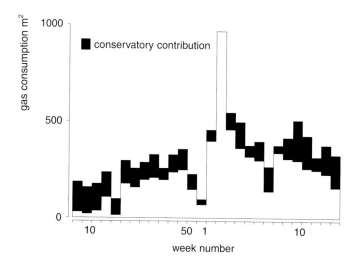

26: *Conservatory energy performance during the heating season*

in the local stock. This equates to £2-3000 per year, and has been achieved at no overall increase in building costs. Furthermore, the calculated saving implies a reduction of approximately 20 tonnes per year in carbon dioxide emission.

User reaction

A questionnaire survey of staff was carried out in 1987, in the third year of building use. Nineteen staff members took part in the survey, including full- and part-time teachers, administrative and cleaning staff.

Impressions at the time were very much coloured by early problems with commissioning of heating, ventilation and control systems; one classroom in particular proved very difficult to heat to an adequate temperature before modifications to the warm-air heating system were carried out. At the time of the survey, over half of the staff said they were dissatisfied with aspects of the environmental systems. A majority wanted changes made to the conservatory corridor; nearly all would have liked heating to be installed in it, and only a quarter found it useful as a supplementary activity area. Almost two-thirds of those surveyed would have preferred a space of conventional design, for example a corridor, in place of the conservatory.

There does seem to have been widespread misunderstanding of the environmental control systems in general and the role of the conservatory in particular. A common complaint was that use of the 'green buttons' failed to relieve ventilation problems; it seems that the buttons were being used in summer when their use would be ineffective. More than three-quarters of staff said they would like more control over the environment, in particular the ability to open windows freely.

LT analysis

LT calculations, carried out retrospectively to demonstrate their application and value, include some simplifications of the project as built. For example, the building has varying ceiling levels – with classroom ceilings following the slope

of the roof between 1.5m and 4m in height – but these have been averaged to give an overall height of 2.3m for the purposes of this exercise (this will tend to underestimate the penetration of natural light into deep plan spaces). An approximation has also been made in respect of orientation – the south-east façade has been considered as 'south-facing', and so on round the building.

It has been assumed that none of the nearby buildings is high enough to obstruct the horizon by more than 15°; there is therefore no need to apply Urban Horizon Factors (UHF). Figures are taken for buffer-space thermal savings on the presumption that the dominant mode of ventilation is from the buffer spaces into adjacent rooms.

Since the east- and west-facing walls are blank, there are no east or west passive zones. Just a small area (the main entrance to the north) has roof glazing, and only two rooms have external south-facing windows. The remaining area of the school is either in a north-facing passive zone, a buffer-adjacent zone (next to the conservatory or atrium) or a non-passive zone in the middle of the plan.

The LT analysis suggests that the conservatory and atrium should be very effective in offsetting heat loss from 'buffer-adjacent' zones; in fact, they may be somewhat oversized.

LT energy-use predictions in terms of primary energy consumption are 52MWh/year for gas for heating, and 59MWh/year for electricity for lighting and ventilation. This is compared with actual energy use recorded in the building during the second heating season which was monitored as 68MWh/year for gas and 64MWh/year for electricity (including water heating).

The LT model prediction therefore shows good agreement with the real building in terms of electricity use. Heating energy at Netley is rather higher than that predicted either by LT or by modelling techniques employed during the design process – largely because of ineffective occupant control of the heating system, and because of the way the building has been used. An example of the latter is the extent to which doors between teaching areas and the conservatory have been left propped open to allow easy access between the two; a frequent general comment made about the building was that the linear layout of the school 'hindered communication with colleagues and contact with other classrooms'. It seems that some staff have attempted to remedy this problem by completely circumventing the environmental control system.

The LT Method can be used to try out modifications to the design, to test whether a better level of energy efficiency is easily achievable. LT analysis indicates that the following might have been promising avenues to explore in the design process:

— A reorientation or redistribution of windows could have minimised north-facing glazing, and consequently reduced heat loss.
— Rooflights could have been used to bring more daylight into the centre of the plan, possibly in place of the large areas of high-level glazing on north façades.
— The buffering effect of sunspaces – atrium and conservatory – in offsetting the heating load of adjacent spaces could have been achieved with less extensive sunspaces. This suggests that a more compact plan, allowing closer connections between teaching areas, might have been devised without compromising thermal performance.

Conclusion

The building has been a success in dramatically reducing energy use without incurring extra capital costs. There is, however, significant occupant dissatisfaction. Some of this can be attributed to a sense of powerlessness when environmental 'controls' do not work as expected. It is clearly important that users should have a full introduction to the working of passive and hybrid systems so they know how to operate them most effectively.

Other causes of dissatisfaction are not directly attributable to the nature of the environmental systems, but may be traced to a feeling that energy efficiency has been given too high a priority during design development to the detriment of other concerns such as flexibility. The use of the LT Method in the development of the project, to test a wide variety of options, could have pointed a way to reconcile such apparent design conflicts.

Bibliography

Baker, N. and Martin, C. (1986). *Netley Abbey School: interim report on monitoring project.* Energy Monitoring Company Ltd.

Edwards, C. (1987). *Assessment of Staff Reaction to Netley Abbey County Infants' School.* Energy Monitoring Company Ltd.

ETSU (1991). Netley School, in *Passive and Hybrid Solar Commercial Buildings: Basic Case Studies.* Report for IEA task XI, ETSU.

Hawkes, D.U. (1988). Energetic design: Netley Infants' School, *Architects' Journal*, 22 June, pp. 32-46.

Martin, C. (1987). *Netley Abbey School: second report on monitoring project 1986-7.* Energy Monitoring Company Ltd.

Martin, C. (1988). *Netley Abbey School: third report on monitoring project 1987-8.* Energy Monitoring Company Ltd.

Department of Electrical Engineering, Norwegian University of Science and Technology, Trondheim
Per Knudsen

Introduction

In the climate of central Norway, it is desirable on a university campus to arrange internal circulation routes between adjacent buildings to facilitate movement around the complex during the dark, snowy winters. In the extension to the Department of Electrical Engineering (ELA) at the Norwegian University of Science and Technology (NUST), glazed atria link the three new blocks to one another and to the three existing buildings, which have been upgraded (Figure 27). Besides their amenity value, these atria significantly reduce energy-use costs for the complex.

The atria are steel-framed and double glazed with low-emissivity units. They are naturally ventilated and heated by radiant panels in the roof, with convectors placed on the glazed façades to counteract down-draughts. The atria were designed to be maintained at a comfortable temperature: studies undertaken during the design phases of the project showed that there was little energy penalty for choosing this level rather than a lower temperature to avoid freezing.

The new buildings are highly glazed – with single glazing – on the façades which face into the atrium. This enables a cost saving to be made which would not be possible in the absence of the atrium spaces; similarly, pipe runs and ducts running through the atrium do not need to be insulated.

27: *View of the ELA building from the west*

Background

The accommodation for the Department of Electrical Engineering (ELA) at NUST was housed in a stone building dating from the early twentieth century. A four-storey brick-clad block was added in 1959. By the 1980s, the department needed to expand very rapidly to cater for the demand for information technology specialists.

The University had strong ideas on how the new development could enhance the social environment of the campus, and act as a demonstration project for energy-efficient design. The departments of architecture and mechanical engineering were involved in design decisions at an early stage, and played an important role in convincing the government funding body that a design incorporating atria would be more cost-effective than one with open streets between the buildings.

The architectural practice of Per Knudsen, based in Trondheim, was appointed to design an extension to house 250 students and 200 researchers.

28: *West elevation*

Built form

The new building on the NUST campus forms an extension to the existing university accommodation for the Department of Electrical Engineering. It is located on the main University campus close to the centre of the city. Three parallel glazed streets run east–west, spanning the gaps between three new office buildings and existing buildings to the north and south. These atria are just over 10m wide and vary in length from 48 to 54m, while the new blocks have a cross-sectional depth of 12-15m (Figure 28). A fourth glazed street runs northwards to give access to new lecture theatres which have been adapted from a pre-existing laboratory block (Figures 29 and 30). The atria have double-pitched roofs and are fully glazed (including the gable walls). The buildings are generally of three storeys in height above the basement level; that is, approximately 13.5m from atrium ground level to eaves. The ratio of atrium width to height is thus around 1.3 (Figure 31).

Heating and ventilation strategy

The accommodation blocks are heated by hot water supplied to radiators from the University's central boiler house. The atria have small convector heaters placed close to the glazing to control down-draughts. Research studies showed that an atrium temperature of a moderately com-

fortable 15°C would not add appreciably to total heating bills, compared with a minimum temperature of 5°C, due to the reduction in heating needs of the accommodation blocks (Figure 32).

Additional radiant heaters are placed in the atrium areas to provide further heating on very cold days. These are positioned in the roof at a considerable distance from building occupants; it is not surprising that they have been found to be ineffectual and are little used.

The original design did not make any provision for overheating in the atrium. Occupants of top-floor offices found that conditions became uncomfortable on hot summer days despite mechanical ventilation of these spaces (Figure 33). This has been rectified by providing automatic controls to existing smoke vents at high level in the atrium to enable them to be used as ventilation openings. With an opening area of 14m² in the roof and 6m² in the gable walls, it is now possible to keep the atrium temperature very close to ambient air temperature – this is adequate for cooling in the Norwegian climate, with a maximum of 10 air changes per hour in high summer.

Daylighting

No explicit modelling of daylighting requirements was carried out before construction. With exceptions for particular cases, the whole of the façades to the new buildings

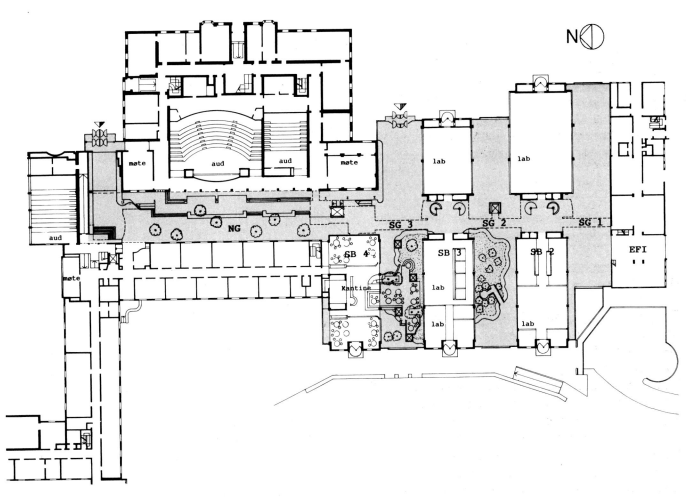

29: *Plan (atria shaded)*

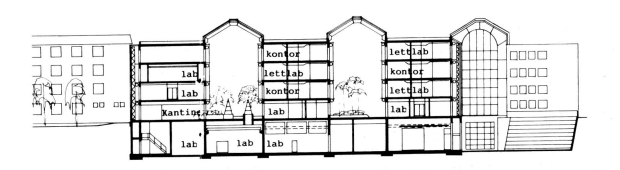

30: *Cross-section*

Energy and Environment in Architecture

34: *Atrium interior at an upper level, showing shading and ductwork obstructing daylight penetration*

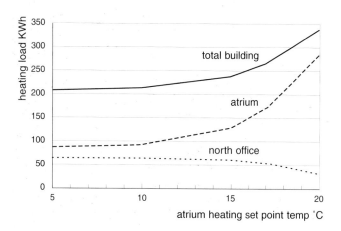

32: *Study of energy demand for different atrium temperatures*

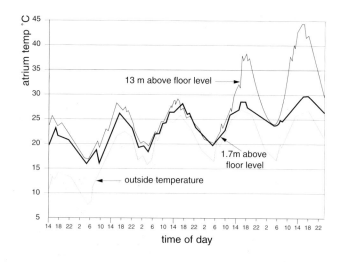

33: *Summertime temperatures at high and low level in the atrium*

34

A			92	DOUBLE GLAZING IN ROOF AND GABLE WALLS, SINGLE IN FACADES.
B			82	DOUBLE, LOW-E GLAZING IN ROOF AND GABLE WALLS, SINGLE IN FACADES.
C			91	DOUBLE GLAZING IN ALL.
D			81	DOUBLE, LOW-E GLAZING IN ROOF AND GABLE WALLS, DOUBLE IN FACADES.
E			100	NO GLASS ROOF, TRIPLE GLAZING IN FACADES.

have a glazing ratio of 30%. The daylighting potential of the office spaces as built is estimated to be 50-55% on the top floor and 30-40% on the floors below. Venetian blinds mounted within the atrium space enable occupants of the offices to block out undesired solar radiation – only south façades are provided with shades in the atrium itself (Figure 34).

The offices have standard artificial lighting without automatic controls – a survey found that in winter 98% of occupants were using artificial lighting even at midday. The figure reduced only to 90% in summer. It is apparent that the daylight reaching the boundary between atrium and office is reduced by the large circular-section ducts which run down the atrium sides just above window-head height; there is clearly potential for further utilisation of daylight within the building.

The atria were originally lit by outdoor lamps to a level just sufficient for circulation. Subsequently, these have been supplemented to provide a suitable environment for study, even after dark.

Energy efficiency

The project formed the subject of a series of detailed energy studies before construction. It was determined that the most cost-effective approach would be to use low-emissivity glazing for atrium walls and roof and single glazing for building façades giving onto the atrium. Double glazing these façades would not save appreciably more energy (Figure 35).

The extension has been extensively monitored since occupation. Comparison between simulated and

36

monitored energy use shows a good correlation between the two. However, it is apparent that several changes made in the use of the building since occupation have had a considerable impact on its energy use. Part of one atrium is used as a cafeteria, with a servery adjacent to it on the ground floor of one of the new buildings (Figure 36). Servery staff complained about the low level of heating in this area, which was intended for intermittent use only. Heat levels were increased to 16°C, then 18°C, but only recently has the building been adapted to close the servery area off from the atrium. Furthermore, the atria are now being extensively used as study areas due to a shortage of accommodation following a large intake of students into the department. This means that all atrium areas are now heated to the higher level, with a consequent steep rise in energy use as predicted by the simulation studies. At current levels of heating, the building consumes 26Wh/m^2 per degree day – this would increase to 30Wh/m^2 per degree day if the atria are excluded from the calculation.

An extensive exercise was carried out to justify the incorporation of the glazed atria in the scheme. It was shown that annual expenditure on running costs and amortisation of capital costs is 14% less for the design as built than for an equivalent design with open streets.

Besides lower energy costs, there is an appreciable saving on construction costs for the building façades which are sheltered by the atria – they are single glazed and do not have to satisfy stringent Norwegian standards for the performance of external walls.

Environmental issues

The atrium areas of the Trondheim scheme are heated by electrical appliances. In most countries, this would imply a high degree of primary energy use – in the UK, for example, heating by electricity uses over three times as much primary energy as heating by gas, and hence generates three times as much carbon dioxide and other pollutants. This is due to the inherent inefficiencies of electricity generation and distribution.

The situation in Norway is quite different. Over 98% of the country's electricity is generated by hydro-power, which produces no carbon dioxide or other pollutant emissions. Electricity is thus 'green', relatively cheap to the consumer, and is widely used for domestic and non-domestic heating applications.

Nevertheless, there is some pressure from environmental groups for greater awareness of energy issues. In particular, Norwegians are conscious that surplus hydroelectricity can be exported to neighbouring countries such as Denmark, Sweden and Germany, and thus reduce those countries' dependence on nuclear- and coal-generated electricity. Central government is supportive of energy-saving measures; building codes are tough by UK standards.

LT analysis

The LT Method is used here to estimate the energy-saving value of the atria. It is assumed for the purposes of this exercise that the building is situated in the northern part of the UK and the atria are unheated; this study does not therefore correspond to conditions in the real building and no comparison with actual energy use is relevant. The study takes the second floor of one of the blocks and calculates energy use with and without the presence of an adjoining atrium space.

In total, it is estimated that the atrium saves 12% in terms of primary energy to service the adjacent spaces; this is despite a rise in energy use for lighting because of the reduction in the amount of natural light reaching the office and lab spaces when an atrium is present. This would be more severe in the case of the lower floors – for these areas, the benefit in energy terms of having an adjacent atrium is only marginal.

Conclusion

The ELA extension building at Trondheim is the latest in a series of similar atrium buildings in the locality (Dragvoll University by Henning Larsen, and Royal Gardens Hotel by Per Knudsen). These have enabled a body of expertise to be assembled on the design of atrium spaces for usability and energy efficiency. The building is popular with its occupants, to the extent that increasing use has forced the building's operators to raise air temperatures in the atria well above the design level. In this case, as in many others, improved energy efficiency has been enjoyed in the form of increased comfort levels rather than in reduced heating bills.

It is perhaps unfortunate that new fire and snow-loading regulations would enforce considerable changes to the design if the building were under construction today, and might make its approach uneconomic. However, the new regulations may induce refinements to the building type in future projects of this nature.

BRF Headquarters, Copenhagen
KHR Arckitekter

Introduction

The BRF Headquarters (Figure 37), near Copenhagen, is an exemplar of how consideration of the thermal balance between lighting and glazing can be taken into account at an early stage in the design process. The building, which is the headquarters for a Danish building society, has a narrow plan depth enabling all office areas to be naturally ventilated with a high level of daylight utilisation. The building fabric is well insulated with triple glazing to office windows.

Energy-efficient lighting is used throughout the building. The design of the building enables internal circulation areas to receive daylighting; the entrance block has a central atrium, and office areas are arranged along roof-lit streets. There are automatic controls on artificial lighting in the top-lit circulation areas which maximise the use of daylight in these zones. External shades to rooflights and side windows can be automatically or manually operated for solar control. The LT Method results suggest that a 29% saving in primary energy is made by making good use of daylight, and in particular by adopting a lower level of design illuminance than the norm for general office buildings.

Background

Byggeriets Realkreditfonds (BRF) is one of the largest property financing institutions in Denmark. In 1982, a decision was taken to relocate the office in a suburban area to enable the company's activities to be concentrated on one site and achieve better working conditions for the staff. Previous accommodation had suffered in particular from

37: *View of the entrance to the*
BRF Headquarters building

poor daylighting, so efficient use of natural light was a pre-requisite of the design. Energy savings were initially a secondary consideration.

The development was shared with another company, Brdr. Hartmann A/S, who initially acquired the site. The same team of architects and engineers designed the whole complex, working closely with BRF's company architects from the initiation of the project. In the final design, BRF occupies 17,000m² with Brdr. Hartmann taking the remaining 4,000m² (Figure 38).

During the course of scheme development, specifications were upgraded due to the growth in BRF's market through the financial boom of the mid-1980s. This allowed a particularly high standard of insulation to be achieved, and investment to be made (for example) in a sophisticated system for lighting control. The aim throughout was to

38: *Site plan*

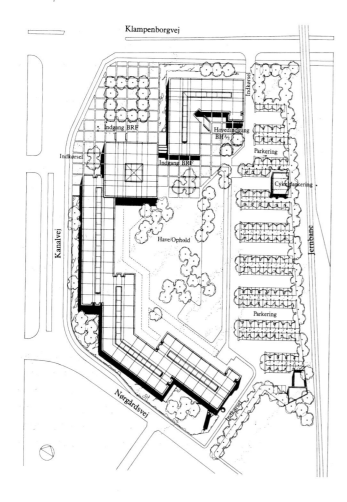

39: *View of central atrium*

Built form

The development is located in Lyngby, a well-established suburban centre 10km north of Copenhagen. The site is adjacent to one of the main shopping streets, with a four-storey shopping centre occupying a site on the opposite side of the dual carriageway.

The building is four storeys high and accommodates a staff of 600. A basement beneath part of the building houses the plant room, while the computer suite is situat-

use natural systems to achieve the quality of an air-conditioned building.

ed in a windowless area on the ground floor. The concrete panel construction has an outer skin of in situ brickwork, with brick-faced cast lintels above the window openings. The building's external appearance is relatively plain, with the design emphasis placed on creating a pleasant and welcoming interior (Figure 39).

The footprint of BRF's accommodation consists of a long thin 'tail' linked to a square entrance block with a central atrium (Figure 40). Besides the reception area serving the building, the entrance block contains communal functions such as cafeteria, meeting rooms and presentation suite. The visual connection between these areas across the central atrium enhances the social function of the space.

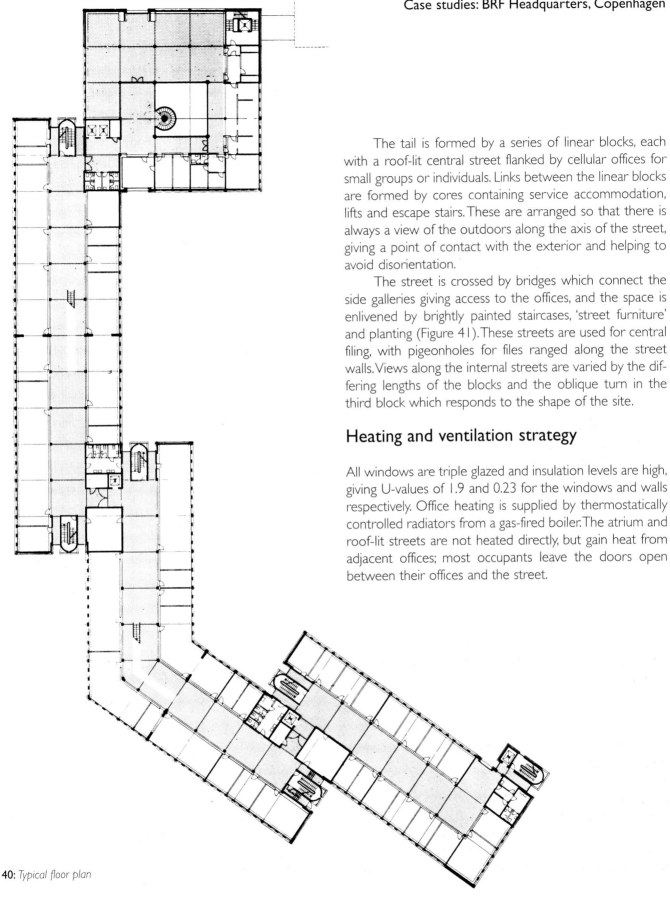

The tail is formed by a series of linear blocks, each with a roof-lit central street flanked by cellular offices for small groups or individuals. Links between the linear blocks are formed by cores containing service accommodation, lifts and escape stairs. These are arranged so that there is always a view of the outdoors along the axis of the street, giving a point of contact with the exterior and helping to avoid disorientation.

The street is crossed by bridges which connect the side galleries giving access to the offices, and the space is enlivened by brightly painted staircases, 'street furniture' and planting (Figure 41). These streets are used for central filing, with pigeonholes for files ranged along the street walls. Views along the internal streets are varied by the differing lengths of the blocks and the oblique turn in the third block which responds to the shape of the site.

Heating and ventilation strategy

All windows are triple glazed and insulation levels are high, giving U-values of 1.9 and 0.23 for the windows and walls respectively. Office heating is supplied by thermostatically controlled radiators from a gas-fired boiler. The atrium and roof-lit streets are not heated directly, but gain heat from adjacent offices; most occupants leave the doors open between their offices and the street.

40: *Typical floor plan*

41: *View of glazed street*

The building conforms to the Danish regulation which prohibits the use of air-conditioning or artificial cooling in normal office spaces. The working areas are therefore designed to be naturally ventilated; all offices have tilt-and-turn windows to be operated by those working adjacent to them. Mechanical ventilation is only provided to internal areas, canteen, etc., and air-conditioning is confined to the computer suite.

The circulation areas in the entrance atrium and office streets are ventilated by infiltration from the offices and other spaces which open onto them. At roof level, double glazing is used, with a U-value of 3.10. Roof panels are openable to increase ventilation rates during summer.

During the period of occupation, it seems that the solar control and ventilation measures have been successful in keeping summertime temperatures comfortable for the building's occupants.

Daylighting

Roof glazing to the atrium and top-floor corridors in the office tail means that daylight is also supplied to internal circulation zones (Figure 42). Excessive solar gain is controlled by external blinds to the windows and rooflights. Blinds to the office windows are slatted to enable a variety of degrees of solar control to be achieved, for example to cut out glare on VDU screens.

The operation of the blinds, artificial lighting levels in the circulation areas and other services are controlled by an energy management system connected to an external weather station. Lights are switched off floor by floor as lighting levels increase, as calculated by a daylighting distribution model incorporated in the computerised energy management system. Even distribution of light between the floors is assisted by the colour of the walls, which is white on the ground floor with an increasingly grey tinge as one ascends the building.

Like the circulation areas, the offices are lit by high efficiency 16W compact fluorescent tubes in specially designed fittings. These are automatically switched off outside working hours and blinds are lowered to reduce U-values during the night; however, manual controls for lighting, shading and heating within the offices can be used to overrule the central system when necessary (Figure 43).

The sketch design included clerestory windows onto the street above the office doors, to further improve the distribution of natural light. However, this zone has been obstructed by an increase in the floor depth of the access galleries running along the street. This provides space for service distribution runs, should a higher level of mechanical ventilation or cooling be required for future uses of the

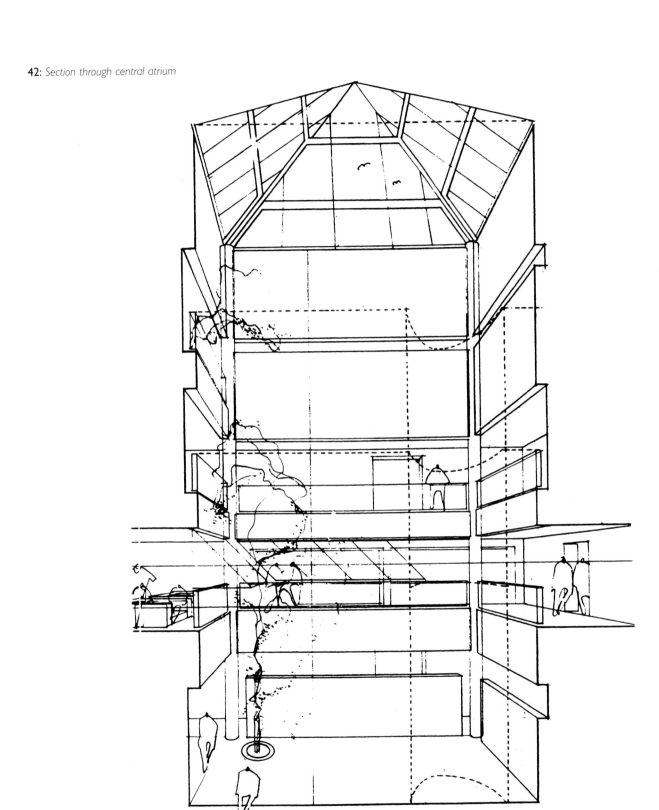

42: *Section through central atrium*

space. While giving additional flexibility in the function of the office wings, this provision has reduced the building designers' options and at present serves no useful purpose.

Energy efficiency

For the first year of operation, the primary energy use amounted to 210kWh/m^2 as electricity for lighting and 90kWh/m^2 for natural gas; a total of 300kWh/m^2 in terms of primary energy. LT analysis has shown that the lighting energy can be reduced from 210kWh/m^2 to 120kWh/m^2 as a result of effective light-switching controls.

Environmental issues

The building has been designed with regard for internal air quality. Floors are finished with birch strip throughout the building to minimise maintenance over the lifetime of the building and reduce the potential for the occurrence of sick-building syndrome; symptoms of this problem have been linked to the use of fitted carpets in offices. The hardwood floors are appreciated by the staff and have not been found to cause acoustical problems, despite their use in circulation areas.

The improvement of working conditions for the company's employees was one of the major reasons for relocation. A comfortable physical environment has been achieved, and (an important contributory factor for occupant satisfaction) the personnel have also attained a high degree of control over their immediate environment, due to the accessibility of openable windows, controllable radiators and adjustable blinds.

LT analysis

In the LT calculations for the BRF building the atrium and glazed street are considered as roof-lit spaces rather than as buffer zones, because they are (indirectly) heated and used in the same way as other internal spaces. Urban Horizon Angles take into account the proximity of the attached building to the north, the office and shopping developments to the west and south, and the open parking space and railway line to the east.

The LT calculation has been carried out twice, first with the design lighting levels of 100-150 lux in the circulation areas and 300 lux in the offices. This can be compared with the second calculation, taking a common lighting-level specification for offices of 500 lux. The results indicate that a 29% saving in total primary energy use has been made by adopting a lower lighting level, and using automatic controls to switch off artificial lights when daylight can satisfy the demand.

Conclusion

The BRF Headquarters demonstrates that an energy-efficient building can be achieved using well-established technologies in a non-intrusive way. The primary concern of the client body and its design team was to create a pleasant working environment, with energy savings a welcome by-product of this aim.

43: *Internal view of a typical cellular office*

Appendices

A.1   Glossary

Terms which have particular significance to the LT Method.

Boiler factor
LT heating energy is based on a boiler efficiency of 0.65. For different efficiencies multiply by boiler factor B = 0.65/(actual boiler efficiency)

Buffer-space
An unheated space between a normally conditioned indoor space, and the outside. Typically a conservatory or atrium.

Buffer-space thermal savings (BTS)
The reduction in heating load due to the presence of a buffer-space.

Climatic zone
Geographical areas which have different temperature, sky illuminance and day length characteristics causing significant differences in LT energy predictions. For LT (version 2.2) these are north and south UK as indicated in Figure 11.2.

Cold radiation
Used to describe excessive heat loss by radiation to large cold surface such as glazing, often causing discomfort.

Cooling energy
The annual primary energy used by refrigeration plant to reject heat from the building, plus the fan power needed to circulate the air.

Daylight factor
The ratio of the illuminance by daylight at a specific point in a building to that which would exist from the unobstructed diffuse sky.

Fan energy
The annual primary energy needed to circulate air for full air-conditioning or for the supply of fresh air only .

Fresh air only
Air for the maintenance of air quality rather than temperature control. Based on 10 litres/second/person.

Glazing ratio
The ratio of unobstructed glass area to total wall area (including the glass) when viewed from outside the building.

Heating energy
The annual primary energy meet demand from conductive heat losses through fabric and ventilation heat loss.

Internal gains
Heat gains from occupants and equipment other than lighting.

Lighting datum (illuminance datum)
The value (in lux) of the internal daylight illuminance below which artificial light is necessary.

Lighting energy
The annual primary energy used by the artificial lighting to meet the lighting datum when daylight is insufficient during occupied hours.

Lighting gains
Heat gains from the use of artificial lighting.

Non-passive zones
Areas of the building without access to the external envelope which have to be permanently artificially lit and mechanically ventilated.

Passive area ratio
Ratio of passive area to total floor area.

Passive zone
Areas of the building which can be daylit and naturally ventilated within two floor-to-ceiling heights of the walls or top-floor areas.

Primary energy
Energy value of fuel at source. E.g. for oil includes energy over-

head for extraction and processing, for electricity it includes heat rejected at power station and distribution losses.

Protectivity
The ratio of the separating wall area to the external envelope area of an atrium or buffer space.

Separating wall
The wall between a heated building and an unheated atrium or buffer space.

Side-lit zone
Passive zone with daylight from the side.

Sky illuminance
The value (in lux) of the illumination falling on the surface specified, from the sky.

Solarity
The ratio of south-facing glazing (between vertical and 45°) to the total area of glazing in an atrium or buffer space envelope.

Specific energy consumption
Annual primary energy consumption per square metre for heating, lighting or cooling.

Roof zone
Zone under roof with the potential for being day lit and naturally ventilated.

Top floor side-lit zone
Roof zone (non-central) with conductive heat losses through both roof and side walls.

Urban horizon angle (UHA)
The average elevation of the skyline from the centre of the façade under consideration, within an angle of 60° in the horizontal plane on either side of the normal to the façade.

Urban horizon factor (UHF)
A factor used in the LT Method by which a heating, cooling or lighting energy total is multiplied to take account of the effect of obstructions to daylight and solar radiation.

Utilisation factor
The fraction of incoming solar energy (on a monthly basis) which is used to displace auxiliary heating.

ion heating energy
The annual heating energy needed to warm up incoming fresh air to room temperature.

A.2 The LT model
In the LT Method, energy use is read off from graphs, printed in this volume [see Chapter 14]. These graphs, the LT curves, are derived from a computer-based mathematical model. The energy flows considered are indicated in Figure 11.1. First the model evaluates the heat conduction through the external envelope, and ventilation heat loss (or gain): using monthly mean temperatures and an average internal temperature with a correction factor to allow for intermittent heating, a monthly gross heating load is calculated. The model then evaluates the solar gain and applies a utilisation factor to this. This factor takes account of the fact that not all of the solar gains available are useful in offsetting auxiliary heating.

At the same time the monthly hours of available daylight are calculated from the average hourly sky illuminance on the façade, the daylight factor, and an internal lighting datum value. This gives a monthly electrical consumption for artificial lighting and a monthly heat gain.

The lighting heat gains and useful solar gains, together with casual gains from occupants and equipment, are then subtracted from the gross heating load to establish the net heating load. If the gains are more than the gross heating load, then the net load is zero. For air-conditioned options it is necessary to evaluate cooling loads. If the gains are sufficient to raise the average temperature above the cooling set point, then a cooling load exists. This cooling load is added on to a fixed energy demand for fan and pump power.

Note that the model assumes 'sensible light-switching', i.e. that lights are only on when the daylighting value drops below a minimum datum value. In practice this would almost certainly require automatic light-sensing switching to realise the full savings. Thus the model already assumes a considerable degree of good design, and evaluates a technical potential performance, rather than the actual performance that would probably be found in a typical, but wasteful, building.

The monthly energy consumption is calculated for a 'cell' and then reduced to the value of energy consumption per square metre. This is then totalled for the year and plotted as a function of glazing ratio. A cell corresponds to a room surrounded by other rooms. This implies a zero conductive heat loss through all surfaces except the external (window) wall or, in the case of rooflighting, the ceiling. Appropriate efficiency factors are applied to reduce all energy to primary energy.

The reason that primary energy is used is that it allows the different 'fuel' inputs for lighting, heating and cooling to be reduced to one common unit. Primary energy is the energy value of the fuel at source. In the case of fuels such as gas or oil used for heating, there is a small energy overhead required for extracting, refining and distribution. There is a rather larger loss of heat energy at the point of use due to combustion losses. This typically results in a value of about 1.5 for the ratio of primary to useful energy.

In the case of electricity, an energy overhead occurs at the power station due to the thermodynamic efficiency of the conversion of heat to mechanical power. This leads to a large ratio of primary to delivered energy of about 3.7 (4). When used to produce heat, electricity converts with 100% efficiency which results in the overall primary to useful ratio remaining at 3.7.

For energy sources which are fossil fuels, primary energy relates well to CO_2 and other pollutant production, and to cost. Problems would arise, however, where a substantial proportion of the electricity is generated by renewable (mechanical) sources such as hydro or wind. It also presents problems where electricity is generated by nuclear sources since the concept of primary nuclear energy is not really equivalent to primary energy of conventional sources. However, nuclear energy is not free from CO_2 production. The energy of construction, decommissioning, and waste fuel reprocessing is significant compared with the lifetime energy production of the plant. Primary energy is calculated here assuming a mix of fuels and electricity generation appropriate for the UK (see also [12.5]).

A.3 LT default values

The model contains more than thirty parameters, most of which are fixed in order to produce the LT curves. These values have been chosen to be appropriate for four building types A–D. These types broadly correspond to schools, colleges, offices and institutional buildings such as hospitals. The main parameter which defines them is the occupancy pattern. Other values, such as ventilation rate and internal heat gains, also vary.

The LT Method can be used for other building types provided any discrepancies in the parameter values are small. For example, large hotels could fit into type D, whilst a light-manufacturing workshop could reasonably be described as type C, provided that internal heat gains lie between 15 and 30W/m^2. When using the curves for types A and B, for buildings without educational-type holidays, the annual energy should be increased by about 30% to account for the extra use. However, for assessing the relative performance of design options, this is probably unnecessary.

The table below lists the values of parameters used in the LT Method which are of interest to the designer.

Default values used in the LT Method:

Site location	Northern UK, southern UK
Orientations	S, E/W, N, Horiz.
Room height	3m
Glazing ratio	0–100%
Glazing bars, framing	20%
Glazing type	Double
Workplane height	0.9m
Reflectances	Ceiling 0.7, wall 0.5, floor 0.25
Illuminance datum	150, 300, 500 lux
U-values	External wall 0.35, roof 0.35, window 2.85
Heating setpoint	20°C
Heating efficiency	0.65
Cooling system CoP	2.5
Fan energy	0.027MWh/m^2 (fresh air), 0.075MWh/m^2 (air-cond.)
Lighting power	6, 12, 20 W/m^2
Occup. and Equip.	10, 15, 20, 30 W/m^2

Default values used in the LT Method:

Building type	Int. gains (W/m²)	Hours/day	Days/wk	Vent. (ac/h)	Light (lux)
A (schools)	20	8	5	2.5	150, 300
B (colleges)	20	11	5	1.5	150, 300
C (offices)	15, 35	11	5	1.0	150, 300, 500
D (institutional*)	10	24	7	1.5	150, 300

* Assuming night set-back and lighting off 23.00–07.00

Holidays (weeks per month)

	Jan	Feb	Mar	Apr	May	June	July	Aug	Sep	Oct	Nov	Dec
A (schools)	1	1	0	2	1	0	1	4	1	0	1	2
B (colleges)	0	0	0	3	0	0	2	4	1	0	0	2

Types C and D - no holiday close down

Primary / delivered energy:
Heating   1.05
Electricity 3.7

A.4 Design checklist

This checklist is not part of the LT Method, but it is included here to remind the designer of all the other factors which will influence building performance – both in relation to energy and occupant comfort and well-being. It is not possible to deal quantitatively with all these other factors at the level of simplicity of the LT Method. Thus, these areas tend to be dealt with descriptively and will be found in Part One.

1   **Site.** Site planning and layout, micro-climate, noise and pollution, landscape and planting, sunlight and daylight access.
2   **Building form.** Plan shape, section shape, floor to ceiling height, proportion of passive zone, orientation, adjacent buildings.
3   **Building fabric.** Construction and insulation of floor, walls, roof, glazing type and areas, thermal mass, cold bridges, vapour barriers, transparent insulation.
4   **Daylight and sunlight.** Glazing area, façade design, glazed area distribution, shading, external reflective surfaces, internal reflective surfaces, views, glare control.
5   **Passive solar.** Thermal strategy relating to climate and building type, glazing area and orientation, distribution, thermal mass, solar ventilation pre-heat, effect on thermal comfort.
6   **Natural ventilation.** Prevailing wind conditions, building shape, pressure coefficients, stack effect, distribution of openings, noise and pollution, minimal ventilation, ventilation pre-heat, structural cooling, night ventilation, physiological cooling by air movement.
7   **Prevention of overheating/reduction of cooling.** Shading, building reflectance, insulation, thermal mass, ventilation gains, lighting gains, casual gains, comfort standards.
8   **Artificial lighting sources.** Luminaires, levels and standards, task lighting, ambient lighting, integration with daylight, zones, glare and visual comfort, controls.
9   **Heating.** Choice of fuel, distribution of plant, emitters, thermal comfort, controls, distribution and storage of hot water.
10 **Mechanical servicing/air-conditioning.** Centralised or distributed air-handling units, duct sizes, heating/cooling recovery and storage, integration with structure, refrigeration type, controls, comfort standards.
11 **Atria/sun spaces/buffer spaces.** Glazing type and area, daylight level, effect on daylighting of adjacent rooms, reflected light, thermal conditions in winter and summer, ventilation pre-heat, heating, shading, ventilation, openable areas, comfort conditions, types of planting and requirements for heat and light.
12 **Environmental issues.** Energy of production of materials, avoidance of CFCs, avoidance of non-renewable timber, choice of fuels to minimise CO_2 and other pollutant production. Building health, avoidance of sick-building syndrome and legionnaires' disease, etc.

Illustration acknowledgements

The authors and publisher would like to acknowledge the following individuals and organizations for permission to reproduce material. We have made every effort to contact and acknowledge copyright holders, but if any errors or omissions have been made, we should be happy to correct them at a later printing.

BRECSU: 1.1, 5.21
Mike Buckley: 2.4, 5.2 and 5.24
Paul Oliver: 3.1
Daylight Europe: 3.6, 3.9, 5.14 and 9.7
Colt International: 3.13
Greenwood Airvac: 3.14
Architects' Journal: 4.6, 5.4 and 5.16, also Figures 4 and 6 in Case Study 1, and Figures 17, 18, 19, 20, 22 and 25 in Case Study 3
Mike Baker: 6.1
BRF (Byggereits Realkreditfonds): 6.8 and Figures 38, 40 and 42 in Case Study 5
M. Cook : 8.2
Daylight Europe: 9.7
Martin Charles: Figures 17, 20 and 25 in Case Study 3
A. R. T. Gardner: 5.16
Norwegian University of Science and Technology, Trondheim: Figures 28, 29 and 30 in Case Study 4

All other illustrations are from slides or photographs taken by the authors.

Index

Page numbers appearing in **bold** indicate figures.

Acoustic comfort 13, 14, **14, 15, 16**
Adaptive behaviour 14-16, 17, **17**
Ahrends, Burton and Koralk 181
Air-conditioning 61, 62, **63**, 218
       comfort 4, 9
       cooling 35-6
       load-reducing strategies 28-30, **28**
Air movement 12, 54-5
Air quality 12
Artificial lighting 12-13, 218
       controls 13, 47-9, **48**, 88
Artificial lighting gains 30, **30**, 34
Ashington, Northumberland 83
Atria 66-7, 80
       and daylighting 67, **67, 68, 69-70**, 70
       design checklist 218
       environmental benefits 66, **67**
       heating 78, 80, **81**, 88
       in LT Method 106, **106, 108**, 109
       LT Method worked example **113**, 114-15
       passive and non-passive zones **64**
       shading 76
       and solar energy 21
       temperature 70-3, **72, 73, 74, 75**
       thermal energy saving 73-4, 75
       and thermal mass 39, 78
       ventilation 76-7, **77, 78**

Boiler efficiencies 86, **86**, 103
BRE Low Energy Offices 2, **5, 7, 27, 41**
BRF Headquarters, Copenhagen 169, 206-12
Bridewell Street, Bristol **28**
Buffer-adjacent zone depth 98, 107, **107, 142, 163**
Buffer-space thermal savings (BTS) **108**, 109, 115, **142, 163**, 214
Buffer-spaces 214, 218
       see also Atria; Conservatories
Building design 5-6, 92, 93
Building Energy Management Systems (BEMS) 19, 86, 88
Building materials **37**
Byggeriets Realkreditfonds see BRF Headquarters, Copenhagen

Cambridge Consultants Ltd **68, 74, 75**

Canary Wharf tower 86, 89
Carbon dioxide see CO_2
Cave dwellings **9**
Cavities, ventilated 31, **32**
Circulation space 58, **60**
Cladding 21, **22**
Climatic zones 93-4, **95**
Clothing level 10, **10**
CO_2 3, 82, **83**, 103-4, **103**
Coal 83, 103
Coefficient of Performance (CoP) 84
Cold bridges 25
Cold radiation 9, **9**, 214
Colleges, LT curves **124-5, 145-6**
Combined heat and power (CHP) 7, 83, 84-85, **85**
Comfort 4, 8, 12, 19
       acoustic 13, **14**, 15, **15**, 16, **16**
       adaptive opportunity and control 14-16, 17, **17**, 88
       indoor air quality 12-13
       thermal 10
       visual 12
Comfort cooling 28-9
Computational Fluid Dynamics (CFD) **53**
Condensing boilers 7, 86, **86**
Conductive gains 30, **30**, 33-4
Conservatories
       LT Method worked example **116**, 117
       and thermal mass 39
Constant volume (CV) systems 87
Convective emitters 87-8
Cooling 107, 109, 218
       reduction 218
       see also Ventilation
Cooling energy 49, 51, 104
Cooling loads 43, 49
Costs **3, 83**, 179, 193
Cross-ventilation 56, 58, 77, 79
Cutty Sark (6) 89, **89**

Darwin College Library, Cambridge **11**
Davis, Langdon & Everest 171, 179
Daylight Factor 4-5, **44**, 67, **68**, 214

Daylighting 6, 7, 42, 218
    and artificial lighting gains 34
    and atria 67, **68, 69**, 70, **70**, 106, 107
    as energy 42, **43**, 44
    and shading 45–6, **46, 47**
    sky as light source 45, **45**
    thermal function of glazing 48, **49, 50**, 51
    and visual comfort 12–13
Delivered energy units 103
Department of Electrical Engineering, Norwegian University of
    Science and Technology (ELA) 169, 196–205
Displacement ventilation 76, **77**
Double glazing 21–2, 34, 50
Down-draughts 10, **11**
Ducts 58, **59**

ECD Partnership 188
Edmond, David 170
Electricity 83, 84–5, 104
Energy conservation 3, 13, 26–30, 42
Energy flows, LT model 93, **94**
Energy performance 2–3, **3**
    factors 4–6, **4**, 92
    low energy strategies 6–7
    management issues 89
    offices 19, **19**
    thermal mass and intermittent heating 39
    see also LT Method
Environmental issues 187, 193, 204–5, 212, 218
    see also CO$_2$
Equipment gains 30, **30**, 35
External solar gains 30–1, **30**

Façades 168, 172–3
Fan coil units 59–60, **62**, 87
Fan power 92, 104
Fans 34, 36, **36**, 55, **62**
Fire safety 60, 75
Form 168–218
Free cooling 36, 54
Fresh-air plenums 58, **60**

Gas 83
Gateway 1 and 2 **63, 79**
Glare 13, 14, 44, 176
Glazed streets 169, 209, **210, 211**
Glazing 10, **11**, 13, 14, 22, 25
    atria 70, **71**

thermal function 22–4, 48–9, **49**, 51
Glazing ratio 49, 99, **99**
Hampshire County Council Architects' Department 188
Hawkes, Professor Dean 179
Heat capacity 37, **37**
Heat gains 30, **30**, 41, 42
Heat loss
    from body 10, **10**
    insulation and cold bridges 24–5
Heat pumps 7, 83–4, **84, 85**, 87
Heat recovery 7, 13, 54, 59, 87
Heat rejection 104
Heating 18–19, 25
    atria 78, 80, **81**, 107, 109
    controls 88
    convective emitters 87
    design checklist 218
    insulation and cold bridges 24–5
    intermittent 38–9, **39**
    orientation and overshadowing 23–4
    production and distribution 86–7
    radiant emitters 87
    renewable sources 83–4
    solar gains and thermal mass 20–1
    thermal balance of glazing 21–3
Heavyweight buildings 39, **39**, 41
    see also Thermal mass
High luminous efficacy light sources 34
Hollow floors **40**, 41
Hospitals, LT Method worked example 117–18, **119**
Housing **17**, 21, **43**
Hydroelectricity 85, 204–5

Inland Revenue Building, Nottingham **38**
Innovation centre, Nantes **71**
Institutions
    LT curves **132–5, 153–6**
    Urban Horizon Factor **141, 162**
Insulation 20, 24–5, 28, 34
    atria 80
    and external solar gains 30, 31
    and ventilation cooling 36
Intelligent buildings 169
Intermittent heating 38–9, **39**
Internal gains 18, 30, 31, 34, 35, 214
Internal solar gains 30, **30**, 31–2, 34
Ionica Headquarters, Cambridge **59**, 170–9

Knudsen, Per 197, 205

Larsen, Henning 205
Light shelves 46, **46**
Lighting 181, 206
     see also Artificial lighting; Daylighting
Lighting datum 214
Lighting energy 92, 104
Lighting gains 214
Lightweight buildings 39–41, **39, 41**
     see also Thermal mass
Local thermostats 10, 34
Louvres 32, **33**
LT curves 99–101, **100, 101**, 103
     colleges 124–5, 125–6
     five-storey office building 112
     institutions 132–5, 153–6
     offices 126–31, 147–52
     schools 122–3, 142–3
LT Data 121
     see also Buffer-space thermal savings; LT curves;
          Urban Horizon Factor
LT Method 92–3
     Buffer-space thermal savings 74, **75**
     cooling energy 104
     default values 216, **216, 217**
     five-storey office building 110, **111**, 112, 114
     four-storey office building with atrium **113**, 114–15
     glazing ratio 99, **99**
     limitations 94
     nucleus hospital 117–18, **119**
     passive zone 96, **97**, 98–9, **98**
     primary energy and CO_2 103–4
     school with conservatory **116**, 117
     sunspaces **106**, 107, **108**
     technical background 93–4
     Urban Horizon Factor 24, 104–7, **105, 106**
LT model 25, 215–16
     energy flows 93, **94**
     thermal balance of glazing 22–3, **23**, 48, 49, **49**
LT worksheets **102**, 103, **111, 113, 164**, 165
Luminous efficacies 42, **43**
Lycée de Blain, France **14**

Maltings, The, Snape **53**
Mean radiant temperature (MRT) 10
Mechanical ventilation 13, 41, 52, 60–2, **61**, 226
     see also Air-conditioning
Metabolic rate 10, **10**
Mixed mode 28–9, **29, 30**, 173
Mixing ventilation 76–7, **76**, 78

Modane, France **70**
Motivation 89

National Farmers Union, Stratford-upon-Avon **31**
Natural ventilation 6, 7, **12**, 52, 54
     analytical techniques **52, 54**
     atria 67, 76–7, **76**
     BRE Low Energy office **27**
     configuration 57–8, **58**
     cooling 35–6
     design checklist 218
     and indoor air quality 13
     night ventilation 41
     stacks and ducts 58–9
     thermal buoyancy 55, 56–7, **57**, 58
     wind pressure 55–6, **55**, 58
Netley Abbey Infants' School, Hampshire **21**, 169, 188–95
Night ventilation 35, 39–40, **40**, 41, **41**
NMB Bank 65, **65**
Noise 13, 14, 16
Non-domestic buildings 24, 26, 93
     energy consumption 2, 3, **3**
     see also Hospitals; Institutions; Offices; Schools
Non-passive zones **97**, 98, **98**, 103
Normal 215
Northern climatic zone 93–4, **95**
     Buffer-space thermal savings **142**
     LT curves **122–34**
     Urban Horizon Factor **136–7**
Nucleus system 117–18, **119**, 180, 181

Occupant gains 30, **30**, 34
Occupants 5, 10, **11**, 52, 65
Offices **6**, 19, **19**
     LT curves 126–31, **147–52**
     LT Method worked examples 110, **111**, 112, **113**, 114–15
     thermal balance of glazing 22–3, **23**
     Urban Horizon Factor **138–40, 159–62**
Oil 83
Orientation
     and heating 23–4
     and internal solar gains 20, 31, 32
     LT curves 103
Overheating 26–30, 41, 49, 218
     cooling load reduction 30, **30**
     night ventilation 39–40, 41
     reduction of heat gains 34–5
     shading and orientation 30–4
     thermal mass 36–9

ventilation cooling 35–6, **35**
Overheating risk 104
Overshadowing 24, **24**

Passive design 6, 8, 82
Passive solar gains 7, 218
Passive zones 51, 64–5, **64**, **65**, 215
    in LT Method 92, 96, **97**, 98–9, **98**
    LT Method worked examples 110, **111**, 112, **113**, 114
Plant design 5, 6, 82, 86
Plants 75, 78, 80
Pollution 13, 82, **83**
Primary energy 19, **19**, 63, 93, 103, 215
Prismatic glass 46, **47**
Protectivity 73

Radiant emitters 87
Radiant heat loss 10, **11**
Reflecting louvres 47, **47**
Renewable energy 83–4
RH Partnership 170, 171
Roof-space solar collectors 21, 22
Rooflights, LT curves 101

St. Mary's Hospital, Isle of Wight 84, **84**, 180–9
Salt tank modelling **54**
Schools
    intermittent heating 38
    internal heat gains 35
    LT curves **122**, **143–4**
    LT Method worked example **116**, 117
    Modane **70**
    Urban Horizon Factor **136**, **157–8**
    ventilation **12**, 54
Security 60
Separating wall 215
Services design 5, 6, 82, 86
Shading 10, 28, 44, 177
    atria 67, 75–6
    and daylighting 5–7, **46**, **47**
    and solar gains 31–2, **31**, **32**, **33**, 34
Shallow plans 6, 7, 24–5, 42, 170
Sick Building Syndrome (SBS) 52, 86
Side-lit top floor areas 98–9, 114
Side-lit zones 96, **97**, 215
Single glazing, thermal benefit 49
Site, design checklist 218
Sky illuminances 45, **45**, 215
Sky view, atria 67, **68–9**

Solar chimneys 57, **57**
Solar collectors 21, 22
Solar energy 83
Solar gains 7, 10, 20–1, **20**, **21**, 80
    external 30–1, **30**
    internal 30, **30**, 31–2, 34
    and thermal mass 38–9, **39**
Solar radiation 10, 23, **25**, **33**
Solar thermal contribution 24, **24**
Solar Utilisation Factor 20–1, **20**, 215
Solar ventilation pre-heating 13, 54
Solarity 73
Southern climatic zone 93–4, **95**
Buffer-space thermal savings **108**, 163
    LT curves **143–56**
    Urban Horizon Factor **157–62**
Space cooling 34–7, **35**, 54
Specific heat 37, **37**
Stack effect, atria 77–8, **79**
Stack extract 58, **59**
    see also Thermal buoyancy
Stack supply and extract 58, **59**
Stratification 77, 80, 87
Sunspaces
    design checklist 218
    see also Atria; Conservatories
Swimming pools, solar heating 83
Switching controls *see* Artificial lighting

Thermal balance point 18–19, **18**
Thermal buoyancy 55, 56–7, **57**, 58
    see also Stack extract
Thermal comfort 9–10, 54–5
Thermal energy saving, atria 73–4, 75
Thermal mass 36–9, **37**, **38**, 41, 78
    and acoustic comfort 13, **14**
    effect on intermittent heating 38–9
    and solar gains 20, 31
Top floor side-lit zones 98–9, 114

Underfloor fresh-air supply 58, **59**
Underfloor heating 80, **81**
Urban Horizon Angle 104, 105–7, 215
    five-storey office building 112, 114
    and heating energy 24, **24**
Urban Horizon Factor 104, **105**, 215
    colleges **137**, **156**
    institutions **141**, **162**
    offices **138–40**, **159–61**

schools **157–8**
Utilisation factor 20–1, **20**, 215

Variable air volume (VAV) systems 87
VDUs 13, **13**
Veiling reflections 12, **13**
Ventilation 41, 52, 53, 54, 63
    and acoustic comfort 16, **17**
    air movement 54–5
    atria 78–80, **75, 77**, 78
    cooling 35–6, **35**, 54
    and indoor air quality 12
    minimum 54
    and thermal comfort 9–10
    see also Mechanical ventilation; Natural ventilation;

Night ventilation
Ventilation dumping 75, **75**, 76
Ventilation gains 30, **30**, 34
Ventilation pre-heating 21, **21, 22**, 74, **77**
Vertical glazing 13
Visual comfort 12–13
Volumetric specific heat 36

Wind pressure 55–6, **55**, 57, 58
Wind towers **60**, 169, 174, **174**
Windows 14, 15, **15, 30**, 37, 42
    and acoustic comfort 13, **15**
Windpower 85